CONNEXITY

CONNEXITY

How to Live in a
Connected World

Geoff Mulgan

Harvard Business School Press
Boston, Massachusetts

Copyright 1997 © Geoff Mulgan

The Author hereby asserts his moral right to be identified as the Author of the Work.

First published in the United States by Harvard Business School Press, 1998. This edition published by arrangement with Random House UK Limited.

First published in Great Britain and outside North America by

Chatto & Windus, 1997.
20 Vauxhall Bridge Road
London SW1V 2SA

Printed in the United States of America

02 01 00 99 98   5 4 3 2 1

Library of Congress Cataloging-in-Publication Data

Mulgan, Geoff.
  Connexity: how to live in a connected world /
Geoff Mulgan.
      p.   cm.
  Includes bibliographic references and index.
  ISBN 0-87584-850-8 (alk. paper)
  1. Mutualism.   2. Individualism.   3. Social
  interaction.   4. Liberty.   I. Title.
HM131.M795   1998
302.5´4—dc21   97-30350
                                              CIP

The paper used in this publication meets the requirements of the American National Standard for Permanence of Paper for Printed Library Materials
Z39.49-1984.

ACKNOWLEDGEMENTS

Many people have contributed to this book. Some of the most important contributors aren't aware just how much I've depended on them, and in other cases I am sure that I am unaware of just how much I've been shaped by a conversation or a book, an article, a television programme or a talk. As for the more direct influences, I am indebted to a large group of people for having inspired and spurred me on over the last few years, through their friendship, their writings or their example. They include Robin Murray, Howard Gardner, Charles Handy, Jane Jacobs, Amitai Etzioni, John Gray, Rosabeth Moss Kanter, Perri 6, Ken Worpole, Charles Leadbetter, Ian Hargreaves, Martin Jacques and, probably most of all, Helen Wilkinson. All the staff at Demos deserve my thanks for their tolerance and patience while I was going through the traumas of writing. Finally, it is only fair to point out that many of the virtues and none of the vices of what has resulted are due to the careful and supportive editing of Jonathan Burnham and Sara Holloway.

CONTENTS

CONNEXITY

INTRODUCTION

IN CLASSICAL TRAGEDIES the hero's downfall is often rooted in his finest qualities. What he does best leads him inexorably to disaster. The argument of this book is that today we may face just such a tragedy. What brings out the best in us is freedom. Freedom allows us to realise our potential, to live life to the full, to imagine and create, and the growth of freedom to live our lives as we think fit, has been the greatest achievement of modern times.

Our problem is that freedom to behave as we would wish, without regard for our effects on others, runs directly counter to the other striking fact of the contemporary world: our growing dependence on other people. The world may never have been freer, but it has also never been so interdependent and interconnected. Only a small proportion of the world's population could now be self-sufficient. The rest of us depend on complex systems to deliver us water, food, justice, energy and health. Far more than its counterpart of a century ago, the modern business depends on distant capital markets, distant consumer markets, distant systems of law enforcement and education. And just as we depend on others, so do our own actions affect others as never before. If we drive a car the emissions affect the living standards of millions of strangers, however marginally. The messages we communicate can influence, irritate or upset strangers we will never meet. Our choices over what clothes to buy determine whether someone on the other side of the world retains or loses their job. Poor regions of the West depend on investment from Korea or

Japan to bring them jobs, just as poor regions of Africa depend on technology from North America to cure new strains of disease. The decisions that firms take can bring prosperity to far-off places, but they can also lead to the destruction of traditional ways of life, and of environmental habitats.

This dawning sense of the connectedness of the world has come more than anything from the environment. The old assumption that the natural environment has an infinite capacity to absorb our waste and pollution is obsolete. We now know that humanity walks heavily on nature, and that the price of an economic system driven by consumer freedoms is being paid in the form of worse air, dirtier water and poisoned land. Today we face a future in which, as a result of industrial progress, global temperatures may rise over two degrees centigrade in the next century; in which, as a consequence, sea levels could rise by over a metre flooding much of Bangladesh, China, the Netherlands and England; and in which the chronic water shortages which already affect nearly half of the world's population could become even more commonplace. These are all startling symptoms of interdependence, and they mean that it is no longer realistic to think of the world as made up of discrete individuals, nations, mountain ranges and forests. Instead it is more like a web of physical connections, made up of rivers that provide water for many different nation-states, winds that carry acid rain, ocean currents that carry toxic wastes and radiation.

These natural connections are matched by the ones that we have made. The world economy has recently gone through another wave of integration, just as it did at the turn of the last century, and global trade has now been joined by global direct investments and the global diffusion of technologies. An ever larger proportion of the world's workforce now depends on distant markets and sources of capital and know-how, and would suffer acutely if these were suddenly cut off. Tying the world together are the communications systems that first spread in the nineteenth century with the radio and telegraph, and now are increasing in scale and scope with the satellite and the Internet, the mobile phone and the navigation system. These too are founded around ideologies of freedom – of free expression and free speech. All are breaking down the barriers, and the friction, that stand in the way of making exchanges. Just as the theory of Gaia showed that we could think of the biosphere as a single organism, the 'infosphere' now has some of the properties of a single, integrated system.

The best word for describing this new situation is an old English one: 'connexity'. It is more accurate than the word 'interdependence', which refers to the symptom not the cause, and it is richer in meaning than the word 'globalisation', which drains the idea of its moral content. The word serves both as a description of the world around us, and as a shorthand for the challenge we now face. Etymologically it links us back to the roots of the word 'connect', which derives from the Latin *con-nectere*, to tie or join together. It is a reminder that the starting-point for understanding the world today is not the size of its GDP or the destructive power of its weapons systems but the fact that it is so much more joined together than before. It may still look as if it is made up of separate and sovereign individuals, firms, nations or cities, but the deeper reality is one of multiple connections.

This connectedness will dominate the lives of our children and grandchildren. The connections spreading around us are only a foretaste of what is to come. Even today, more than a century after its invention, less than half of the world's population has access to a telephone and little more than one per cent of all households use the Internet. Soon, the combination of a rapid rise in the world's population, continuing advances in technology and sharply falling communication costs, will make the world a far more interconnected place than it is today.

In this book I ask a simple question: are the achievements of freedom and the growth of interdependence compatible, or are we doomed to a classical tragedy in which our love of freedom destroys our capacity to be interdependent?

The optimistic answer sees freedom and interdependence as like twins, or like two organisms coevolving in tandem rather than in tension. It emphasises just how closely freedom and interdependence have been linked in the formation of the modern world. It argues that freedom to trade and travel makes people aware of their common interests, that it locks them into benign bonds that help them respect differences, and that abjure the use of force. The optimists point also to the explosion of new knowledge coming from science: the rise of new fields like microrobotics and nanotechnology, the rapid advances in older fields like biotechnology and neuroscience, as more scientific work is done each year than in the five centuries preceding this one. Technologies, they promise, can solve the problems of the environment, guarantee secure supplies of water and food, and help us to learn how to live together.

But the optimistic accounts, which remain the conventional wisdom across most of the Western world, and certainly amongst its more prosperous elites, skate over the profound tension between freedom and interdependence. To be meaningful, freedom entails being able to leave the family or the community, to act against its interests. Freedom has to mean the chance to behave in antisocial ways, and that naturally brings with it tensions of a kind that are felt in every home, every relationship, every firm, every association. Everyone knows from their own experience that within any relationship we feel both the desire to opt out and the pull of habit and duty, the temptation to follow our own desires and the knowledge that our own well-being depends on the well-being of others.

This tension is inherent in every area of life. But there are special reasons why it is coming to a head now, at the turn of the millennium. One is the difficulty of adapting to a more fragile global ecology without major changes in industrial and personal lifestyles involving sacrifices, particularly by the prosperous nations that have become most accustomed to their liberties and luxuries. Another is that new communications technologies like the Internet thin our sense of obligation to others, enabling us to hide behind pseudonyms, or surround ourselves with more fleeting transactions that demand less in terms of understanding and intimacy.

In politics the tension is rising because one of the most common reactions to a more connected world is retreat into the simpler, bounded identities of fundamentalist religion and nationalist politics, and into ideologies that deny the claim that interdependence brings any new obligations in its wake. In business the tension is rising because as firms become more powerful they seem ever less willing to accept the responsibilities that come with that power, concentrating instead on serving their shareholders and maximising their short-term profits to the exclusion of any other goals. In our culture, attachment to the value of autonomy is developing faster than any matching cultures of interdependence which would demand new habits of self-restraint.

The clearest sign of all of the heightening tension between freedom and interdependence is that in much of the world today the most pressing problems on the public agenda are not poverty or material shortage (although these remain acute for large minorities even in the richest countries), but rather the disorders of freedom: the troubles that result directly from having too many freedoms that are abused rather than constructively used. There are simple examples of this, like the fact that people with sufficient spending power tend to overeat, to eat too much salt, fat and sugar and to use drugs, whether alcohol, barbiturates or opiates, in ways that fail to make them happy. Freedom of choice all too often ends with compulsive and self-destructive behaviour.

But these are just the simplest cases. Others, like personal relationships, are more complex. For many, particularly women, the right to break away from an unhappy marriage was a great advance, but freedom in family life leaves huge costs in its wake. Today, in the UK and the USA, nearly half of all marriages end in divorce. Millions of children suffer from the deficit of parental attention that tends to result if parents value their own careers and pleasures more than their responsibilities to their children. Much the same could be said of the relationship between employers and employees. There never has been a golden age of mutual trust and loyalty, but

5

in a fluid and open global market the pressures seem to make employers more casual in their treatment of their staff and employees less willing to make any commitments back: both see their relationship as short-term and instrumental.

Then there are the direct costs of an excessively individual-istic society. It costs more if everyone travels in a private car and is willing to spend long spells in traffic jams; more if everyone wishes to live alone, or to live in a house large enough to accommodate the children of a previous marriage at weekends; more if people have to protect themselves against actions of others which in another society might be prevented by mutual moral suasion. In each of these cases, we are paying the costs that arise from the advance of a narrow and stunted idea of freedom.

Such problems remind us that societies rest on more than freedom. They also depend on order. By 'order' I do not mean primarily the physical power of armies and police forces, although without these we can rarely sleep safely at night. I mean something more pervasive: the presence of things we can rely on, frameworks within which life can be lived, like the rules that preserve safe streets and independent media, and that guarantee against poverty in old age.

Today it is hard to focus honestly on the question of order. Our attitudes have been so shaped by the centuries-long battles to win freedoms from kings and the church, and to liberate the powerless from oppressive orders, that it is hard to acknowledge that what was once the solution may now have become the problem. We have grown so used to strug-gling against authority that it is not easy to acknowledge that any institutions – whether they are firms or families, sports teams or nations – need some basis of authority if they are not always to take the line of least resistance, but rather to act for the long-term.

Coming to terms with this is particularly hard for liberal-ism, which has become the world's dominant ideology at the very moment when its standard formulations are no longer adequate to the world it has helped to bring about. John Stuart Mill declared that only harm to others justifies the restraint of freedom. This has never been an easy idea to turn into practice, since it begs the questions of what counts as harm, and who is to decide what counts as harm. But in an age when decisions are so much more intimately inter-connected, it becomes virtually useless as a guide for action. Liberal ideas provide a defence against bullying and power, but in practice freedoms rest on order as much as on individual liberties.

For people brought up in a liberal culture the question of order inevitably appears to look backward: it is about returning to a traditional hierarchy in which everyone knew their place. But the question really looks forward: it is about how to create the conditions for a fuller freedom, in radically new conditions, how to achieve what the Japanese call *kakumei*, the renewing of rules and order.

It matters whether or not our society produces orders, because without them we stand to lose many things, like the sense of continuity with the past, or the cultivation of everyday moral habits and trustworthiness that make life so much easier. Those regions of the world where order is decomposing – like parts of West Africa and Central Asia, and many urban neighbourhoods across the Western world – are prone to levels of violence, hunger and fear that make any sort of life a perpetual struggle. But these are just the extreme examples. Everywhere, psychological stability and fulfilment depend on the existence of a reliable social order. If the world around us is disordered, we have to devote more psychic energy to coping with it, and are left with less to devote to our own goals.

Not that order is always a good thing. Schopenhauer put the reasons well in his famous parable likening human society to a community of porcupines. In the winter, he wrote, they huddled together to keep warm, but the closer they came to each other the more they pricked each other with their quills. The porcupines then drew apart until they could find an appropriate balance between warmth and pain. The point is a simple one. We need the warmth of human connectedness, but the warmth often comes with the pains of intimacies and emotions, and of being trapped in unhappy situations, and that is why we need a balance between individuality and commonality, what pulls us apart and what brings us together. Any discussion of order needs to respect that balance. No one wants a world so ordered that there is no room to breathe, create, or differ. History has already provided enough examples of orders that destroyed the human spirit, orders that George Orwell summed up with his image of a boot stamping on a human face for ever.

But with some important exceptions this is not our primary threat today. The problems that most trouble electorates and that most tax the abilities of governments – problems that range from crime to unemployment, family breakdown to ill-health, political distrust to lack of care for the elderly – all stem more from a narrowly defined freedom than from its absence.

How should we think about solving these problems, and how could we bring freedom and interdependence into harmony? To understand the world and act on it, we need workable concepts. Alchemists cannot mend nuclear power stations and astrologers cannot guide rockets to the moon. Today's attempts to steer the world are being systematically skewed by the use of outdated concepts that dominate economic and political thought – ideas that made sense and contributed to progress in an earlier period but have now become barriers.

Nearly all of these concepts share two common features: they define social units in terms of their separateness rather than their connections, and they think in terms of untrammelled powers and sovereignty. So, for example, ideas based on nationalism, national sovereignty or exclusive identities of religion or ethnicity all divide the world between us and them. From the legitimate view that we need to belong to, and take pride in, larger entities, they draw the illegitimate conclusion that one identity can demand an exclusive attachment. In this way an idea that suited an age of clear-cut territorial boundaries is transposed into an environment in which it no longer makes sense.

The same weakness infuses liberal politics which imagines

the individual as a self-sufficient entity, not formed by society, and owing nothing to it, but rather heroic in his or her isolation, and defined by a series of claims that can be made on society. This is the flaw, too, of orthodox economics which is founded on the sovereignty of the individual as consumer, and the firm as trader – again, treating the separate boxes as primary. Business often mirrors this delusion. Many of the manuals of business ethics, for example, assume that the responsibilities of the business extend no further than the integrity of its own transactions.

Taken at face value, such ideas point to the sort of pathological individualism that David Hume once summed up by his chilling comment that it is rational 'to prefer the destruction of the world to the scratching of my finger'.

None of these concepts belongs to a world of interconnectedness. Because they treat the outside world as residual, they have no clear sense of limits. Because they pretend that it is possible for the individual, or the nation to exercise an unbounded sovereignty, they inevitably lead to failure, disillusion and damage. Their advocates remain articulate and vocal, but in important respects they have become prisoners of the past.

The result is an odd symmetry between the personal and the institutional world. Very few institutions today act with full competence, by which I mean being both fully aware of the world around them and fully able to act in response to its opportunities and threats. Instead most sense themselves to be inadequate and prone to underachievement. No governments now stand as unambiguous models for others to copy, and the companies that are praised as models one year all too often stumble the next. The big institutions that appear allpowerful from the outside look out on to a world that is hard to comprehend and that appears to be changing at a bewildering speed. Individuals too, perhaps more than ever, behave as if incompetent to perform the tasks they face. If in the past the roles of being a parent, a citizen or an employee were relatively predictable, today they entail much more choice, and much more negotiation of a mass of conflicting information and values. How to be in a relationship, or carry out a job, how to manage others, care for children or be a good friend: all of these are difficult challenges and on each there is now a mountain of advice, much of it contradictory. Together these contribute to the sense of being 'in over our heads', unable to match our capacities and our tasks, in a world where no one is quite in control.

The personal and institutional dimensions of the inadequacy of the present social order reinforce each other. The failure of the social order amplifies our sense of impotence, and many people's behaviour in reaction, seeking solace in drink or drugs, or cutting themselves off from public life, leaves governments feeling powerless and unloved.

What should be the responses? For many individuals the simplest one is to turn inwards, to focus on an insulated sphere of intimate life, and block out the complications. 'Cultivating your garden', both literally and metaphorically, is one way of coping with a climate change over which you have no power. The same is true of anyone who digs deeply into a particular interest: a profession, a discipline, an art form, or simply having fun. For many institutions too there is a similar response: faced with complexity it is easier to focus on a simple mission, or a few measurable outputs and to disregard everything else. Businesses certainly find it easier to focus ruthlessly on the bottom line when times are tough. These responses make sense, literally. But added together they exacerbate the problems of a world that is failing to produce sufficient order. The same is true of another common response, fatalism: if your world is uncertain and subject to distant forces, then it may be almost rational not to prepare for the future, not to save money or master knowledge that may anyway soon be obsolete. But while fatalism might make sense for the individual, it becomes a sort of madness if aggregated to the level of a whole society.

During the course of this book I make the case for a very different response to a more connected, and fast-changing world. Our primary responsibility today is to find ways to live with interdependence, not to deny it. For governments, that means a sharp change of direction. In a world where governments no longer exercise much direct sovereignty either over their defences or over their economies, the best service they can perform for their citizens is to help them to be stronger, more responsible, more capable of making decisions and understanding the world in which they live. Narrowly this means providing them with skills to make them employable: the habits of being disciplined and flexible, creative and adaptive, able to speak many languages and work with many different technologies. More broadly it means helping them to look after themselves and to care for others, cultivating life skills and emotional intelligence rather than just the analytical intelligence that older educational systems valued so highly. But there is also a moral dimension, in that a more connected world brings with it a moral duty to consider the effects we have on others, and a need for moral fluency that goes beyond simply learning codes of right and wrong by rote. For moral as well as practical reasons we even have to think in a different way, understanding the world as made up of complex systems rather than linear relationships, ecologies rather than machines.

To the extent that we can change mentalities in these ways some of the tensions between freedom and interdependence can be contained. After all, free parents automatically try to do the best for their children. Good neighbours naturally do what they can to help their community, and for most people maturity involves learning that true freedom involves us in a web of mutual obligations. But the Western tradition has lost its sense of the balance between part and whole. It has focused solely on the interests and sovereignty of individuals, standing apart and above the systems in which they live, and for men in particular it has fostered a myth of robust separateness. By contrast, a more realistic ideal of strength would define it not so much in terms of self-sufficiency, but rather in terms of the capacity to internalise interdependence, and to cultivate fulfilling relationships based on commitment. A more useful ideal of freedom would tie it to the achievement of well-being and shared goals, rather than the absence of restraints.

Societies are better placed to cultivate mentalities than modern liberalism admits. But the focus on mentalities, however, only takes us so far. Only saints and geniuses can fully internalise the state of the world, and, as the English philosopher Henry Sidgwick put it, take the point of view of the universe. The prevalence of empowered and responsible individuals is a necessary but not a sufficient condition for squaring freedom with interdependence in an environment made up of many connections. The corollary of the imperative to take care of mentalities is that we need to reshape our institutions and systems to better fit a connected world, not because they can create love or virtue, but rather because they can make the climate warm or cold.

A first step is to question institutions not just about their efficiency and accountability but also about their external effects. Do firms, for example, make their employees better able to function as parents or citizens or do they leave them exhausted and paranoid? Do schools help children to make judgements and decisions or only to pass exams? Do welfare systems produce confident outward-going people, or dependants who are passive and depressed? Do rituals, like marriage vows, treat women as submissive subordinates or give new meaning to reciprocal obligations? Such questions take us to the fine grain of social connections and the mentalities they foster. We know for example that the best predictor of antisocial and criminal behaviour is a lack of healthy bonds within families and social institutions. We know that the quality of secure attachments, from early childhood onwards, is critical in providing the capacity to play a full and generous role in the life of a community. We know that children find it easier to act morally if they receive consistent messages from families, schools and the media.

Translating this knowledge into practical policies is rarely easy. States have often lost the authority to shape cultures and mentalities. If they lack integrity themselves then they are in no position to place moral demands on others. Nor are the methods available for shaping cultures and behaviour simple. Although there are many examples of successes – like the campaigns against drunk driving or unsafe sex, or the programmes that inculcated democratic values in post-war Germany or post-1989 Eastern Europe – there are also plenty of examples of failure. Some of the attempts by well-meaning professionals to intervene in family life have been disastrous. But there is much that governments can do to make it easier for people to act as responsible citizens. Governments that keep the streets safe, that guarantee a baseline of economic security and that preserve personal privacy are more likely to encourage generous behaviour than those that do not. Governments that act early to prevent social exclusion through crime and unemployment, and that enforce laws that are seen to be fair, make it much more likely that people will be committed and engaged in the lives of their community than ones that are corrupt, short-sighted and mean spirited. Governments that make it easier for their citizens to save for themselves, to help their children to learn, to recycle their household waste, or to act as volunteers and mentors, inevitably shape the feel, the psychology of their society for the better.

Anyone who doubts the importance of cultivating mentalities should take note of the failure of both of the twentieth century's dominant political systems to grasp the point. It is a great paradox that both communism and capitalism have corroded the mentalities on which they depend. Communism needs people to be generous, altruistic, honest and virtuous but instead makes them suspicious, secretive, selfish, more inclined to hoard than to share. Capitalism needs people who are willing to work hard for the sake of it, who will bring up children without material reward, who will respect others and trade honestly. Yet instead capitalism all too often makes people instrumental, selfish, short-sighted, hedonistic, and so undermines the very qualities it needs in order to thrive.[1]

The advocates of the virtues of the free market and the planned society tend to take mental frameworks for granted. But unless someone – whether governments or civic organisations, religions or parents – can cultivate the mentalities needed for a system to function, it will atrophy into mutual distrust.

During the course of this book I make the case for a simple, but powerful idea, that underpins both the culture and the institutions of a connected world. Reciprocity, the idea of give and take, of the golden mean, is the most important idea for a developed democratic society, and it should underpin our social morality. It is an idea that goes with the grain of more educated, assertive societies that are less tied to tradition and deference. It is an idea that makes it possible to draw on the commitment, sense of membership and intimacy that clubs can offer in areas as diverse as health, learning, and savings, in place of the impersonality of the state and the mass market.

For governments, the principle of reciprocity demands a different way of governing. Instead of depending on blueprints and plans, and top-down command and control, more complex and highly educated societies work best when leaders provide a framework of predictability, but leave space for people to organise themselves in flatter, more reciprocal structures. Instead of edicts and commands, governments need to learn how to use new tools, like covenants and citizen contracts, bidding mechanisms that encourage partnerships, disaggregated tax systems that make a more direct link between taxes and the services they finance, and programmes aimed at achieving cultural change rather than social engineering. Beyond the state, since many of the older institutions which used to help societies to cohere, like churches, large firms and trade unions, are in decline, our challenge is to develop new forms of connection, and new shared institutions that draw on our innate sociability and our instinctive dispositions to act ethically. In business, for example, we need to encourage models of organisation that reconnect ownership and responsibility. Contemporary capitalism all too often detaches businesses from having to consider the ultimate consequences of their decisions. Means have become divorced from ends. Capital markets separate owners from any knowledge or responsibility for the uses made of their capital; buyers are detached from any awareness of where products come from; currency traders gamble with other people's money without any personal responsibility for their actions. The principle of reciprocity, by contrast, demands that wherever possible we should reconnect responsibility and power, means and ends, and restore business to its place within society rather than apart from it.

What does all of this imply for politics? There can be no doubting the continuing importance of politics since it is through politics that laws are made, that common moralities are upheld, that typically half of all wealth is spent, and that patronage and largesse are given to everything from inventions to charities. It is through politics that the benefits of capitalism, of technology and knowledge, have been widely distributed and if you look around the world, the presence of stable and effective government is a much better predictor of prosperity than the presence of natural resources, skills, the strength of the family or even the presence of an entrepreneurial culture.

The problem, however, is that politics is held in lower esteem than it has been for a very long time. Most of the world's population is now governed by states that call themselves democracies, and that have adopted the principles of equality, liberty and the rule of law. Politics stands at the top of societies where previously there might have been dictators, monarchs or religious leaders. Yet for all that there is remarkably little confidence in politics, particularly in the countries that have been democracies for longest. Politics looks bypassed by the powers of a global economy, communications systems, and science. It seems locked into heavy-handed, bureaucratic forms of government, and where once it seemed the best means of asserting human freedom from nature, today politics just as often feels like a force of nature weighing down on the individual. Its mechanisms – the parliaments, parties, manifestos and professional politicians – hark back to an earlier time and define themselves by concepts that have become, as Ivan Illich put it, 'plastic words' drained of meaning.

However, these are not good reasons for dancing on the grave of politics, but rather for thinking much harder about how to revive it as the least worst means we have for making collective decisions. In societies made up of well-informed and confident citizens, politics can no longer be organised with the tools that suited a more deferential, hierarchical age. Today, with ubiquitous and instant communications, there is no longer such a need to rely on full-time representatives, meeting in permanent parliaments in capital cities. Instead, democracy can become more of a permanent conversation, using a plethora of new tools such as deliberative forums, advisory 'juries' of citizens, and chambers chosen by lot, as well as technologies that allow for much more intensive communication between decision-makers and those on the receiving end of decisions. Tools of this kind tackle head-on the tendency of existing forms of politics to encourage infantilism – where leaders retain a monopoly of power and knowledge, leaving citizens simultaneously dependent and resentful. The most effective solutions make politics more reciprocal, turning it into a continuing dialogue of discussion, explanation and decision, drawing on the distributed intelligence of the society, rather than depending solely on an elite.

Fortunately the principle of reciprocity is in tune with much of what is happening across the world. A more connected culture does indeed become more attuned to difference, more at ease with discussion, more open. Even in international affairs, which might be expected to be the last redoubt of secretive, hard forms of power, the most successful orders are turning out to be those based on mutual transparency, trust-building and common responsibility, rather than might. In the economy, the harbingers of the future are those businesses that combine a clear ethos with multiple reciprocal connections, and that share ownership amongst the employees who are the true source of their value.

The life of man, according to Thomas Hobbes, was solitary before it became nasty, brutish and short. Today it is anything but solitary. We will soon share the planet with as many as ten billion others as the world's population grows faster than ever before. Our lives are tied up with others, and the cumulation of events such as the accidents at Chernobyl, two world wars, and the simultaneous experience of moments like the first moon landing has reinforced the fact. Within a lifetime or two, if the technological futurists are to be believed, there may even be direct connections between people's minds, transcending the idea of separate selves and suojects.

At the moment, some of the features of connexity may appear to be relevant only for a privileged minority, and it is true that the thickest connections are experienced only by about a billion people, in North America and Europe, Japan and the tiger economies of East Asia, and in the middle classes of China, India and Latin America. For the rest, more basic needs remain paramount. But even the poorest people on earth share the same climate as the richest and, looking ahead, few are likely to remain insulated long from the pace of change in technology and culture. In any event, it will be in the poorer areas of the world that an already densely packed planet is set to double its population during the course of the next century.

This new reality defines the greatest political and ethical challenge of our times. The facts of connexity do not automatically make people more tolerant, responsible, or understanding, but they do constitute a new environment that demands a creative response. This book can only offer a few suggestions about what that response might be. But the central argument is straightforward. Just as in our own lives we hope to make the transition from dependence on family, through independence in our teens and twenties, to chosen interdependence with partners, children and friends, so do societies go through a similar transition. Traditional agrarian societies have some of the properties of childhood, in that they place people in dependence on authorities, both temporal and spiritual. Modern societies are the equivalent of adolescence, since they value above everything else the freedom to make yourself, to escape and to satisfy your desires. The emerging societies that take stock of connexity, by contrast, are becoming adult through accepting that they live in a web of mutual interdependence. From the differentiation that has marked the great flowering of freedom and creativity, they are evolving towards a higher integration.

What is the alternative? The tragedy would be if our fixation on a narrow idea of freedom blinded us to how freedom could develop into something more. Then, as in the classical tragedies, our finest qualities really would bring about our downfall. Fortunately, unlike the Greeks, we no longer believe in destiny. Life is too indeterminate for that, and we are still able to make our own history rather than being condemned to become its victims.

I

THE AGE OF CONNEXITY

FOR PEOPLE LIVING in the eighteenth century, Robinson Crusoe was a fascinating figure. He could live alone untouched by the outside world. On his desert island he was sovereign. He symbolised the idea that while man had been born free, in the industrialising states of Europe he was now in chains.

Today there are few if any Crusoes. There may be a handful of remote uninhabited desert islands, a few regions without a satellite dish, and large expanses of the Antarctic and Siberia untrodden by humans, but to find terra incognita, or rather terra incommunicado, you must now go to another planet, or to the bottom of the ocean, and even there you will probably find exploration, mining, or imaging robots beaming signals back to their bases. For the vast majority of people, the basic fact of the modern world is that it is connected. Nowhere is remote in the way that so many places were remote a century, or even a generation, ago.

The simplest dimension of this connectedness is communication: today nearly a billion homes can talk to each other within a few seconds. Global positioning technologies can precisely track positions anywhere on the surface of the planet. Mobile phones can be carried up cliffs and into deserts. But there are other vital dimensions: global climate change, the decay of the ozone layer and the pollution of the oceans all bring the world's peoples closer together, if only because decisions made in one place shape other places. The result is an odd and novel situation. Remoteness and isolation

19

were once the condition of the poor. Today it is only the super rich who can easily escape other people, and even they depend on armies of assistants to protect their privacy.

This degree of connectedness was not planned. No one had a blueprint for shrinking the world. The merchant adventurers and pirates, railway barons and shipping magnates who pulled it together were motivated by profit and glory, not by visions of a global village. Few of the technologists who designed the machines that have connected the world had any clear idea of what they were creating. When Alexander Graham Bell invented the telephone he thought it would be used for piping music from concert halls into homes. When Marconi invented the radio he saw it as a way of sending messages from ships to shore. Many of the early pioneers of the computer found it hard to imagine the world needing more than a handful, and as recently as the late 1970s the chairman of one leading computer company could see no reason why anyone would want one in their home. Very few of the designers and engineers of new technologies have been good at predicting the needs their inventions would meet. There is something protean about communications technologies which attaches them to previous unseen needs, like the demand for communication from housebound women in New England in the 1890s or Japan in the 1980s, or the hunger for communicating about sex that was revealed by France's Minitel, and later by the Internet.

There have been several milestones along the way. Looking back we can point not just to the first telegraph, telephone, or communications satellite, but also more recently to the invention in 1974 of the TCP/IP interconnection protocol that allowed networks to be connected and enabled the Internet to get off the ground. Looking forward, the great milestones may include the full integration of television into the Internet, so that it ceases to be a one-way medium, and, further ahead, the implant of a serial port for plugging a computer or network into the human brain itself.

The cumulative effect of these changes has been a drastic recasting of the landscape, both social and mental. For most of human history the world was an archipelago. It consisted of millions of islands – villages, families, homesteads, wandering bands. Occasionally the people living in them would meet others, but most of their lives were spent looking inwards, with their energies devoted to their own daily necessities, such as finding food, looking after the children, or protecting against predators. Their compartments were their universe, and only rarely would some larger unit, like a kingdom or a church, make demands on them. The same was true of the economy. Small numbers of traders linked the great cities but most economic life was local, face to face and small in scale.

Today the world is more like a cacophonous city. Continents are crisscrossed with roads and railways, airports and distribution centres. Telephones, computers, faxes, television sets, mobile devices, even electronic tags on consumer goods, jewellery or clothing, can all be connected together, so that the world sometimes seems like the marketplace of a medieval city, a buzz of messages, letters, newspapers, complaints and requests, small advertisements and bombastic slogans.

Within this city, things are more visible, or at least visible in a new way. In villages there are few secrets, but the scope of public knowledge is very narrow. Today we can find out about the sex lives of political leaders, or the peccadilloes of tycoons. Distant wars can be watched in real time on television. Satellites can observe troop movements and, even now, can almost make out individual faces from thousands of miles above the earth. Few state secrets remain secret for very long, and we may now be entering an era when much more personal information is widely available over networks and on smart cards and when, however painful this may be, it will be beyond the capacity of most individuals and organisations to control who knows what about them.

Just as personal lives become more porous, so do cultures. Every culture today is mongrel, impure. Images – like the Coca-Cola logo – are recognised by a majority of the world's population, as are the world's leading stars of film and music. Items as diverse as jeans, chopsticks, curry, karaoke machines, footballs, cocaine and business suits have gone global. The popular culture produced in the 1920s and 1930s by East European migrants in Hollywood, and by the fusion of black American music with English, Scottish and Irish music in Memphis in the 1950s, and Liverpool and London in the 1960s, has probably done more than anything to unify the world, and in the next decade there will be roughly two billion teenagers taking part in a global culture of fast food and songs, clothes and symbols that they will not share with their parents. Much that was different is becoming standardised, but at the same time connexity makes it easier for bits of culture to be combined, hybridised and transformed so that no one can be quite sure what is authentic and what is not, or where an idea, a tune, a turn of phrase was born.

The porousness of societies has made us used to odd juxtapositions. The most advanced medicines, for example, depend on plants from remote rain forests (like the rosy periwinkle of Madagascar which produces the drugs with the best known treatment for leukaemia). The richest streets in the world in Manhattan lie only a few miles away from Harlem where life expectancy is lower than Bangladesh. It used to take weeks to travel from a hot climate to a cold one, or from one time zone to another, but now it takes only a few hours. Within big cities, the most advanced businesses stand next door to people living in conditions little advanced from a century ago, hi-tech smart homes only a few minutes' walk away from shanty towns. In most wealthy countries distinct cultures coexist in ways unimaginable a century ago, mainly because of migration by so many people from the former colonies. Elsewhere, over many decades, we have grown accustomed to stories of primitive forest peoples coming into contact with everything from pop music to communist propaganda (the French historian Fernand Braudel tells how even though the tribal peoples of North Borneo could not understand the words the Maoist propagandists directed at them, they nevertheless changed their music in response to the rhythms). We take for granted the juxtaposition of the jet plane on the tarmac with a stone age tribe beyond the fence, the global firm within the barrio, the traditional singer with the digital recording studio. Guerrillas wear Western fashion T-shirts. Militia-men proclaim traditional values over the World Wide Web. In Chechnya, the armed resistance who were caricatured as backward bandits used mobile phones to get the better of the Russian army. In Mexico, the Chiapas guerrillas used the Internet to mobilise support against their government.

Connectedness makes it possible to bypass things, to 'disintermediate' or cut out the intermediaries. The guerrillas can bypass their own government and speak direct to the world's media. Businesses can raise capital directly from capital markets rather than depending on local banks. Sellers of insurance, music or software can reach their clients without going through local branches. The schoolchild can access databases without the help of their teacher. Even religious hierarchies can be bypassed. So, for example, when a milk-drinking Ganesh was seen in Delhi on a Thursday in September 1995, it was reported worldwide the next day, and replicated in many other temples across the world the day after, in what one newspaper called 'the first example of global religious fervour propagated by mass telecommunications'.

Each of these examples shows that we now need a different map of the world from the old ones that coloured in landmasses according to their political masters. Today the links matter as much as the territory, and our maps should show the volume of trade, of messages, or of movements of people. We need maps that can measure the ease of communication or travel in terms of how long it takes to send a message or to move a thing between two given points – giving us a map of the world made up of isomorphic lines, rapidly coming closer together over time, until most parts of the world are within twenty-four hours of each other in physical movement, and a few microseconds in terms of the movement of information.

The principal effect of all of these changes is simple. Behaviours that were once of no concern to other people are now everyone's business. 'No man is an island' is no longer a moral comment but a statement of fact. Nuclear weapons first made this evident, when it was realised that a decision taken in

Washington or Moscow could spell not just the devastation of their own countries (wars have often done that) but an end to civilisation as a whole, perhaps even to any advanced form of life. The Chernobyl disaster brought the same point home to a new generation in the 1980s, as reindeer in Lapland and sheep in Wales were poisoned by radiation let loose by human error in the Ukraine. At the end of that decade, the mounting evidence of global warming and the appearance of a hole in the ozone layer proved that the behaviour of a relatively small proportion of the world's population could change nature, not just locally but as a whole. Chiming in with the times, the development of the Gaia hypothesis by James Lovelock and Lynn Margulis offered a theoretical framework for thinking about the biosphere as a single living entity, and one that would long outlive humanity.

Sometimes it seems as if this is all new. But the rise of connections has not been sudden. In earlier periods, too, very distant peoples were bound together, albeit by more delicate and tenuous threads. The great religions brought large swathes of the world into contact, sometimes with extraordinary speed. Islam took only a century to spread from Mecca to Spain, Buddhism a few centuries from India to China. The great civilisations of Rome, Persia and China connected vast interiors with roads, messengers, shared rules and languages. As far back as the fourth century BC, records show, to take just one example, merchants from Carthage in North Africa, Massilia (now Marseille) in France and Elea in southern Italy combining to import perfumes and oils from Africa and Arabia into Alexandria, in an early form of multinational enterprise. Nevertheless, it is only in the last few hundred years that the majority of the world's people have been pulled into a single orbit. Each of these earlier systems was broadly self-contained. While the occasional trader came from China to Europe, and every empire fought wars on its edges, each major power could be mapped as a series of concentric circles around the centres of power, with the more distant areas scarcely controlled at all.

It is only now that it has become meaningful for the first time to talk of a single world system rather than a series of separate ones. It is only this century that technologies have made real-time communication possible by undersea cables, radio and satellites. And whereas past civilisations often wreaked environmental havoc on their own land – for example, the overcultivation of arable land by the Anasazi in the southern United States and by the first inhabitants of what may be the world's oldest city, Uruk, in present-day Iraq – until this century it was impossible for a civilisation in one part of the world to influence the climate of another. We are now in a novel situation. The speed and scale of the changes underway make history an imperfect guide. No one knows what possibilities and risks are being generated.

In any case, we are still in the early days. It is more than a century and a half since the invention of the telegraph, a century since the invention of the telephone and half a century since the invention of the computer, yet by most criteria their influence remains partial, even immature. We are still at a point when the users of the Internet are equivalent to the drivers of the Model T Ford, enthusiasts who are willing to lie on their backs fixing the engine, while the great majority wait for the technology to become easier to use, seamless and trouble-free.

The history of technologies shows that it usually takes at least fifty to sixty years for them to diffuse fully throughout a society and economy. Some of the barriers are technical, but more often their most important uses have to wait for organisational and social innovations. The full use of the internal combustion engine, for example, depended on new ways of planning cities, with suburbs and supermarkets, heavy investment in autobahns and highways. The full use of electricity depended on new models of dispersed production, and the willingness to let women use labour-saving devices in the home so as to be free to work outside. In their first few decades these new technologies did little to boost productivity because

25

people used them in traditional ways: for example, factories, which had been built compactly on many floors to take advantage of steam power in their basements, were only belatedly replaced by sprawling horizontal structures when electric engines became the norm.

Even if the pace of change has speeded up, information and communication technologies may be at most halfway through the same cycle, and they too are only just beginning to make much impression on productivity. Few machines can communicate with each other. Few make it easy for people to communicate with them: the formal text systems of e-mail for example are much harder to use than the telephone. It is still not possible to use networks to access the information we really need, such as whether we are about to be sacked, or whether our partner is on the point of walking out, although access to financial indicators and low-cost surveillance technologies might help (with all of the disorientating effects that cheap bugs and cameras would bring in their wake). Yet it is only a matter of time before the technical barriers are overcome. Digitisation is making it easier to carry the same signals through different mediums and to interconnect different networks. Radio technologies mean that all communications can become mobile, and personalised (so that before long we will be given a communications number at birth). Smart interfaces are enabling technologies to mimic human interaction, with a 'high touch' character using voice operation and handwriting rather than keyboards. Virtual reality is achieving levels of sophistication that may indeed make it a substitute for viewing a building, learning surgical techniques, going to the shops, or investigating a holiday. Soon all of the functions that have the prefix 'tele' attached to them look set to come to maturity: shopping, voting, work, design, insurance, diagnosis, learning.

The harder barriers to overcome, however, are the social ones. As with the car and electricity, social and cultural barriers can be much more obstinate, and it is not surprising that people react defensively when their livelihoods are threatened. Communications technologies have the potential to revolutionise almost every area of human life – but to do so means unsettling the wealth and prestige of powerful professions and organisations. So, for example, the idea of turning the teacher into a counsellor, a helper at the gateway to technologies rather than a transmitter of knowledge, is seen as a threat by most teachers, just as the prospect of giving nurses access to smart diagnostic systems is seen as a threat by most doctors. Business leaders are naturally threatened when their most junior staff are more competent with technologies than they are, politicians naturally fear the instant demands of interactive technologies, and husbands and wives have good reason to fear the ease with which their partners can find out from their bills whom they called, where they ate, what they bought. Few are entirely at ease with the idea of a world where the physical aspect of city life disappears into the background as time is spent instead communicating through terminals and mobile devices, a world where there are only virtual congregations and asynchronous activities.

The fact that even now services as various as designing a car or watching a security camera can be performed on a screen or other terminal from anywhere is bound to be threatening to people who are less confident and less able to market themselves. Local services have already been squeezed by the rise of call centres that manage reservations for hotels or aeroplanes in ways that make their site invisible to the user (British Airways, for instance, organises reservations through Bombay, the Best Western hotels through the Arizona Women's Penitentiary). And it is only natural that the older ways of organising things resist the new, putting up protections and barriers.

Looking ahead, however, just as the car has had to make an accommodation with the train, the pedestrian and the bicycle, so will communications technologies that appear to cause the death of distance have to make an accommodation with physical proximity. Many of the things we need to live are still very material, and still very much dependent on geography. Daily life rests on the provision of water, clean air and food, of schools to teach children and neighbours to look out for them, parks to walk in and streets to feel safe in. Perhaps more surprisingly, the production of high-value-added activities, such as design, software and culture, depends more than ever on local roots, or rather what economists call 'agglomeration economies', the benefit of being close to others doing the same thing, so that in places like the City of London, Silicon Valley and Hollywood astronomical rents are paid for the privilege of taking part in a community of gossip and interpersonal networks.

In fact history tells us that it is misleading to see physical travel and virtual connectedness as alternatives. Throughout the twentieth century physical mobility and communications grew in tandem rather than as substitutes. The spread of the telephone accompanied that of commuter railways and trams, the radio accompanied the spread of cars and aeroplanes, the television that of motorways and jets, and everywhere the graphs of traffic movement move in parallel with the graphs of communication usage. In the same way, and contrary to common sense, the consumption of electronic culture often generates demand for the real thing: as the UK's Open University discovered, the experience of distance learning increased demand for face-to-face learning, just as the market for rock records boosted the market for rock concerts, and the growth of video-conferencing ironically boosted the market for hotel conference centres. Connexity tends to be cumulative. Each new medium of communication does not displace its predecessors so much as complement them.

The connectedness of the world can be understood through the physical character of the technologies and flows. But it can also be understood as a state of mind, the mentality of the cosmopolitan, the non-parochial and the global. Not all of its characteristics are attractive. When people have fewer repeated contacts with others they tend to behave in less ethical and less cooperative ways. When they have to come into contact with many different cultures they lose some of their capacity to spot dishonesty and deception, and therefore tend to trust less. When communication shifts ever further from face-to-face conversation towards text-based messages over electronic networks, one of the consequences is that people become less polite and less sensitive. There is more anger and indiscretion, more of the communicational equivalents of road rage.

But the mindsets of a connected world are also full of hope. There is good reason for believing that when people communicate they don't fight, that opportunities and horizons are expanding, along with tolerance, awareness and knowledge. Connexity is undoubtedly breaking down many of the barriers and separate identities that have been the main cause of human suffering and war, and nurturing a new, more open type of human being.

This optimism is not fanciful. A connected world defies the rules of zero sum games, where an advantage for someone else means a disadvantage for me. This is most apparent in economics. In an economy based on material objects everything is shaped by trade-offs. More of one thing means less of another. An economy based on information and knowledge behaves very differently. It may cost nothing to disseminate information: two people can use the same chemical formulae at the same time, but they cannot both drive the same car. Whereas material industrial processes tend to change in straight lines, informational ones often look exponential, with runaway changes that seem to feed themselves. The earliest example was the evolution of the human brain itself, which grew because of the cumulative adaptive advantage it conferred, an advantage that was different in nature from having bigger teeth or muscles. Something similar may be happening as economies move from the material to the immaterial. When economists tried to analyse the sources of growth in the 1950s they found that technological change accounted for 80 per cent of it. More recently the new growth theories developed by Paul Romer have shown more rigorously the primary role played by ideas and knowledge in driving economic growth. The implication is that scarcity is no longer as much of a consideration as it once was, and the most valuable resources may be very cheap (Korea's payments for intellectual property, for example, cost it only one-thousandth of gross domestic product during its period of fastest growth). Moreover, whereas in an economy based on material goods all resources are scarce and finite, the cost of reproducing immaterial things such as television programmes or software falls to zero, and the apparently firm link between costs and prices fades.[1] There are many other examples of this kind of positive, cumulative pattern. Trust tends to breed trust. Mutual understanding increases the more it is used. Love fosters love.

Some earlier thinkers had a sense of these immaterial properties when they argued that more connected systems would automatically have benign outcomes for humanity. Adam Smith and Bernard de Mandeville in the eighteenth century both suggested a link between a multitude of individual choices and a general interest. Divine providence ensured that the pursuit of self-interest would, through the connections of the market and the implicit actions of an invisible hand, contribute to the general good. Alexis de Tocqueville argued that the experience of freedom makes people better able to join together in common civic activities, and that this in turn makes them better able to exercise their freedoms. More recent theorists have suggested that free societies learn through their conflicts how better to resolve, to negotiate, to empathise with another's point of view. In other words the really strong, organic community develops not by suppressing differences to achieve consensus, but rather by acknowledging and resolving them.[2]

This positive sum character even applies to politics. Greater connexity tends to mean less oppression because states are now subject, albeit weakly and unevenly, to the moral force of world opinion over how they treat their citizens. Their citizens in turn can denounce them, or find outside help. These facts are cumulative: the habits of communication and negotiation, which underpin democracy, are hard to unlearn. Within societies too, the habits of association foster virtuous circles of self-organisation. Without them many of the simplest tasks become impossible: as Lech Walesa put it, making capitalism out of communism was like making a fish out of fish soup.

In each of these examples, our societies are beginning to behave in ways that run directly counter to the laws governing most natural ecologies. Instead of being characterised by equilibrium and limits, more and more of the systems we live with have runaway properties, in which changes feed on themselves rather than being cancelled out. The properties of this connected world can be summed up in three laws. The first was originally stated by Gordon Moore, co-founder of Intel, the dominant chip-making firm. He forecast that the number of transistors which could be built on the same size piece of silicon would double every eighteen months, and subsequently his 'law' has been generalised into the claim, borne out by experience, that the cost of computing power halves every eighteen months. A second law is attributed to Robert Metcalfe and states that the value of a network rises exponentially relative to the square of the numbers using it, because each new person connected to the network increases its value for everyone already on the network. The third we could call Kao's law, from John Kao, the Chinese-American business thinker, who made the less quantifiable claim that the power of creativity rises exponentially with the diversity and divergence of those connected into a network: in other words its capacity to innovate or create depends on dissonant and complementary ways of thinking, not on consensus.

Together, these three laws suggest some of the economic sources of the distinctive ethos and dynamics of connexity. There is the sheer speed of change, because costs can fall and capacities rise so much faster than in more materially based industries. There is the economic drive to maximise connections, and there is the value attributed to multiplicity, complementarity and difference: after all, who wants a relationship with someone who is exactly the same?

*

What about the quality of our connections? There is clearly little virtue in communicating with someone if the quality of the relationship is so low that you cannot know what to believe, or cannot rely on that person to provide help when it is needed. One of the constant criticisms of new communications technologies is that they make for more acquaintances but fewer friends, for more holiday romances and less true love, for superficial and ultimately unsatisfying relationships.

Psychology has cast light on this issue through its analysis of 'theories of mind'. These refer to the ability to grasp what someone else is thinking and feeling, and to believe in the reality of the other person's mental states. Our capacity to have beliefs about other people's beliefs, and beliefs about their beliefs about our beliefs, has been described as intensionality, while the different layers of understanding, the ability to understand other people's feelings and thoughts about us, amount to 'orders of intensionality'. Small children do not have this ability, in that they cannot imagine another person having thoughts and beliefs different from their own. Machines have the capacity to be aware of their environment, but lack the understanding of their own self which intensionality rests on, and they are very far from being able to imagine themselves into the thought-worlds of people.

There have been many attempts to map this basic feature of human sociability. The American philosopher Daniel Dennett designed a series of sentences that run up to eight orders of intensionality (A believes B about C who believes D about A and so on) which have been used by psychologists to test how far people are able to think in multidimensional ways.[3] Their first finding has been that this capacity appears to be learned. There is a critical moment around the age of four and a half when children discover that other people can have different beliefs from their own, and when they consciously learn to understand, and to influence, the beliefs of others. Amongst adults the capacity to understand appears to have a limit of four or five 'orders of intensionality': beyond that our minds lose the thread.[4]

What relevance does this have to connexity? Whenever we

communicate with someone else we make some assumptions about them: about their beliefs, their wants, their prejudices. A society in which people live good lives is likely to be one where there is high mutual understanding, where people automatically pick up signals and nuances, where they understand how another person relates to a third. In our own lives these are all the things that make us feel secure and happy, living amidst webs of subtle mutual understanding, and many of the strains of modern life arise because of deficient understanding, deficient communications and failures to empathise.

The great fear of connexity is that it replaces relationships based on high orders of intensionality with relationships based on low ones. Text-based systems miss out on the nine-tenths of any emotional message which is non-verbal. Economic exchange requires little understanding of the needs and cares of the other party. Anonymous messaging systems positively discourage real intimacy. Transient, mobile life-styles discourage deep understanding. Television encourages us to understand fictional neighbours better than real ones.

As we shall see, the story is rarely so simple: the telephone, for example, has dramatically increased the scope for mutual understanding, particularly amongst women. Connexity has brought far greater flows of information about private, intimate secrets, whether the love affairs of the powerful or the spending patterns of the average consumer. Some find this threatening, but others revel in a more honest and confessional culture that opens up to awareness emotions and resentments that are otherwise suppressed. The important point, however, is that connections and understanding do not automatically rise in tandem, because whereas connections can be multiplied by technology, understanding still depends on time and, longevity aside, time remains a painfully finite resource.

We could point to a hundred other effects of connexity, from music to fashions, knowledge of agricultural methods to weather forecasting, some of them enriching understanding, some arguably stunting it. But the key point is this: more than ever before, people are joined together, physically and mentally, in terms of their lives and their life chances, and what they say and do, as well as in terms of their destiny. This is the new fact that defines the challenges, and the hopes and fears, of our time more than anything else.

2

THE LOVE OF FREEDOM

THE CONNECTED WORLD has its own distinctive ideologies and dreams. Earlier eras dreamed of the kingdom of God, or of absolute equality, but the most compelling dream of an age of connexity is freedom. At Louis Armstrong's funeral Duke Ellington suggested one version of it. He commented that Armstrong 'was born poor, died rich, begat a great new form of art and hurt no one along the way'. It is a marvellous description of an ideal of human freedom, of starting from little and creating something, giving rather than taking. It sums up what freedom can mean today: mobility, creativity, and walking lightly. It was a suitable epitaph for one of the first figures to take advantage of a global system for distributing music by records and radio, who broke out of the oppression to which his birth seemed to condemn him.

Louis Armstrong's life, like those of so many of his contemporaries, showed how intimately connexity and freedom have been interwoven. Freedom allows new links and connections to be made. Ideas, trade and communication all thrive on a certain looseness, a lack of tight control, and they in turn promote a sensibility that values freedom. The same is true of technology. Those societies that have tried to rig the uses of technology have stunted them. Stalin blocked the plans for a Soviet phone system on the not unreasonable grounds that it would be used for counter-revolution, and only permitted it later under strict controls. The upper classes in England resisted the telephone on the very different grounds that it would disrupt protocols by allowing strangers to barge uninvited into homes or offices. But it was only when the restraints were lifted that technologies were able to thrive, to meet needs that the elites had scarcely imagined, and to liberate people from old rules.

Repeatedly over the last few hundred years, a circle has been set in motion whereby freedom has promoted connections, and connections have promoted freedom. In the case of jazz musicians, the abolition of slavery had made it possible to escape from the landlords of the South, the railway had opened the way to the bright lights of the city, and the self-confident culture that was hammered out there had inspired subsequent generations to think of their lives in a different way.

For millions of the children of slaves, of downtrodden factory workers and peasants, the steady liberation from dependence on religions, kings and traditions has been like a growing-up. The gradual awakening to independence and maturity, and open horizons, leaves people free to make their own relationships, and to reject those that are unhealthy or unsatisfying. So close is the fit between freedom and connexity that the words that most often use 'free' as an epithet, are all about connections: trade, love, speech, assembly, association, even jazz.

Freedom remains a remarkably hard idea to pin down, and Isaiah Berlin once wrote that historians of ideas had found more than two hundred senses of 'this protean word'. But there is, nevertheless, a clear core to the contemporary idea of freedom, and that is the idea of choice. A connected world may be baffling, confusing and unsettling, but it is open and alive because it widens your capacity to choose. If you can travel, or communicate, you can also make new allies, friends and partners. If goods and services are more mobile you can choose not to rely on the local shop or the local farmer. If you can chat on-line all night to strangers in Bolivia or Bosnia you are less likely to end up marrying the boy next door. If you can put together your own scanned images, pictures, and gossip, instead of relying on the top-down messages of the television, you can feel a richer sense of self.

By the same token, connexity means more knowledge about other lives, places and possibilities, and this is always the starting-point for freedom. If you don't know that things can be otherwise, the very idea of freedom is meaningless. In this sense modern freedoms are products of modern media: magazines and newspapers, mail-order catalogues and bill-boards, as well as telephones and telegraphs. All of these have been the practical means by which people became accustomed to making regular choices about what to wear, who to marry, what to eat, how to travel – and all have contributed to making more mobile, fluid, urban societies in which it is normal to come across people with different backgrounds and trajectories, and normal to choose from a range of options. This sense of choice even affects religions. Where once whole populations sometimes converted from one religion to another, today it is a matter of personal choice. Affiliation to a dissident, nonconformist religion may lose you your friends but it is unlikely to lose you your life, and even though the great majority still hold to the religion of their parents, they do so more out of inertia than necessity.

A more connected world also brings more opportunities to escape, above all from oppression by those close around – landowner or father, priest or magistrate. The idea of leaving is not new. Many of the great religions begin with someone leaving their family. But during the nineteenth and twentieth centuries, the expansion of networks of communication and travel has been accompanied by rises in each main indicator of exit – divorce, migration, religious disaffiliation. All have increased, and so left the idea of loyalty reduced to a mere shadow of what it once was. Again, networks amplify this, helping consumers to opt out of loyalty to a supplier, or helping an employee to find new clients. Perhaps it is no coincidence that for the first time ever the world's dominant civilisation is one that was shaped by the freedom to get away – from the landlords of Europe and Russia to the great plains of the USA.[1]

The allure of escape is obvious. It makes it possible to be different, to be an individual. City air makes people free and one of the peculiar features of Western culture has been its celebration of the creative dissenters, the innovators, the people who made something of freedom and carved originality out of the jungle of conformity. In practice it is hard to do this on your own, but a more connected world makes it easier for the dissenter to find an echo, to discover like-minded people. Stubborn, difficult, questioning characters can secure a niche, rather than being hammered into sameness.

Conversely, connexity makes it harder for those in power to contain new ideas. Boundaries and borders are more easily bypassed. Mobility and fleetness of foot circumvent formal channels of control, which is also why each new technology of communication – like the television, the Internet, the press – has been seen, at least in its early stages, as a simple agent of freedom, a new front line against tyranny. Indeed, in one account, communications networks are literally 'technologies of freedom', guarantees against oppressive states, since anyone with even a small radio in Saudi Arabia or Myanmar can still find out about the actions of their rulers,[2] and even the poorest political organisation can use e-mail to mobilise its forces.

Freedom is never absolute. The dominance of a local power may simply be replaced by the dominance of a less visible, more distant power. Subordination to something tangible may just be replaced by subordination to a system. Hundreds of millions remain trapped in environments which offer them little choice and little scope for escape. Freedom of expression can coincide with massive new concentrations of power over images in the hands of a few media conglomerates, and the self-employed can be slaves to work in more ways than the employee. Power works in subtle ways to internalise oppressions. But the idea of exit, of freedom to leave, is central to our culture and wholly dependent on the existence of connections.

This has one other, crucial, ramification. If you no longer automatically take your identity from your origins, you can make it yourself. If it is no longer given by your race, your parents, or your village, you can define yourself as you like, even choosing your own name, and inventing your own history. You can submerge yourself in another given identity – perhaps as a member of a religious cult, a follower of a sport, a member of a subculture – or you can make an entirely distinctive identity out of the materials around. On the Internet you can create and mimic identities: a child can play at being an adult, a man can play at being a woman. You can invent a persona with its own history, prejudices and style.

This idea of self-creation is a novel one. It influences how we think about many things. It changes the meaning of morality, because it implies that the self is the only authority capable of creating or decreeing moral rules. It changes how we view children, because it seems to deny the right of the adult to exercise power and authority over the child. It changes perceptions of aesthetics, because it implies that aesthetic principles are there to be continually created and destroyed. There is no longer any need to carry your past and genealogy as baggage.

To be free also means to be powerful. The word freedom came originally from the barbarian conquerors of Rome, for whom it was one of the virtues of the warrior, and certainly not something to be widely shared. Freedom was a privilege of elites, nobles, and later of the bourgeois in the self-governing towns of medieval Europe. No wonder that, as the saying goes, freedom for the pike is not freedom for the minnow. Even within modern liberalism, John Locke, in his *Essay Concerning Human Understanding*, argued that freedom could be understood as power unfettered, an idea of power that derives from human will, and going further back Orlando Patterson has even suggested that the Egyptian pharaoh Akhnaton deserves credit as the originator of the idea of freedom, because for him the act of breaking free from the constraints of the other gods and the priests of Amun was the first great blow on behalf of humans casting off their own myths. In the cosmology within which he lived, freedom from other gods made him the first man ever to exercise (or imagine exercising) power without limit. Patterson warns that 'it is important to remember that freedom had its first explicit, intellectual – if not ethical – expression in the power lust of an ugly, artistic tyrant'.[3]

In modern Western culture this idea of freedom as power has obvious persistence. There is an intimate connection between belief in individual freedom and the philosophical belief in humanity's God-given right to dominate nature and other creatures, or to pursue desires. But the link to power does not have to be malign. Viewed from the perspective of psychology what matters is the capacity to take control internally and to harness the self to moral or transcendental aims. To be free means having learned enough control over your psychic energies to direct them to the goals you choose, and above all to goals that deliver fulfilment, leading the self to greater awareness, complexity and integration. Bringing up a child, creating a garden, supporting a group of friends or learning to write poetry would all be examples.

This view of the individual is not peculiar to modern Western psychology. It can be found in every major tradition. Each of the world religions has within it a set of ideas about psychic development that go far beyond the idea of independence, or of power over others. We can draw from them the idea, or at least the hope, that human consciousness, whether within the lifespan of the individual or the much longer lifespan of the species, is on a progressive path to realise its full capacities, a path away from the limited lives of the past and towards greater awareness and achievement.

These ideas of freedom, the freedom to choose, to exit, to shape your own identity, and to be empowered, add up to a reasonably coherent view of the world. Together they constitute the ideology of the first generations to grow up against a backdrop of connexity, the nearly two billion teenagers in the world by 2001, a large minority of whom will become familiar with computers, virtual reality and videolinks, and a common, if highly fractured, culture. Theirs is an ideology that favours tolerance, pluralism and diversity, and that defines the self as a choosing, self-determining entity, not subject to fate, or blind destiny, but rather able to make its own life, and even its own morality.

The rise of this set of values can be found confirmed in every study of contemporary populations. In the work of

Ronald Inglehart, the World Values Group, and the many other researchers of values in academic and commercial life, the evidence is abundant. The long period of peace and prosperity that has come since 1945 has steadily eroded the attachment to traditional values, organised religions, authoritarian political ideas and even nationhood, and replaced all with a profound attachment to autonomy, as well as fostering other values like the attachment to authenticity, the blurring of gender roles and hedonism. Each decade of prosperity and relative security seems to deepen these values not only in Western Europe and North America, but also in Turkey and Eastern Europe, the tiger economies of East Asia, and the burgeoning middle classes of India and China.[4] Freedom has come a long way from its origins in the privileges of Teutonic rulers. It has been democratised, and belief in freedom has swept through all classes, affecting women as much as men, the poor as much as the rich.

The conventional history of the West painted a story of cumulative progress as peoples evolved ever closer to self-government and away from dependence on traditional forms of power. While technological and economic progress liberated them from dependence on the land, and later from settled industry, battles in the realm of politics led to a steady accretion of formal freedoms, underpinned by the rule of law. At the end-point of this history is the view of the individual as surrounded by a panoply of legal and philosophical principles that bristle like defences against tyrants and bullies: freedom of speech and expression, freedom in relationships, freedom in the workplace. These guarantee the right to walk away, the liberty to act according to whims, to do almost anything so long as it doesn't harm anyone else. The power to exit, which was once so dangerous, since leaving the community meant the likelihood of death, is instead enshrined as a universal principle.

Such a history presents the idea of freedom as very new, but there are also very ancient origins that make the idea part of our humanity rather than an abstract construct. The mental capacity to communicate with others, to make plans and to

41

construct mental models, also enables people to be curious, to reach out and try to make patterns out of unknown things. This capacity to reach beyond the everyday and the functional is surely one of the psychological foundations of freedom. It explains why it is meaningful to talk of someone being mentally free, even in a jail. Indeed, this impulse to seek new experiences may not be peculiar to humans, it may have a general evolutionary advantage since it ensures that the mind is always open to new chances to secure food or energy. Melvin Konner suggests that many animals have an internal state which is 'a vague mixture of anxiety and desire – best described by the phrase "I want", spoken with or without an object for the verb' – a suggestion which shows both why the sense of freedom is so endemic, and why satisfaction is so hard to secure.

There may also be an equally ancient social origin to the attraction to freedom. In any community some people will try to find ways to coopt the physical or psychic energy of others to their own ends. The source of the idea of freedom may lie in our refusal to submit to this kind of power, the stubborn desire to be independent. This capacity to resist must have had an evolutionary advantage, certainly in any society governed by language and social rules rather than just physical force. If a male gave in too easily to a dominant male, you could be fairly sure that his genes would not be passed on. If a female gave in too easily to a stronger male she would lose the capacity to choose the best genes for her children. In some species there might be little point in trying to get the better of a stronger rival, but primatologists have shown how amongst the more intelligent apes, less dominant males will try to manipulate situations to get the better of dominant ones, and that the more intelligent the species, the greater is the room for manoeuvre. In this sense freedom is the accompaniment of intelligence: it is the way we try to stack the odds in our favour.

An evolutionary disposition towards freedom helps to explain why prehistoric societies were so hostile to the accumulation of personal power. As one writer put it, where power existed in prehistory it was almost 'totally confined to the use of "authority" on behalf of the collectivity'.[5] The most important divides were between insiders and outsiders, not the powerful and powerless, and within the small group authority was never fixed, and never permanently unchallengeable. This is true in any animal group, but more so where intelligence is present, and where with smart actions two weaker parties can cooperate to dominate a stronger one.

So our sense of freedom is in part associated with intelligence, with guile and cunning against dominant forms of power. To the extent that this is true, freedom has always been comprehensible only as a mirror of the changing forms that power has taken, as the way we think of resistance to domination by others. Slavery brings forth the slave revolt. The rise of techniques like the stirrup – which gave power to the horsemen and forced farmers to employ other horsemen to protect them, only to find that their protectors turned into masters – encouraged the association of freedom and the longbow. The rise of the machine encouraged the association of freedom with Luddism.

Against each of these forms of power, freedom remains easy to define. Psychologically it means not having your psychic energy controlled by another against your will. Physically it means being in control of your body, of where it is and what work it does. This simplicity explains why to anyone who has been unfree, held back, or imprisoned, it has an extraordinary magnetism. It is a beautiful idea with a clear aesthetic draw. We can all project possibility on to it, and in a world of rich communications, everyone encounters many more possibilities, many more ideas of what life might mean, than in the narrow constraints of the traditional community.

Perhaps the purest expression of freedom in this sense is the idea of self-sufficiency, embodied in the image of the freeman or yeoman, the farmer secure and independent behind his fence. This was the ideal that Thomas Jefferson seemed to have in mind in many of his writings, and one that has influenced historians seeking the roots of contemporary individualism.[6] In eighteenth-century America it was indeed possible to be independent in this way. You could provide your own defence with a musket, your own food and your own entertainments, with only tenuous links to the outside world.

Indeed, the ideal of self-sufficiency goes back further still. Part of its appeal is that it reminds us of our original nature, that of a mobile nomad, rather than a peasant or wage-earner tied to one place. Nomads used more of their mental capacities and arguably had a fuller life than their successors. We have some evidence that they were healthier, lived longer, and grew taller, and certainly historical records show that more recent nomads were, and still are, contemptuous of immobile farmers dependent on rearing sheep and pigs. If modern anthropologists are right, earlier gatherers and hunters only worked a sixteen-hour week.

The idea of nomadic mobility is surprisingly prominent in our culture. For a settled society the traveller, tramp and hobo are potent symbols of freedom. Even in a highly materialist society, freedom is not only about acquisition, but also about having 'nothing left to lose'. This may be why the car has become the quintessential symbol of freedom, since it gives the individual complete and effortless mobility. The fact that it depends on a highly constructed social order of overt rules, signs and internalised behaviours (an order which sometimes breaks down in anger or drunkenness) in no way diminishes the pull of the ideal which is conventionally portrayed in a car driving through open landscapes, deserts, mountain ranges and rolling hills.

The nomadic freedom symbolised by the car exerts an even more intense pull in a world saturated with information technologies. Networks and free-flowing information liberate people from the bonds of settled agriculture and industry. In cyberspace there are literally no physical spaces and no fixed identities; instead, the experience of the user is that of the disembodied free agent, or the 'nym', (an abbreviation of pseudonym), the identity which is not attached to a name. He or she is able to roam at will, to take on and make up new identities, and in the subcultures associated with networks all restraints – including property rights – are seen as tyrannous, and contrary to the spirit of free, frictionless exchange. Each generation of technology is giving a sharper expression to this ideal of individual freedom, with networks now offering the personal newspaper, the interfaces customised to the individual's own interests, not to mention increasingly intelligent digital agents acting as servants.

Appropriately, in the world of communications the idea of negative liberty finds its most ardent advocates. Users place themselves in the tradition of the great fighters for liberty. John Milton's impassioned polemic against censorship, the *Areopagitica*, the American First Amendment, and Thomas Paine's *The Rights of Man* serve as the sacred texts for the nomadic free spirit who, with the help of information, is once again freed from the constraints of place and fixed relationships.

But the irony is that just as the car's independence rests on a complex system of maintenance, roads and fuel supplies, so does any system of complex communication have to be highly organised. Technical specifications determine precisely which bits mean what; loads have to be managed and signals routed to prevent overload; sophisticated arrangements are needed to ensure that users pay for their use; rules have to be enforced to protect intellectual property, so that the system does not destroy the incentives for people to improve it.

We are left in other words with a striking and apparently widening gap between the categories with which we think about our place in the world and the reality we depend on. There can be no attractive vision of the future that does not involve widening the scope of freedom. But for now, although the drive to freedom helps to inoculate us against oppression, in the narrower form that it has taken it also makes it harder for us to accept the facts of interdependence.

3

FREEDOM'S LIMITS

GEORGE BERNARD SHAW once quipped that the only thing as bad as not getting your heart's desire is to succeed in getting it. The same may be true of freedom. At the very moment when the world has the means to extend freedom to every corner, to realise the dream of opening up human potential to new chances, its limits have become far more visible.

When Isaiah Berlin made a famous distinction between negative liberty which he defined as the absence of restraint, and the positive liberty of being in control, he saw the negative idea of freedom as marking out human civilisation's greatest achievement. Negative liberty certainly lies at the heart of contemporary liberalism. The true test of liberty is non-interference, and above all non-interference by the state or community when the individual is doing something wrong or even self-destructive, so long as it does not harm others. So we should be free to take drugs in the privacy of our own home, free to mutilate our own bodies if that is what gives us sexual pleasure, as well as free to make music or to start our own magazine. For business the same principle applies: what matters more than anything is to be free from regulations or taxes.

Choice has become the highest value of all. In economics, the consumer is sovereign, and it is legitimate for businesses to meet consumer demands, however bizarre. In politics, politicians promise to empower individuals (never groups), and flatter their electors with the language of choice. There is even a spiritual dimension to the cult of independence which finds its purest expression in some of the new age religions, which claim that the only truths lie within the self, in intuition or the inner voice, or what the Theosophist Annie Besant called 'the inner government'. This self-ethic states that we should distrust society's rules and knowledge, and take notice only of inner wisdom and experience.

For many people these ideas are genuinely empowering. If they have been dependent or crushed, the idea of independence helps to evolve the self beyond childlike subordination: being your own master is certainly preferable to being anyone's slave. It is good to be able to guide your own mind and to be aware of your deepest feelings. But the idea of a pure individual independence, according to which everyone is self-sufficient, and can follow their own desires, make their own meanings and even their own morality, is so far from human reality that it soon becomes destructive.

The simplest reason is that we remain social animals – perhaps obsessively so. Our sense of well-being, our desires, our fears, all are bound up with the people around us. We understand ourselves not from inside but from the clues given us by other people and by institutions. This may be why in many non-Western societies the opposite of slavery is not freedom but inclusion, and the greatest fear is not so much oppression as exclusion, being cut off. It is also why you are more likely to be healthy if you have strong relationships with family and friends, and why for most people isolation means being less than human.

A society which too loudly proclaims individual independence soon becomes an unpleasant one to live in. In a densely populated society it is hard to enjoy freedom if you can have no certainties about how others will behave. Freedom to walk the streets, happiness in a relationship, contentment in a job, all of these depend on confidence – that the streets will be safe, your partner will not suddenly walk out, you will not be suddenly sacked. For the same reasons, free markets rest on rules guaranteeing property rights and enforcing contracts, and policing against fraud.

Just how much we depend on the social order becomes

more visible in large, complex, interconnected societies than in small ones. In a small community, subtle social pressures tend to maintain conformity and to punish antisocial behaviour. In larger ones, the rules have to be made explicit and formal, backed by professional policing, and it is a characteristic of more heterogeneous societies that greater liberty is always accompanied by the growth of professions whose main job is to maintain order: lawyers, accountants, security personnel and even traffic wardens.

The subtle relationship between freedom and order that has exercised thinkers for a long time. Greek philosophy oscillated between an obsessive concern with social status and *arete*, and the contempt for social order of Socrates and the Cynics. As we shall see the tension between the two ideas has framed much of the Western philosophical tradition. But when, to take just one example from many, Orestes comments in Sartre's *The Flies* that we should live by 'no other law but mine', most have accepted that this is not a definition of freedom but of hell.

One of the reasons is that such an idea of freedom is blind to any difference between right and wrong. In the past it was taken for granted that there was a distinction between liberty and licence. Freedom would have little meaning if people were dominated by their instincts and passions. In Renaissance times, autonomy meant being self-possessed, that is to say, having a mastery and discipline that warranted respect (and it was because of this view that the professions came to be seen as models of autonomy by contrast with mere managers, since professionals had the means to control their own work). For the pioneers of modern liberalism, too, like John Locke and John Stuart Mill, it was self-evident that greater freedom rested on a moral and religious base and would be inconceivable without it. They presumed a society made up of active, participating people, governed by religious faith. Without another force to guide it, freedom would result in formless chaos.

The same considerations applied to democracy. Edmund Burke wrote that 'men are qualified for civil liberty in exact proportion to their disposition to put moral chains upon their own appetites', and John Stuart Mill that democracy depends on citizens' self-restraint and their 'willingness to direct their energies into common projects'. He stood in a long tradition of seeing freedom in terms of the domination by a higher rational self of the lower passions (which could be more easily exploited by demagogues and dictators), and like many others he believed that the widening of freedom would tend to make people more moral, and more caring. Where many of his contemporaries warned that if people were given more freedoms they would fritter their lives away, and if democracy was extended the dismal result would be dictatorship by a philistine mob, he believed that freedom and engagement would grow in a virtuous circle.

Since then, however, liberalism has shrunk and become thinner. It has largely lost its other dimensions. They are seen as part of its religious past, not its secular present, which is above all about defending diversity and individuality, not virtue. Over time the legalistic definitions of freedom have hardened, and gained institutional force at the cost of its other dimensions. If we see liberty only as a set of legal rights, then what was once a common good, a shared tool for progress, becomes an increasingly bitter zero-sum game. It is as if the defining battles of liberalism, which were fought not to assert virtue but rather to escape from excessive conformity and restraint, have diluted its moral richness into a thinner, sourer substance.

We have made individual choice into a totem, and by doing so have blinded ourselves to its limits. For the truth is that our capacity to choose is fundamentally flawed. We carry with us a legacy of our evolution in a radically different environment on the savannahs and grasslands of Africa which profoundly shapes the choices we make. This is why children who have never seen spiders and snakes are frightened by pictures of them, it is why adults cannot avoid hunger and sexual desire, and why we feel the adrenalin rush when a murderer appears in a film. In the same way many other responses that were appropriate in the environment in which early humans took shape are painfully inappropriate today. A simple example is addiction to salt or sugars: the past need for salt to replenish bodies that were partially evolved in the sea (the salt is needed to maintain the electric potential across cell membranes necessary for the heart to pump blood) now leads to excess consumption. The same is true of sugar. We respond to genetic programming to seek out what were scarce and vital foods in the past and end up with obesity and gluttony. Another example is chronic drug dependency. The inability to cope with mind-altering drugs makes us prone to addiction, so that what starts as the pursuit of pleasure ends as imprisonment (like the rats that starve themselves to death as they endlessly stimulate their brains' pleasure centres in laboratory experiments). Other examples of inappropriate choices include men asserting territorial control in dense urban areas (testosterone and dominance grate in a highly rational, organised world), or women wanting to mother large families in overpopulated societies. Evolutionary psychology also explains why people are attracted towards negative thoughts and outcomes. In a dangerous past this predisposition prepared people to flee and avoid harm, but today it fuels an unhealthy attraction to violence and disaster, in ways that tend to be addictive. Lionel Tiger argues that a host of instinctive drives towards dominance, sex and social interaction were useful to survival and thus tended to become pleasurable, but are now out of place (as Tiger puts it, in his paraphrase of Santayana, 'those who do not learn from prehistory are condemned to repeat its successes').[1]

To accept that people are shaped by their genes does not mean the end of freedom. Nor does awareness that genetic impulses will lead people to be selfish legitimate viciously competitive social arrangements. The laws of physics tell us that water flows downhill, but they do not stop us from building pumps to take it uphill. Knowledge just tells us the limits of what we can do.

Understanding these limits is important because so much of the Enlightenment tradition was founded on a belief that human beings are endlessly malleable, and able to exercise their reason to achieve anything. Today this elevation of the human into a secular deity seems faintly absurd. Darwin demonstrated that humans are not special, Freud that conscious reason is not all-powerful, and now evolutionary psychology reveals the profound architectural flaws in our makeup. So instead of faith in freedom we are left with the inclination, as Paul Ricoeur wrote, to demystify the illusions around us by 'exercise of suspicion',[2] and, rather than seeing the human as a *tabula rasa*, capable of choosing to be anything, to accept the internal limits to human nature, limits that mirror the external ones set by the natural environment.

If anyone is in any doubt, they need only think of the more mundane limits to their own exercise of freedom. Simply to survive, we now have to keep track of so much more information about the relationships in which we are immersed, relationships with lovers, children, relatives, former partners, friends, employers, doctors, teachers, as well as governments. The range of choices that the typical individual has to make about how to manage relationships, careers or eating habits is far wider than in the past, if only because we can no longer simply draw on tradition as a guide. Instead each set of choices is accompanied by competing theories, interpretations and advice. It is this that gives modern life the character that Robert Kegan described as being 'in over our heads'.[3] Like a curriculum that is too hard for the pupil to master, the effect of an excess of mental challenges is to leave people feeling inadequate, as if they are perpetually underperforming. Even if they triumph in one domain they may be wholly inadequate in another. The successful executive may be a disastrous parent, the charismatic politician a poor lover, the perfect father an inadequate son.

More choice may do as much to harm and to hinder mental well-being as to help it. Stress, anxiety and lack of self-esteem all follow. There are answers to these problems, both individual ones that better prepare people to be independent and social ones that give shape and reliability to choices. But an expansion of freedoms and choices may reach a peak after which the returns diminish and even become negative. This is well understood within art forms. Creative artists nearly always seek to work within a framework of disciplines and grammars. Without them, what looks like freedom ultimately turns out to be nothing more than formlessness and meaninglessness.

But the most fundamental limit to the narrow idea of freedom is that it assumes a clearly bounded self, with its own beliefs and desires, and a full capacity to make choices. Such a distinct concept of self provides a simple building block for economics and politics. Unfortunately it has only limited utility. It cannot explain how values and beliefs are formed; it cannot account for how people feel part of larger wholes, like families or nations. Worse, it leads to unnecessary conflicts, which is why many of the people concerned with healing the pains of modern society – marriage psychologists, industrial relations mediators, educational theorists and family therapists – are rejecting it. If the self is bounded and wholly independent then interests are fixed, and any negotiation or communication starts from a fixed position, rather than being a way for two parties to evolve together to a new accommodation. The idea of a separate self is also being rejected in other fields: in the realm of art and ideas, for example, the idea of the genius creator is being modified as attention turns to the far broader river of culture which expresses itself through individuals as much as the other way round.

The alternative is to see the self as less of a given, less complete and less whole.[4] The more open self finds it easier to deal with others, to understand their perspectives, fears and aspirations. Its own beliefs can be treated less as fixities, its interests as less surrounded by boundaries. By thinking in this way the task of negotiation is not just to compromise between selves but rather to transform them. Maturing means accepting your incompleteness, your permeability to other people. It means being wary of believing what you think (since what you think may change, indeed should change), of investing all of your psychic energies in what you want, wary of seeing yourself as separate when in all likelihood many of your preferences come from outside you. This idea of a more open self is spreading in psychology, as well as in philosophy and literature. It may not be much easier to live with than the idea of the self as sovereign, but it offers a more productive goal than the fantasy of a complete and separate ego. Its significance is that it suggests that our narrow idea of freedom doesn't only fail to match the facts of how the world is ordered. It also doesn't match our own evolving sense of how we are ordered.

Freedom is a distinctively Western concept. In Japanese, for example, the best translation of the word 'freedom' is *jiyu* which had previously meant licentiousness. The Chinese word for 'freedom' was also used primarily to mean licentiousness, sometimes to mean living alone and only rarely for the Confucian virtue of an absence of ego. For us, by contrast, living in a very different environment, the idea of freedom marks out a distinctive set of values, and an ideal that remains crucial to our sense of a progress beyond conformity and submission. But in order for it to be useful we need a far richer definition than that of independence. Although aesthetically a narrow view of freedom makes perfect sense on its own, in human societies it only makes sense in conjunction with other things, above all power and self-control, a sense of right and wrong, a framework of order, and a sense of the limits of the choosing self. Without the power to use freedom you remain vulnerable to oppression. Without an order determining the behaviour of others you remain vulnerable to uncertainty and unpredictability. Without a sense of your own limits, freedom becomes brittle, selfish and ultimately unfulfilling. Freedom in other words only works in partnership with other ideals, not on its own. It is the classic example of an idea, and an ideal, that is thought about outside systems, yet lived, very differently, within them.

4

MARKETS WITHOUT FRONTIERS

IF FREEDOM IS the dominant idea in the newly connected world, its most important structure is the market. Once the great networks of roads and messengers were shaped by their role as tools of power, holding together empires. Today they serve the exchange of goods and services. They can be used to buy everything from news reports to satellite images of a mountain range on the far side of the world. If the world is connected as never before, it is primarily because of the cumulative growth of systems that permit exchange: the higher systems of footloose capital and commodities markets, and the exchange markets that now trade $1 trillion each day, fifty times the level of world trade; the lower levels of distribution and marketing, supermarkets and job exchanges; and, right down in everyday life, the markets governing the sale of labour time and domestic services.

The steady expansion of this market system – and it is in many respects one system, even if it is made up of many sub-systems – has been one of the most important changes of the twentieth century, in the long run more significant even than the world wars. During this period it has steadily absorbed more parts of the world, more people and more activities within its sway. In Japan, which is today the world's leading economic power, as recently as the 1860s only 5 per cent of the population were engaged in wage employment. At the end of the twentieth century, some 90 per cent of the world's population lives within a market system, compared to only 40 per cent in the 1970s and perhaps 10 or 15 per cent at the beginning of the century. With falling transport and communication costs, and falling tariff barriers, the majority of countries now trade with the majority of others, and in most developed economies a third of private-sector output is traded. The best measure of the market's sheer reach is that there are now world prices for so many goods and services, where in the past there were only local prices. Some markets remain local: only 1.5 per cent of the global labour force works outside its own country, and half of this in the Middle East and sub-Saharan Africa. Even in the European Union only 2 per cent of EU nationals work in another member country. But taken as a whole, the spread of markets means that, from California to China, it is relatively easy to sell things, to trade, to establish an enterprise, to take out profits and to employ others.[1]

The physical extension of the market system is remarkable enough in historical terms, but just as important for the character of daily life is its intensification. Capitalism brings with it a dynamic which dictates that more things, and more types of things, can be bought and sold at the end of each decade than at the beginning. A society based on the pursuit of profit gives every entrepreneur an incentive to transform activities and things into marketable commodities, usually by packaging them and restricting access to them. A valley can be turned into a park with a toll for entry. A spring can be turned into bottled water. Helping behaviour, such as childcare or delivering meals to the elderly, can be turned into formalised, organised, commercial services. Looking ahead, the most revolutionary impact of new communications technologies may come from their capacity to run transactions rather than their capacity to share information, since it will be technically feasible for people as a matter of course to market their time, to rent their cars, houses and power tools, and to carry out these transactions over networks with other individuals rather than through the organisations of the formal economy.

This tendency towards intensification is not always unchecked. Every society outlaws some kinds of exchange. The economist Arthur Okun once described America's Bill of Rights as a series of definitions of things which could not be exchanged. The Bill of Rights included prohibitions on such things as slavery, and in every society there is a longer list of things which it is deemed inappropriate to exchange. In most modern Western societies that list would include children's labour, public offices (which were bought and sold until relatively recently), slavery, votes, criminal justice, freedom of speech, military service, jury duty, basic physical protection, and prizes.[2] Some would argue that one of the definitions of human progress is that it lengthens this list, and brings fairer principles to the distribution of these various goods than the market criterion of simply having enough money. In this view, reducing the sway of money is the next stage of civilisation, rather as earlier phases of civilisation sought to reduce the sway of physical force in determining who had access to goods, wives or justice.

But these limitations on exchange run against the grain, the momentum for making exchange more free. In a more inter-connected world it becomes harder to constrain what can be bought and sold. Restrictive rules may apply in one jurisdiction, but this merely increases the incentives for others to be more liberal. Even money itself is becoming harder to control, as new forms of e-cash are created on networks, allowing a company like Microsoft to make payments in the form of future claims on its own products, rather than in dollars or yen. Together these forces explain why, even though within most societies many types of exchange are prevented, within the global system as a whole more things can be bought than ever before – including everything from old masters to high-technology weapons, private jets to heart transplants, the genes of a rare plant in a tropical rain-forest to a popular tune – and why the world is dotted with havens: tax havens, free-trade zones, data havens, as well as societies that deliberately turn a blind eye to trade in narcotics, prostitutes, university degrees, copyrights and child labour.

In the perpetual conflict between rules to restrict exchange, and the dynamic to widen it, the latter has tended to win for the simple reason that restricting one type of exchange tends to require restrictions on others. For example, if a state wishes to prevent its citizens from buying abortions it may also have to prevent them from purchasing air tickets to visit a nation which ignores this prohibition. If it wishes to prohibit access to pornographic images it may also need to police the use of technology necessary to access news, or chemical databases. The central issue in other words is that the agencies for restricting exchange tend to be territorial, and limited in their sway, whereas the means of carrying out exchanges tend to be global and extensive.

All structures carry their own systems of belief. Usually these beliefs are the things that seem most obvious and common sense to the people living within them. Markets are no exception, and the beliefs most closely associated with them are formalised in the theories of modern economics. The great achievement of economics has been to develop a science that appears to be about how people achieve well-being and prosperity but is really a science only of external relationships and of the exchanges that people and institutions make. In economics what matter are the choices people make in buying or selling, not their motives, or the physical properties of things they trade. This focus on exchange leads economics to view exchange as a good in itself, since it is only by exchanging things that we can maximise our welfare (in economics every hermit is a heretic). It makes the discipline uninterested in subjective feelings of happiness or internal fulfilment except in so far as they are 'revealed' through decisions to buy and sell. So, although in most contemporary societies there is more work done unpaid than paid – usually the domestic labour of bringing up children, cooking and cleaning – in orthodox economics this kind of work literally counts for nothing. It only becomes visible when the market turns the informal labour of the household into a service bought in: a cleaner, nanny or cook.

This myopia becomes apparent if we look at the nature of exchange itself. If you are taking part in an exchange you see only the immediate conditions, the bread you are being offered and the price-tag attached, or the price attached to your labour. It is rational for the individual to concern his or herself solely with the transaction, since an individual is virtually powerless to influence the whole system, the conditions of supply and demand which are determined by the aggregation of millions of individual decisions. It is only through other routes, like politics, that you can influence these broader conditions. Strictly speaking the economy is structured in such a way as to make it unlikely for the individual to internalise the interests of the system, to reconcile the needs of the part and of the whole, in each individual choice. Instead the interests of the system appear, literally, to look after themselves.

The focus on the moment of exchange, and not on the system as a whole, has been profoundly absorbed into the worldview of modern citizens. Education is a good example. In the past the goal of education might be to discover knowledge, to achieve wisdom or to develop a well-rounded character. Today the dominant rhetoric of policy-makers concerns itself with designing education systems that can cultivate marketable skills and competences. Their ideal pupil is one who can enter the labour market with confidence, and succeed in a career. Work is another example: for much of the industrial era the dominant image of work was of the employee, working for much of their life for a single firm, and with a single set of skills. In the post-industrial era by contrast the dominant image is of the individual as a seller of packages of labour time to a range of different purchasers. The most desirable attributes are not loyalty or commitment, but rather flexibility, adaptability and the willingness to sell yourself. Even our attitudes to old age have been reframed through the prism of exchange: provision for old age is no longer a question of carefully managing relationships with children, or even of voting for a paternalistic government, but rather of purchasing wisely a set of financial products that will deliver returns in twenty or forty years' time.

The corollary of the dominance of the exchange mentality

is that exchange is not just the primary means of securing things that in other eras would have come in other ways: food, shelter, and long-term security. It is also the main means of inclusion: without being able to sell your labour, and without the cash that comes from successful exchange of labour, you are effectively excluded from participation in most forms of communal life. Whereas earlier generations of the unemployed might have thought of themselves as unlucky, today those without jobs are more likely to think of themselves as literally valueless.

If the ideas of exchange are embedded deep in everyday culture, they are also predominant in high politics. The institutions of free trade have proven more effective than those designed to prevent or contain war, and more diplomatic activity is now devoted to managing trade than to the management of security. Any nation considering serious restrictions on trade is threatened with the status of a pariah (unless it is a dominant trader). The same is true of any jurisdiction that seeks to impose serious restrictions on the flow of information.

Barely a century after economics took its modern form, deep in the interior consciousness of our culture, *Homo economicus* has become not just a rational calculator of advantages, but something more: a person who conceives of him or herself as made up of a series of exchanges – time for money, money for goods and services, commitments for commitments – so that ultimately every relationship, even the most primordial, can be defined by a contract. Marriage can be turned into a contract specifying hours of domestic labour and the division of shared assets; parenthood into a formalised set of mutual obligations (the parent giving time and money to be reciprocated when the child becomes an adult) and citizenship defined as a series of rights and obligations connecting the individual and the state.

The rise of economic exchange and the mentalities that surround it generates one of the most powerful images of connexity: a world made up of a lattice of contracts and reciprocal flows that can absorb any person (even the mentally disabled may have something to sell), any place, and any type of activity. The universalism of this image makes it extraordinarily powerful, and apparently inclusive, since when one becomes a buyer or seller the old labels of status and class become irrelevant. Where money is concerned everyone can be equal.

Records of stocks and sales make up the bulk of the earliest written records. But if we look further back into prehistory the things that were exchanged appear to have been marginal rather than essential. Archaeologists have found extraordinary patterns of shell deposits, carved stones and amber from known sources spread out over large distances. Cro-Magnons appear to have roamed further, to have cooperated more widely, and to have been more nomadic than the Neanderthals they displaced. There may also have been trade in more utilitarian things, such as tools, or clothes and food that have since disappeared, but most of what remains are luxuries, symbolic goods, trinkets satisfying curiosity rather than need, and showing good will, suggesting that the origins of exchange lie more in the deep need for sociability in human nature, the fear of loneliness and isolation, rather than in the calculation of direct material advantage.

Stephen Jay Gould writes of 'coopted epiphenomena': some organs began with different uses from those into which they evolved – fish fins became reptiles' legs, limbs became wings. Exchange was not essential to our evolution, but the same mental capacities that allowed us to communicate, to gather and to hunt also suited us for exchange.

People appear to be strongly shaped to understand the rules of social exchange. In a series of seminal studies, Leda Cosmides and John Toobey showed that people of widely differing backgrounds all had an apparently powerful intuitive capacity to detect cheats in social contracts – people who take benefits without paying the cost. We automatically compute that we owe something back when we receive a gift, and that one favour deserves another, and much of our moral language sounds very like a calculus, in which we owe obligations, and in which evil deeds require us to repay a debt to society. In Matt Ridley's words, part of our brain 'is a ruthless and devastatingly focused calculating machine. It treats every problem as a social contract arrived at between two people and looks for ways to check those who might cheat the contract.'[3]

It was not hard to extend this capacity to dealings with strangers. But without the restless, outward-going curiosity of the human brain, exchange would have remained marginal. Clearly our distant ancestors were prepared to take risks (because dealing with strangers must have been risky) even when there was little direct reward in terms of food, shelter, security or finding a mate. The same seems to be true of the evidence of the coming together of widely dispersed groups for annual festivals, sometimes to build great works, but apparently more often for symbolic purposes: exchanges that are more easily understood as expressive, part of curiosity and play, part of a sense of self and community, rather than understandable in utilitarian terms.

In his classic study of games Johann Huizinga suggested that many contemporary institutions originated not in meeting needs but rather in play.[4] Armies developed out of the ritualised festivals whereby neighbouring bands would come together for competitive games (echoed in the medieval contests and jousts). The festive exchange of gifts lay behind the more formalised markets of the town and city. The forms of justice derive from the 'trials' in which contestants confronted each other with their cases, politics from competitions of rhetoric. In each case what began as curious exchange became steadily more formalised, more functional, more codified, but always in each incarnation able to feed off its origins in play, so that those engaged would still be able to derive pleasure and fulfilment from their work as a soldier, an advocate or an entrepreneur.

The capacity to exchange things can make a good claim to be one of the defining features of human beings. All animals try to maintain a territory, a space in which they exercise some control, within which they protect their young. Some mark it, others prowl it. But no other species systematically exchanges things, beyond a few dozen signals, and none seems to engage in the systematic exchange of objects, or the passing of things and ideas down through several generations or along convoluted supply lines.

Yet although exchange has such a long pedigree, and is so distinctively part of what marks humans off from other creatures, it has never had an entirely comfortable position within cultures. Somehow exchange is felt to be lacking in virtue. 'True' labour involves transforming matter and engaging with nature. Production and reproduction give something to the world whereas exchange only shuffles the elements. It has often been seen as a luxury that does nothing to provide the basics of life and survival – protection, shelter, sustenance – and its moral status is at best ambiguous. Since most early trade was indeed of luxuries, of wine, spices, silks and gold, this view was not unreasonable. What is more surprising is its persistence. Adam Smith may be remembered today as the prophet of a market economy based on exchange, but in *The Wealth of Nations* he repeatedly condemns the consumer goods of his times as 'trinkets and baubles', and frivolous machines. Part of his conception of the invisible hand was as a deception that encouraged people to work in order to gain essentially worthless things that did not make them happy. In his other great work, *The Theory of Moral Sentiments*, he writes of riches leaving him 'as always as much as sometimes, more exposed than before to anxiety, to fear and to sorrow: to diseases, to danger and to death'.[5] In the same vein, and perhaps less surprisingly, his contemporary Jean-Jacques Rousseau attacked the *colifichet* – the useless luxuries of the embryonic capitalism around him – and Robespierre attacked the Paris mob for looting shops for sugar and coffee, which he called *chetives marchandises* (pitiful merchandise).

Today, there are precise parallels in the denunciations of the trivia on the Internet, of junk food, junk mail and junk things. The early uses of every communication technology tend to be relatively frivolous or marginal, arousing the hostility of mainstream culture, rather as the anthropologists were baffled by the mysterious complex mechanisms whereby the Trobriand Islanders exchanged red shell necklaces and white shell bracelets (known as the Kula). Yet what was once marginal has now become central. The trivia paved the way for the essentials, and today, without markets and exchange, little of our civilisation would survive.

5

THE LIMITS OF EXCHANGE

THERE IS A long-held philosophical belief that different domains of human life should operate according to their own rules. What is appropriate for matters of health is not appropriate for matters of war; what suits learning does not suit the management of the home. There are local rules and, in Jon Elster's phrase, forms of 'local justice', defined by the particular situation or environment rather than by general rules. So general principles of social justice break down when societies are devising rules for distributing such things as access to dialysis machines or military conscription.

It follows that money should be kept in check, so that its power operates only in relevant domains. Pascal wrote that 'tyranny is the wish to obtain by one means what can only be had by another', and Marx that 'love can only be exchanged for love, trust for trust'. But money has always tended to seep across boundaries. Even in the most legalistic democracies, powerful monied interests can often buy laws, and technology assists the flow of money, as it does of all kinds of information. Money talks and is persuasive precisely because it can so easily slip across apparent boundaries. It turns things into commodities that are defined not by their intrinsic qualities but by their nature as things to be exchanged. As Karl Marx wrote in one of his earlier books, 'there came a time when everything that men had considered inalienable became an object of exchange, of traffic, and could be alienated. This is the time when the very things which till then had been communicated, but never exchanged; given but never sold,

64

acquired but never bought – virtue, love, knowledge, conscience – when everything in short passed into commerce. It is the time of general corruption, of universal venality.'

The fundamental objection is that money appears to govern the relationships between things – between labour, goods and services – when it is really governing relationships between people. The market system has become phenomenally sophisticated at managing what could be called first-order exchanges – like buying a car, a loaf of bread or a television set, in which it is unnecessary to have any continuing relationship with the partner to an exchange. But it is less sophisticated at second-order exchanges which, like most human relationships, depend on reciprocal understandings. And it is deliberately blind to the environment in which it is located. This moral blindness can be justified as a necessary focus. Most of the many manuals written about business ethics argue that the moral issues involved in any exchange concern only the legitimacy of the exchange itself. Around this exchange a clear line is drawn. The morality of business stops at the transaction, and business should not concern itself with the system of which it forms a part. Indeed, in some accounts it is illegitimate, even immoral, for people engaged in business to subject their decisions to concerns about the impact on the wider society. Instead there is a moral division of labour: the business of business is honest trade, and other concerns are the responsibility of other institutions, of government or charity. This moral view echoes the principles of Adam Smith: so long as each transaction is carried out with honesty and integrity the system will look after itself.

In her book *Systems of Survival*, Jane Jacobs provided an important insight into the division of responsibilities between business and other institutions.[1] There is and always has been, she argues, a natural symbiosis between the systems of exchange and the systems of territory and power. Both depend on each other for survival. The latter derive from the behaviour which we share with animals, the search for food and the protection of territory (and we might add the search for a mate). Rather than originating in play, she suggests that the rules we associate with armies and police forces, government bureaucracies and organised religions, aristocracies and courts, all come from territory and the animal instinct to security. All, she points out, are concerned with 'protecting, acquiring, exploiting, administering or controlling territories', and together they add up to what she calls a 'guardian syndrome'.

Where the guardian syndrome values hierarchy, loyalty, prowess, ostentation, honour and exclusivity, and upholds rights and duties associated with position or status, the syndrome associated with trade values thrift, industry, optimism, voluntary agreements, honesty, invention and collaboration with strangers, and rights and duties associated with contracts. Both share some of the same basic virtues, such as cooperation, energy, patience and wisdom. But beyond these they become starkly different, in fact often contradictory. In matters of protecting territory, it is legitimate to lie – but not in trade. In trade anything is saleable, but the idea of selling a position, or a secret, is anathema to the guardian syndrome.

Both syndromes can be found in any culture and any period of history. We can characterise one as embodying the virtues of an internal, inward-looking culture based on the land – with expression in the royal families in the past, and in everything from armies to environmental movements today – while the other embodies the values of the outward-looking, the cosmopolitan (deriving from the Greek *cosmos* and *polis*, meaning universal people or world citizen). It finds its natural habitat in cities, where it is essential to be able to trust in contracts. Neither stands alone, and in fact both syndromes are interdependent. The traders have to be able to pay for monarchs to defend them and their trade (the English navy, for example, was first financed by merchants to clear the seas of pirates), and to police against corruption and fraud. Financiers, chemical companies and software houses need a state to guarantee their property rights, and, metaphorically at least, outside every auction room stands a policeman. Conversely, the guardians depend on taxes levied on the wealth created by commerce.

Each mentality, each moral system, has its own different styles. The guardian style is more interested in sacrifice and service, the trader in material advantage. The guardian view sees a social order in terms of roles and solidarity, the trader in terms of the accumulation of self-interest. The guardian prefers continuity, whereas the cosmopolitan mentality tends to be more relaxed, at ease with change and difference.

We can imagine many examples of these different styles. Norbert Elias, for example, wrote about how French courtiers, who had fixed and clearly defined relationships with other aristocrats, would meet others only with extreme caution because a misjudged word could have permanent consequences.[2] The same is true of village life and indeed of any closed community, which will tend to have a long and unforgiving memory. These are the very opposite of the fleeting relationships of the marketplace (and of the 'city air that makes for freedom' in the medieval phrase). Similarly whereas one syndrome prizes conformity and adherence to norms, the second values dissent and innovation, fashion and change.

There is much that can be disputed in Jane Jacobs' account. She ignores what may be one of the most important distinctions between the guardian and the trader mentality: the guardian's sense of humility, piety and awe in the face of nature, a perspective quite at odds with the pragmatism of the buyer and seller. She warns against mixing elements from each syndrome (governments running firms, armies running wars industriously, businesses becoming involved in largesse), but lacks a metatheory from which to decide what are legitimate combinations and what are not. But her strangest conclusion is that the two syndromes are steadily symbiotic, and that there has been no fundamental change in the balance between them.

Instead, the most striking fact about the trading syndrome is that it has spread, not just in terms of volumes of trade, but also as an ideal, a way of living and thinking, a body of tasks and powers. Over time the traders have usually outstripped the guardians and coercers (although when the bourgeois merchants became too confident they elicited the classic guardian response of a communist system built on a coalition between secular priests, bureaucrats and soldiers). I have already suggested some of the reasons for the relative success of the traders. The guardian syndrome tends to favour stasis. It is concerned with control within a boundary, maintaining a status quo. Its mentality involves seeing the world as a zero-sum game – as it always is in struggles over territory – in the manner of mercantilist economics. Its ethos is to distrust all others but to favour loyalty above all else, respect for hier-archy and obedience, and to do this because life is a struggle of winners and losers. This view was well put by Francis Bacon, when he wrote that 'the increase of any state must be upon the foreigner, for whatever is gained is somewhere lost'.[3] A few centuries later Heinrich von Treitschke described it even more starkly. He wrote that 'your neighbour, even though he may look upon you as his natural ally against another power which is feared by you both, is always ready at the first opportunity . . . to better himself at your expense . . . whoever fails to increase his power must decrease it, if others increase theirs'.[4]

By contrast the exchange syndrome tends to promote dynamic, cumulative activities. Its power and reach tend to grow. A sum of capital expands, the web of trading partners widens, the range of products diversifies. The syndrome embraces change, division, recombination and has no place for fixity and loyalty. Such a dynamic property is one of the consistent features of money, as it is of many processes which are essentially about information (money is never more than a signal that someone else will respect its purchasing power, even if it is made of a precious metal). The more it is used the more capacity it gains: if money circulates twice in a month instead of once, twice as many economic activities become viable. In the same way some kinds of knowledge have this cumulative capacity – the more they spread the more valuable they become, just as the more we act in the light of trust, the more trust we get.

Sometimes the key to this kind of cumulation has been missing – if traders feel the need to spend their surpluses in the form of largesse, or if perpetual war blocks trade, or monarchs too consistently devalue the currency, then the system will remain relatively static. But, once galvanised, the growth of exchange appears literally limitless, especially when helped by roads, canals, railways, telegraphs, undersea cables, aircraft, satellites, whose cumulative impact has been to accelerate the speed of circulation of inventions, products and ideas.

The division between the guardian and the trader mentalities is mirrored in the geography of the world. If you looked at the world of a few centuries ago you saw empires, walled cities and armies. The great struggles were battles for territory. Today the boundaries are still there but instead you see economies, and the centres of power are not walled, but rather the hubs of creativity and exchange, the economic dynamos of industrial regions like the area south of San Francisco and Greater Tokyo, Singapore and Hong Kong, London and Paris, EmilioRomagna and Catalonia, Seattle and Bayern.

Their rise has accompanied a decisive shift in the age-old balance between what could be termed the 'edge' places, those that specialise in exchange, and the places that think of themselves as centres, defined by their boundaries. The edge places can be found throughout history: they are the hubs, entrepôts, port cities. They see themselves as a web of connections, not as a territory. They could be found dotted around the Mediterranean in the time of the Greeks and Phoenicians. The Chinese established them across East Asia, the Arabs down the Gulf and the east coast of Africa to Zanzibar. More recent examples include Hong Kong and Singapore, the Hanseatic cities of the North Sea and Baltic, Venice and Genoa, Amsterdam and London. They were often not only creative, and absorptive (good at absorbing immigrant people as well as ideas into their mainstream), but also often unstable, subject to the crime that tends to be associated with competition from outsiders who are willing to accept lower wages. Creative cities like Athens in the fifth century BC, or Florence in the fifteenth century, used their surpluses to pull in outside talent, and to feed off the outsiders' sense of dissonance with the system, just as technologically innovative cities, like Manchester in the eighteenth century and Glasgow in the nineteenth, exploited their distance from the mainstream to draw on the energies of self-taught inventors and entrepreneurs working in relatively egalitarian cultures.[5] The majority of these cities have traditionally been found on the edges of landmasses; often their geography makes them literally 'edges'.

Such places, which thrive on their capacity to connect, to buy and sell, have always stood in marked contrast to places of the interior. Their culture has tended to be liberal, cosmopolitan, sceptical of absolute certainties, restless, outward-going and chance-taking. It is rough, piratical, pragmatic. By contrast, in the landmasses you find the cultures of the centre. These are built around great empires, huge bureaucracies, absolute religions and ideologies based in grand imperial capitals like Persepolis, Rome, Beijing, Moscow, Babylon, Baghdad. They aspire to stasis and immobility, quite unlike the mobile, changing cultures of the peripheral edge cities. This immobility has been reflected in architectures and urban design, with grand buildings that symbolise hierarchy, cathedrals, palaces, boulevards. Their cultures (and economic surpluses) have supported great luxury and sophistication. Otherworldliness is made manifest in the sacred geometries of squares, pyramids and the centres for mysticism. Politics and power are ostentatious, tied up with protocols, rules and rituals establishing a continuity with the past, and imperial power is organised through the exercise of control over open plains and spaces.

The dialectic of the edge and the centre has been a consistent theme in history. Each has its advantages and its disadvantages. The Greeks found this as they were defeated by the Romans but in some respects triumphed in culture. The Venetians fought against the Ottomans and the Hanseatic League, the Vikings against the Russians, the Phoenicians against the Egyptians. In practice the lines of distinction have rarely been wholly clear-cut. Some civilisations have made the transition from one culture to another. The Phoenicians evolved into the Carthaginian empire. The Greek cities spawned the imperial descendants of Alexander. Almost every empire has had both its interiors, usually based on relatively conservative agrarian populations, and port cities attracted to new ideas, lifestyles and experiment (think of Russia and St Petersburg, France and Paris, Spain and Barcelona). Other edge cities became great empires. Venice, Genoa and later Britain and the Netherlands were all small edge societies that through superior technology and the marriage of arms and trade created empires.

More recently the world has seen a fascinating shift in culture in the United States of America. In its formative years it was an exterior, mobile, trading society. Each grouping in the new colony was allowed to be self-governing, and to raise its own taxes, mainly because the British lacked the resources to support it. The American ideas of liberty, taxation and representation, scepticism about government, the faith in cash and commerce, all derive from this early history. But over time, while the constitution has remained intact, its very success has encouraged the transition from an edge to a centre culture. What began as an exterior mobile culture became a continental empire. The Monroe doctrine in the early nineteenth century marked a turn away from the earlier anti-imperial instincts of America's founders. By pushing back the frontier all the way to the Pacific, what had begun as a federation of coastal regions became a vast landmass, and subtly, almost unnoticed, its new physical shape seemed to encourage a more interior mentality: fundamentalism in religion, and imperial and military sentiments that manifest themselves not just in the urge to trade around the world but also in the urge to be a force for order, even a policeman, around the world.

In the US these two characters remain in balance. There are

sharp tensions between the cultures of the interior and those of the edges in New York and Los Angeles, the big cosmopolitan cities, with their lack of certainty, their willingness to trade and compromise, their indifference to war and ritual. Much the same was true in Britain when its eighteenth-century, piratical, thrusting character evolved into the nineteenth-century love of the land and continuity, the attachment to the symbols of monarchy and parliament that made it the heart of a great global empire rather than a buccaneer nation. China is the clearest example today of this tension, as the tiny entrepôt of Hong Kong is experienced both as a desirable source of wealth and as an acute threat by the vastly greater landmass of the People's Republic.

This last example is indicative of a dramatic change in the relationship between edges and centres. As with the guardians and the traders, there have always been elements both of symbiosis and of conflict. The empires need to be able to buy things; they often want trade routes to pass through them so that they can be taxed. Equally, edge cities have often sought protection from an empire, and thrived best in the shadow of a hegemonic power like the Roman Empire or the Caliphate. But each step towards a more global, interconnected system stacks the cards in favour of the edges, which are no longer defined by their geographical position. As more things are traded, the places specialising in exchange gain relative to those that do not. They become the natural hubs for telecommunications and financial markets, and amass specialist trading knowledge, while the warrior nations can no longer afford the technology needed to win wars. In a global economy that is more and more dependent on information, every society has to be concerned about whether it has sufficient edges, whether its culture is good at identifying useful things and absorbing and adapting them. Certainly this failure to cultivate an edge is one of the explanations for the collapse of communist economies. They had no shortage of trading ingenuity but it was all absorbed internally, in making the system work, and holding on to territory, rather in successful external exchange. Most nations have now learnt the lesson. While trying to cultivate the spirit of enterprise to create wealth, they now see the conquest of territory as a burden, not as something to aspire to.

The relative decline in the importance of war in some parts of the world is casting attention back to the role of the city region and city state as more natural units of commitment and production than territorial nations and empires. If territory is a less reliable source of power than connections, then the city comes back into its own. Many of its natural characteristics – the emphasis on the exterior of human personality, on change, and on tolerance (and the pleasing fact that, other things being equal, the more we know about each other the more we tend to understand and sympathise) – become economic as well as social values. And far from being made obsolete by communications technologies, the cities' character as centres of sociability becomes more important because, in the words of urban geographers, each programmed interaction needs to be backed by an unprogrammed one, a less formal interchange in a bar, a restaurant or someone's home. Trade, exchange, and the cities of the edge all thrive amidst connexity. Even more than before, they become specialists at syncretic creativity, merging elements into new forms, and benefiting from the ways in which the new ideas emerge on the edge of things, not at the centre.

It is a striking feature of the modern world that nearly all of its creative geniuses were in important senses marginal people, people who had gone into exile. Howard Gardner points out that what he calls the seven 'creators of the modern era' all travelled widely, and all but one ended up living in a country different from that of his or her birth.[6] Freud went to Paris and London, Einstein to the US, Picasso to France, Stravinsky to the US, T.S. Eliot to London, Gandhi to England and South Africa, and only one (Martha Graham) remained in the country of her birth. We could add to that list figures like Karl Marx, Ludwig Wittgenstein, or James Joyce. It appears easier to see a clear reality at one remove from a culture (and the exceptions, like Immanuel Kant, who famously never left his home of Königsberg, or Charles

Darwin, who scarcely moved after his travels on the *Beagle*, stand out precisely because they are exceptions).

It would be wrong to celebrate this syncretic cosmopolitan culture uncritically. Cities have always been denounced for being unfriendly, acquisitive, superficial. Edges tend to be weak on commitment and belonging, community and loyalty. They live more on the surface, without profound spirituality, without silence and contemplation. They naturally care less for the physical environment, the diversity of species and the tranquillity of the landscape. But the important point is that the long-run rise of connectedness and exchange means that the places that were once exceptional, the ports and markets, are now in a sense ubiquitous, present in a telephone, a computer, in a global culture where selling is normal, accepted and unashamed. And this edge culture, like the culture of exchange more generally, has the advantage of its dynamism, always searching out new connections, new things to trade and new forms of knowledge, in the search for the potent alchemy that enables a new place or a new firm to make something out of nothing.

Alongside the division between moral syndromes and places there is another kind of division, a division of roles. In every traditional society the majority of tasks involved working with physical things to transform them: soil and plants to grow food, wood and metal, stone and water. Only a relatively few specialists were concerned with managing relations with the outside world. The shaman interpreted the signals from the natural world and the gods, the diplomat dealt with other states, the merchant with goods. But these have always been relatively few in number, and even to some extent strangers in their own societies, albeit viewed with fascination.

Today this weighting of roles is reversed. The proportion of any population working directly with physical things in the most advanced societies is usually well under a fifth (and most of those ostensibly involved in manufacturing things are in practice working through machines rather than directly on the thing itself). What has happened is a shift from a game with nature, about extracting resources, or making products, to what Daniel Bell called a 'game between persons'.[7] There are still large numbers involved in direct care for others, and these roles have something in common with cultivating land, but the majority of new jobs involve manipulating symbols and abstractions, and working with others towards what to previous generations would have seemed like very abstract ends. In this work, ever fewer people work solely with mechanical machines: most spend their working day interacting with computers and with other people who may be consumers or suppliers, or co-workers joined together in groups and on projects.

The shift to a game between persons brings with it a change in skills. The labour market now places a high value on the 'interpersonal' and intrapersonal skills, the capacity to think into another's mind, to empathise not just to serve. Qualities are as important as qualifications. At the peak of this new kind of labour is the expanding army of intermediaries and interpreters dealing with the myriad of human relationships. They include the lawyers and accountants, journalists and managers, entertainers and consultants, therapists and experts. Some work as lubricants of exchange. The original meaning of entrepreneur is someone who brings two parties together, and many of the most highly paid tasks involve brokering in some sense, whether in relation to money, health, materials or knowledge. Others work as interpreters. These are the specialists who analyse the raw facts of the news, consumer data, fashions, cooking and gossip. Every market, however sophisticated its technologies, still depends on human judgements to help it function, to make sense of the raw data. The rise of information does not lead to secure and certain citizens, but rather fosters an infinite regression of interpretation. We have more information about health, or products, or how to bring up children, but also layers of interpreters of the information, and interpreters of the interpreters.

We value more than ever the ones who are not *parti pris*, who retain an independence, and these interpreters are part of the world of exchange, since without advice about how to engage in buying and selling we fear being taken advantage of, and without counselling or mediation we may get trapped in unhappy situations or irresolvable conflicts.

The intermediaries and interpreters have skills that are not bound to one spot, or embedded in a single culture. Instead, their accumulated knowledge, and their capacity to make judgements (especially those that cannot be captured in an expert system or program), makes them mobile, marketable in a global market. This fact tends to be reflected in payment scales. Occupations like corporate law, accounting, consultancy, even surgery, tend towards the pay structures seen first in Hollywood films, with astronomic pay for a relatively few stars, a base of more average rewards, and a large pool outside of people wanting to get in. More generally, the 'skyworkers', the managers, administrators, consultants and designers working in glass and steel towers, have grown powerful relative to the 'groundworkers' , the park wardens, cashiers, train drivers and waitresses working at street level.

These new inequalities are different from traditional ones. Just as the edge cities allow for greater mobility than the more rooted centre cultures, so are the professions based on knowledge and judgement more open to social mobility. The capacity to exchange, or to make sense of things, does not depend on status or accumulated capital. A world in which power over physical things is less important than power over symbols or knowledge is also more open, because it renders at best temporary any absolute hierarchies of culture, truth and authority. One symptom of this openness is the lack of mystique that surrounds roles that were once obscured by deference. Power has lost its equation with respect, and today, amidst a marketplace of facts and interpretations, presidents, kings and chairmen of companies can no longer count on any automatic respect. Those with power are liable to be seen as shallow egos, seeking vainglory, and many who might in other times have wanted to become leaders seek recognition in other ways. Theodore Zeldin puts it well: 'Traditionally respect was converted into power but it has now become desirable for its own sake, preferred raw rather than cooked'.[8]

We can sum these points up as follows: the rise of exchange has left us with an unprecedented density of institutions, cultures, and people whose *raison d'être* is exchange and transformation, taking something and turning it into something else, as opposed to concern for land, territory and direct engagement either with material things or with others as people to be cared for. The centre of gravity of societies has shifted away from those occupations which favour continuity towards occupations which favour change, unpredictability, spontaneity, innovation, creativity.

For these new elites creativity is a cardinal virtue. Over the last few decades it has become conventional wisdom that an information revolution is taking economies and societies out of the industrial age, just as the steam engine took us out of an agrarian one. But the dominance of exchange means that we need to think beyond these categories. The Nomura Institute in Japan, for example, classifies the four successive eras of economic activity as agriculture, industry, information and creativity, on the grounds that the focus on creativity is the natural evolution of rich information environments, where there are large flows of creative interaction in groupware, Inter- and Intranets. It is only the unexpected, the unpredictable, the combinations that make something new, that count.

The idea of an age of creativity combines the values of the traders and the edge areas with the technological capacities of the present. Its ethos values novelty, syncretism and change as goods in themselves. It sees as heroic the modern enterprises – like Netscape or Oracle – that create value out of nothing, or rather only out of ideas.

What follows from the rise of these new roles that cluster in the global cities, the hubs at the centre of networks? If the conventional view that exchange fosters benign interdependence was correct, they would be well regarded, but just as the rise of exchange has heightened the fault-lines between the trading and the guardian mentalities, so has it sharpened the divides between people whose roles are secondary ones of analysis, interpretation and mediation, and those who work in more primary occupations. Some of these tensions are about pay. The more mobile occupations can claim pay levels by virtue of prevailing rates in international markets. Many of the people working in more primary occupations, such as care, teaching or police, depend on pay rates set by governments, and tend to find these pressurised downwards.

At the same time information technologies have been used to automate unskilled repetitive jobs rather than more complex jobs, wiping out millions of manufacturing jobs that used to be available for working-class male school-leavers at just the time that the other main source of employment – the army – has shrunk as well. Women – who have always been more adaptable to shifts in the labour market – have coped better, but in most of the advanced economies a large rump of unemployed men has not unnaturally come to resent the open markets that have so suddenly devalued them.

Unemployment is just one symptom of a bigger change in how we organise time and work that the new economy has brought. For a century or so, the economy demanded less time from its citizens. Working hours fell by 40 per cent between 1880 and 1990 in the typical Western country. Citizens cashed in their votes to demand some of the rise in productivity in the form of time. It was possible to imagine a future in which leisure time steadily increased and unemployment disappeared. But with the acceleration of globalisation since the early 1970s this dream evaporated. While the less skilled found themselves unemployed, the highly skilled were under more intense pressure to work longer hours. While a third of working-age men are now estimated to be out of work or underemployed worldwide, the elite of brokers, professionals and officials work around the clock, partly because complex, knowledge-based jobs are harder to divide up: five people working thirty hours a week is less efficient than three people working fifty hours a week. A century ago overwork was a sign of poverty (and Mark Twain famously quipped that if work was so great the rich would have hogged it long ago). Today it can be a sign of wealth and prestige.

Polarisation of time has become one of the marks of a more connected global economy. It creates huge strains both because persistent unemployment corrodes the legitimacy of the exchange system (as well as leading to unhappiness, ill-health and crime) and because overwork destroys communities and families.

Fred Hirsch called it the 'economics of bad neighbours'.[9] If the economy demands more time there is less for chatting with the neighbours over the fence, or playing with the children. If jobs are more demanding, then there is less spare energy to put into keeping a political party going or volunteering for a charity. If being a consumer demands time to read consumer magazines and to drive to far-off shopping centres, that must mean less time for something else.

This new economy of time highlights a more subtle division. A world of global networks brings tensions between the mobile participants in a global exchange system and those whose first sense of themselves is as rooted: connected to their families, to a place, to a landscape. The tension manifests itself in many ways. There are bitter clashes over free trade, usually over whether openness of exchange should take precedence over the preservation of community and jobs. Tax also becomes a point of conflict, because the mobile can usually avoid the taxes of territorially based jurisdictions, holding their money offshore or threatening to divert resources to jurisdictions with lower taxes. There are battles over the extent of political power, since those without money naturally try to convert their votes into resources whereas those with marketable skills seek to minimise political claims on their money.

Connexity has heightened these tensions because it has so rapidly amplified the mobility of some groups. They move geographically with the help of cheap air travel, economically with the help of more organised international labour markets, and financially with the help of new instruments that allow them to earn their money at one remove from tax authorities. According to one estimate, a majority of the world's private banking is held in trust in offshore unsupervised tax havens, and the Cayman Islands alone has more funds under management than all the New York banks combined. For firms too the scope for mobility is far greater than in the past – the US Congress estimated that it was losing $35 billion each year through multinational firms using their internal pricing policies to avoid taxes. Given that overall public spending levels have tended to be static in most Western countries, this inevitably means that a higher burden of taxation is being imposed on the immobile, those left behind.

Within each society the battle takes a different form, but there is always a consistent shape to the argument. On the one hand there is the defence of a distinct way of life, embedded in a culture, jobs and a landscape. On the other, there are universal and abstract principles of free exchange and the insistent claim that in the long run these benefit everyone. Both sides use very different types of argument. One is rational and instrumental, the other about belonging. As such, they cannot easily be resolved or compromised. Although it is possible to imagine that the relative weight of those engaged in mobile occupations, in acting as intermediaries and interpreters, will continue to grow, it is hard to imagine that there will ever be a majority of the population engaged in these activities.

Many of the thinkers of the past assumed that greater trade would automatically make people more aware of the outside world, and more concerned with its well-being and security. Alexis de Tocqueville believed that the pursuit of free interests would bring people into contact with others, and that this would in turn stimulate concern for them. But the irony of the rise of an exchange culture is how little it promotes awareness of interdependence. The sense of humility and awe in the face of the complexities of human society and nature is lost in the absorption and excitement of trade.

You can gain a sense of this in any account of traders. The very people most engaged in trade often seem to be least concerned with the behaviour of the system as a whole. People involved in trade have often imbibed the moral division of labour I described earlier, according to which all that matters is the morality of the exchange itself, since the system is outside the loop. Their mentality becomes that of the 'spot' market, rather than that of continuing exchanges. Their myopia reflects the fact that it is easier to organise simple exchanges within a minimum of parameters. To keep track of a market in one-dimensional goods, like money or coffee beans or microchips, or of an international system based on a sport with fixed rules, is a simpler proposition than to manage relationships based on many dimensions. Most fulfilling human relationships are multidimensional, and full of intensionality (the cumulative understanding of motives and feelings). But whereas first-order exchanges are rapid and clear-cut, these second-order exchanges, involving understanding, require a commitment of time and a leap of trust that they will be worthwhile. In other words they are costly. They are hard work, and so less attractive than exchanges whose virtue is precisely that you do not need to worry about the concerns of those you trade with, and so can economise on emotion.

Together these two tendencies, the neglect of territory and of fulfilling relationships, loom like a shadow behind a system based on exchange. The majority of people in the economically advanced societies of North America, Europe and East Asia have benefited from the rise of market systems of exchange. They have less fear of hunger, of lack of shelter, more luxuries and more chances to stretch themselves. But however successful the market, it rarely breeds stable contentment. The anxiety remains just below the surface, and can even be measured in the evidence that levels of reported happiness have remained stagnant even while economic output has doubled, and in the even more abundant evidence that the main sources of human joy come from relationships, and from activities like dancing that are acted out rather than bought.

Interestingly, such anxieties become visible more in fiction than in philosophy. The characteristic fictional dystopias of our time involve myopia, systems collapse, and the neglect of nature, whether their direct source is environmental disaster, the perverse effects of media on behaviour, the proneness of financial systems and computer systems to sudden crisis, or the vulnerability of the population to unknown viruses. Many of the most compelling fictions portray a future where the market system has gone awry. Global corporations that dominate the new information and genetic technologies act beyond the reach of governments that have shrunk to impotence. Societies are racked by deep-seated social divisions and pervasive fatalism, and in the economy the lines between business and organised crime have evaporated.

These stirrings in the subconscious are warnings that even in its moment of triumph capitalism remains unbalanced and incomplete. The values that served it so well in the past may no longer be adequate in a world where its greatest threats do not come from outside, but from within.

6

FALLING APART AND STICKING TOGETHER

THE WORLD IS once again learning that societies need more than free choice and free markets. Interest is returning to older questions of social order: what makes societies hold together, what makes people take care of each other, what persuades people to accept common rules?

In the century or so after the birth of modern democracy these questions were not the most compelling ones. Most people lacked even the basic material needs of shelter over their heads, food to eat, and clothes to wear. Poor health and nutrition shortened their lives, while pervasive war and low-level violence made it hard ever to feel secure. Today poverty remains acute for much of the world's population, not only in the poor south but also in the cities of the richest countries. But for most of the people in Europe, North America and East Asia, and for increasing numbers in China, India and Latin America, the most pressing problems have changed. Poverty has been largely alleviated. The threat of starvation or chronic disease has become distant. In much of the world even the danger of invasion has become remote.

Instead, the characteristic problems of our times are very different ones. They are likely to stem from success rather than failure, too much growth rather than the lack of it, too much choice rather than too little, insufficient capacities to use freedoms rather than too few freedoms. Drug addiction, criminality, terrorism, loneliness, unemployment, family breakdown and the weakening of community – these are the problems that dominate the headlines of newspapers and arguments in kitchens and bars, and that most defy the dominant ideas based on freedoms and rights. Whereas the troubles of the past manifestly arose from the absence of rights and freedoms, each of these problems is, at root, a matter of order, of orders that have gone wrong and are out of kilter.

All human life needs orders. We are sustained by the natural order of sun, oxygen and foods, and die when that order breaks down. We depend on social orders that protect us from being attacked. Our livelihood depends on economic orders that ensure that we are paid for our work, that contracts are kept to, and that the money we use retains its value. Without the cooperation that order makes possible, human groups and societies would never have been able to gather food, look after children or fend off attackers.

Fortunately, we are well designed to function within social orders. We are born with the traits that are needed for a healthy social order, including mutual understanding and respect, sympathy, a sense of fairness and an instinctive grasp of reciprocity.[1] The virtue of these predispositions is that they make it possible for social orders to thrive without surveillance cameras and jackboots; we are well made to police ourselves.

Our natures make social orders possible. But every social order also needs rules – rules that prevent free-riding and parasitism, abuse and violence. Montesquieu wrote that republics are based on men's virtues and tyrannies on their vices, but it would be more accurate to say that a good order both cultivates good inclinations and reins in ones that are unhealthy either for the individual or for the social group. This is what parents do when they bring children up well, and what schools do when they tap into an individual's potential while preventing them from behaving violently or selfishly to their peers. This dual character, reinforcing some dispositions and discouraging others, is also common to all religions and cultures. It can be found in the Buddhist eightfold path to eliminating desire, the biblical Ten Commandments, and the Code of Hammurabi. Conceived carefully, a social order makes it possible for moral rules to be internalised not only through conscious understanding but also through the habit and repetition which turn constraints into preferences.

Each age has its characteristic ways of combining the formal and informal rules that go into any social order. The feudal order matched the church and the military state. The industrial age built on the compartments of the nation, the class and the firm. Our great difficulty today is that there is much less consensus about the kind of order that is appropriate for connexity. In a culture of individualism and expressive freedom, it is easy to see order as a burden, the opposite of the values of autonomy and self-fulfilment. The self-restraint that religions encourage is at odds with hedonism and consumer choice. Many of the traditional sources of order, like the authority of organised religion and the experience of the elderly, cannot sustain their claims to legitimacy. Tradition no longer equates with wisdom because so many traditional forms of knowledge are now obsolete. Experience may even be a barrier to understanding a radically new situation, and with many information technologies the young, even the very young, are strikingly more competent than the old.

Often our culture seems to wish social orders away. The typical heroes of today, as portrayed by Hollywood, are rugged individuals who save the planet solely by their own courage and guile. We like to believe that we could, if we wished, opt out of society and into another life: quieter, simpler, and insulated from the pressures of the world. Yet for simple reasons of arithmetic and space only a small minority ever could opt out, but even for them, this would only be an option because the societies around them are so successful at preserving a modicum of order: at keeping the countryside free from marauding bandits, preventing plagues, or providing a failsafe system of high-technology medicine or communication. The paradox is that even the most self-sufficient are in some respects parasites on everyone else.

Why should we be concerned about social order? Some of the reasons are timeless, but some are recent. One is that the ties binding our societies together have become looser. The clearest symptom is that the typical size of households has shrunk, first in the Protestant countries and more recently in Catholic, Buddhist and Confucian societies as well. Families and friends have become less able to provide people with money, care and moral support and as a result people have become ever more dependent on organisations and on the state to provide for them. We have also become more dependent in other ways. Simply to survive, modern urban societies have to be more tightly organised than their predecessors to supply the water, food, energy, waste disposal, and information needs of a greater number of demanding citizens. The centrifugal forces towards disorder are strong, but they are matched by powerful centripetal forces that encourage people to pull together.

We also have psychological needs for social order. Few can live a fulfilled life unless societies protect the space within which we can pursue our own goals, insulated from threats. Faltering social orders show up first in psychic problems and mental ill-health. Uncertainty and anxiety are disabling. People who feel insecure find it harder to give. The lack of some basic regularities in life makes it necessary to devote our psychic energy to simple things like not being attacked, not losing a job, investing in a pension or negotiating a difficult relationship. We are denied the space or time to develop our potential in other ways, or for that matter to give to the communities to which we belong.

Benign orders by contrast release energy for other goals, and they do this by making life predictable. Peter Drucker understood this well when he wrote that organisations depend on trust and that 'trust is mutual understanding. Not mutual love, not even mutual respect. Predictability.'[2] Predictability can be boring and oppressive, but it is not coincidental that reported happiness levels are often highest in relatively poor regions where family structures remain stable and religious faith still thrives.

There is also a new reason why order is so important. Modern societies have been extraordinarily successful at managing the risks that afflicted the past. The dangers of being murdered in modern Britain, France or Germany are less than one-tenth what they were in the Middle Ages. The danger of dying from infectious diseases has been much reduced. The threat of invasion has been largely eliminated in much of Europe and North America. Yet in their place new types of risk have arisen: those produced by technology itself, particularly when technologists push at the forefront of scientific understanding in the case of genetically engineered organisms, toxic wastes, or food processes. Some now fear, for example, that the epidemiological transition, which made degenerative illnesses, like cancers and heart disease rather than infectious ones like TB or malaria, the major cause of death, could go into reverse as new strains of drug-resistant viruses and bacteria take advantage of population density and mobility. There are the risks produced by complex market systems, such as derivatives, that can wipe out savings accumulated over many decades. Social conflicts born in other countries can turn up today in the form of bombs on the streets of any of the world's cities. Insidious threats may come from cults and militias that brainwash children, or release toxic gases on subway systems.

No social order can guarantee certainty, but its capacity to reduce malign and unpredictable threats is its most important value from the point of view of the individual. In highly connected societies this value grows rather than dwindles, because connexity multiplies the number of unpredictable factors – from global markets to new viruses – that may threaten our well-being.

But it doesn't follow that we should simply try to return to some past tradition or hierarchy. One of the greatest flaws of traditional orders was that they left much of the population subject to chronic unpredictability, arbitrary violence and sudden poverty, which is why historically there has been such support for the advance of freedoms and the rule of law. Instead what we need are ways of generating social orders

that provide a proper balance between freedom and interdependence, risk and safety, for the great majority.

The question of how orders are created, and how they survive, is the oldest one in social science. More than five hundred years ago Ibn Khaldun sought to explain what held
together the complex desert and urban societies of medieval
North Africa, and the classical founders of modern sociology
set themselves the task of explaining what bound industrial
societies together. The mystery was not why societies fall
apart but rather why they cohere.

Sociology and anthropology have collected many examples
showing just how easily social orders can unravel, even without invasion or disease. Studies by Margaret Mead of the
Mundugumor in New Guinea, by Fortune of the Dobu of
Melanesiato, by Colin Turnbull of the Ik in Uganda, by Cora
Dubois of the Alor in the South Pacific, all tell a similar, and
similarly dismal, story of just how readily the social order can
break down and then stabilise at a new equilibrium of mutual
distrust and hatred.

It used to be common to romanticise traditional, pre-
agrarian societies. They were seen as at one with nature and
with each other. Europeans usually looked to Africa or the
Pacific, Americans to the native Americans, to serve as vessels
for their hopes about the virtues of human nature. They saw
modernity as the outcome of the decay of an older, more
benign order, that was replaced with the chaos of the mills,
the smokestacks and the teeming cities. But the more recent
historical evidence has wholly undermined this idyllic view,
and shown that even in the most apparently harmonious
'primitive' society there may be an underlying reality of
danger and disorder. Murder rates are a good indicator. The
Gebusi in New Guinea, for example, have a murder rate fifty
times that of the USA. The Inuit had a far higher murder rate
than Canada as a whole even before alcoholism took its toll,
and the Kung San in Southern Africa murder three times as

many per capita as North Americans. In troubled times the death rates could escalate far higher.

Civilisation does indeed involve making order more structured, but Freud's view (in *Civilisation and Its Discontents*) that 'civilisation is built upon the renunciation of instinct' was as misleading as the inference that lack of restraint would produce a happier and more harmonious way of living. Instead, civilisations come into existence and survive only because they build on underlying dispositions towards order, at the same time as they rein in antisocial instincts.

The tools they use are many. They include fear (the favourite of Thomas Hobbes), self-interest (as expressed through liberalism's idea of the social contract), shared memories and concepts (the preferred explanation of the sociological tradition of Emile Durkheim), daily routines (brilliantly analysed by Erving Goffman among others) as well as the rule of law.

The problem for contemporary politics, however, is that so many of the older social glues look less likely to work today. Fear is always a brittle means of preserving order, but today even the police and army know how easily dictators can be overthrown. They waver in front of angry crowds because they know that the tables may soon be turned. Nor does faith act as much of a glue. The moral authority of religious leaders is bound to be flawed when some religions have had to give up the pretence that their cosmologies and histories are anything more than illuminating fictions (and the ferocious assertion by others of their monopoly of truth may in the long run harm them even more). Shared categories are less likely to act as glues when so many media cut across the boundaries of societies, and when the sheer scale of flows of culture from around the world – news, scandals, pornography, horror, militates against a shared culture. Habits and laws may retain their pull (even if lifestyles are becoming more diverse), but they must do so in an environment where no one needs any more to believe in the permanence of their social order, or in its sacred underpinnings.

*

It is not surprising that many people feel their societies are dis-
solving, and that the language of social cohesion, bonds –
glues and fabrics – has once again become so prominent. But
how should greater cohesion be achieved in a new environment in which information flows more easily, in which freedom is in the air, and in which boundaries are more porous?
Part of the answer lies in clearer thinking about precisely what
we mean by a social order. The classical view of social order
saw it as something static: it was analysed in terms of fixed
structures, fixed categories or contracts, and held in place by
the coercive power of the state and the army, with a monarch
perched at the top of society. The modern view, by contrast,
sees social order as something more like the health of the body
or the human brain, which needs to be continually generated
and regenerated, eliminating parasites and cancers and producing new forms and new complexity. A good order in this
view is one that is flexible enough to adapt to rapid change,
but reliable enough to provide a space within which free individuals can pursue their very different life goals. So we might
want police who can keep the streets safe, but also let people
get as drunk as they want in bars and nightclubs. We might
want flexibility in how work is organised, doing away with
the five-day week or the eight-hour day to make it easier for
two parents to do their jobs, but against a backdrop of a stable relationship between employer and employee. Or we
might want a society that could cope with extending the principle of marriage to gay couples, without sacrificing the ritual,
semi-sacred qualities of marriage itself. These examples are
reminders that orders should be able to adapt, while matching inflexibility on some things – like laws, contracts or violence – with flexibility on others.

The need to balance deliberate design and the naturally
adaptive character of healthy societies was rarely understood
by social engineers. Too many reformers believed that social
orders could be designed, as in a blueprint. The role of political theory and political parties was to crystallise a vision, and
then to implement it through laws and regulations that would
make a permanent settlement. The American Constitution

was one such settlement. The Marxist-Leninist states imposed others. Hayekian neoliberals, in their counter-revolution against social democracy, also tried to replace one blueprint with another, in which the social order was remade in the form of a web of contracts and markets.

But healthy social orders are not like this. They evolve as much as being built. They may benefit from the reflection provided by theories and visions, but they are too complex to be encompassed by them. This is why the best theorists as often follow practice as lead it: giving shape to the changing day-to-day realities of family life, the firm or legal practice. It is why the best legislators understand that all healthy orders function in many registers, with space for fun as well as morality, for some chaos as well as order, whereas the worst are those, like Adolf Hitler and Mao Zedong, who have a vision, define it in a blueprint, and then single-mindedly stick to their principles through thick and thin.

Friedrich Hayek may have at times taken up the stance of a classic revolutionary, seeking to impose his own worldview on all around him, but he also explained as well as anyone the limits of constructed orders. Since our minds construct reality from the shifting data we receive from experience, he argued, we cannot know the contents of other people's minds, and social knowledge cannot be concentrated in a single supreme mind. States that seek to create order therefore tend to become more coercive: their ignorance guarantees that their achievements will be out of line with their aims, and so they command, standardise and systematise, undermining societies' capacities to organise themselves.

As an historical prediction Hayek's argument was wrong, mainly because he understood the state as a single mind, in the image of a monarch, whereas the modern state is better understood as a flotilla of different minds and practices that is part of society rather than standing above it. But his basic point is correct; governments cannot easily legislate social orders because the best have a spontaneous side to them, like the market, languages and common law. They adapt because they generate information through the choices people make, rather than through commands from on high.

But it does not follow that they exist without authority, or plans, as is sometimes implied in the more naive accounts of spontaneous order. Even language has its lexicographers. Someone has to define the laws, to set the rules governing public goods and spaces, although their later evolution requires a healthy interplay between those who set the rules and those who live with them.

Few social orders have evolved without any conscious construction. Sometimes orders have been given shape by a defining conflict like the class struggles in Sweden in the 1920s, or as a response to the trauma of defeat, as with Germany after 1945. Sometimes they are produced by a conquering elite. Sometimes they are born out of revolutions, as happened in America in the 1770s, France in 1789, the Soviet Union in 1917 and Iran in 1978. The act of creation is rarely simple or painless. Instead, like an information pattern, or the ordering of a crystal, a new social order requires an enormous amount of energy to create it, but then needs much less energy to remain in being. This is why orders survive, and why it is only after great effort, revolts, revolutions, that they shift. A social order is in this sense the respect paid to the power that has produced it, as it makes routine the habits of going along with power rather than challenging it.

This need for substantial inputs of energy to make orders has a close parallel with individual psychology. In order to function we all have to be able to read and interpret the social world – the meanings of a smile, a relationship, a love or an enmity. In early childhood the infant has to create from nothing a sense of order, constructing workable hypotheses about who is friend or foe, what is internal or external. Once shaped, this sense of order frees psychic energy for other tasks.

The same is true of the intermediate institutions between the individual and the society, that are created and set moving with some effort, but then maintain their momentum with far less energy. They help to simplify the world, to generate rules of thumb, to make relationships and obligations more transparent. And we also use them to think. As Mary Douglas put it, 'individuals really do share their thoughts and they do to some extent harmonise their preferences, and they have no other way to make the big decisions except with the scope of the institutions they build.'[3]

Which principles should we want to see expressed in a social order? Democratic societies are underpinned by a simple idea, the principle of reciprocity, of equal, fair and symmetrical treatment. In later chapters I spell out in more detail why the principle of reciprocity has become such a feature of a connected world, and how it can be understood as a meta-principle above the trinity of 'liberty, equality and fraternity'. For our purposes here the significance of reciprocity is that it implies a very radical break with the ways in which social orders were shaped in the past. Traditional orders, and many modern ones, have been based around asymmetrical rather than symmetrical relationships: different obligations and authority belonged to the status of a king, a lord or a bishop, than to that of a peasant or merchant. In meritocracies, differential rights are conferred on people who are judged to have superior talents. Even in apparently egalitarian communist societies some are decidedly more equal than others in their army-like command structures. Today, however, those asymmetries are being folded over. There is no universally accepted God to decree why one person should be superior to another; it is less likely that those who lead are wiser, more informed or even better educated than the rest; what constitutes merit is more contested; and authority is more contingent, not so much a stock that is passed down from generation to generation as something that has to be repeatedly created. So today, if a Pope has authority it is not just because of the office he holds, but because he lives out the principles associated with the office, and because his statements touch on public hopes and fears.

What follows from the principle of reciprocity is a requirement that social orders be explicable, rather than mysterious like older orders. If something is restricted, the restriction has to be explained. If a behaviour is discouraged – smoking in public places, owning dangerous knives, having children at too young an age to look after them well, or making fraudulent insurance claims – then it needs to be clear, not just to the majority, but also to the minority whose behaviour would be constrained, why that behaviour would lead to damaging effects for the community as a whole. For all of these reasons a healthy order has to communicate far more: upwards from citizens about their needs and their views of the boundaries of tolerance, and downwards from legitimate authorities about why particular rules should be followed. Such flows of information can have a very material effect. As Amartya Sen showed in his classic studies of famines, it was the presence of a free press as much as anything that made democratic India so much more effective at alleviating famines than the authorities of secretive communist China.[4] The principle of reciprocity also has another implication. A reciprocal society is likely to be a fairer one, more concerned with how decently people are treated rather than only with their outcomes. It is likely to find social exclusion more unacceptable, since that means preventing large minorities from taking part in reciprocal exchange. For the same reasons it is also likely to be healthier than a society which is only successful at generating wealth. Surprisingly, a country can be twice as rich as another without its people being any healthier. The reason is that our sense of self-esteem, the psychological precondition for being able to exercise freedom, is socially dependent. One survey found a fourfold difference in death rates from heart disease between senior and junior office workers in government offices in Britain, and all the major known individual risk factors for heart disease explained less than half the difference. The difference was better explained as a result of the stress the juniors experienced because of their subordinate position. Other studies have shown clear links between levels of social integration and mortality, and even murder appears to correlate partially with levels of income inequality.

Because people think of themselves as connected to others, even in a rich society being relatively poor is damaging: while stress is useful in that it prepares us to respond to threats, 'the effects of chronic stress, which is a frequent concomitant of low social status and the lack of mutually supportive social relations, appears to be something our bodies are not used to'[5]. In other words, a social order which does not promote reciprocity is, literally, bad for our health.

An old Arab proverb warns: 'Me against my brother; me and my brother against my cousin; me, my brother and my cousin against the world.' This is one view of order: that it revolves around concentric circles of family and group, with weakening bonds at each stage. The closer the scale of the social order, the stronger its pull (which is perhaps why it is so rarely remembered that in Leviticus the injunction to 'love thy neighbour as thyself' is followed by the call to 'love the stranger as thyself'). There may be good genetic explanations why this should be so if the basis of altruism and helping behaviours lies in the evolutionary imperative to give shared genes better chances to reproduce. Certainly the language of social order often draws on the imagery of family bonds. Leaders call themselves 'fathers of the nation' and peers are addressed as brothers and sisters in an effort to coopt the unthinking trust and mutual help that family life entails.

There has been remarkably little serious consideration of scale in social science. There were some attempts in the past to define the optimum size for groups, such as Plato's definition of the size of the *polis* in terms of the numbers (around five thousand) who could gather together in the *agora*. But these have been the exception. By contrast other sciences have developed sophisticated ways of understanding the links between size and form. In biology, for example, D'Arcy Thompson's descriptions of how plants and animals adapted their form to larger sizes and weights have framed the common sense of several generations of biologists.[6] But most social science has seen big things just as magnified versions of small things, rather as in medieval times children were seen as miniature adults, not as fundamentally different.

Yet no social order can be understood without reference to its scale. The bonds that hold a community together in a small village no longer function in a city. The norms that govern a clan no longer suit a nation. The rules that determine behaviour on a communications network bringing together tens of millions of people from different cultures have to be different from those operating within a single institution.

What are the right scales for people to live well together? Some of the vices of large scales are well-known. In big societies, other people can come to be seen only as barriers to our own freedom. In big cities, researchers have found that people walk faster, avoid eye contact, and fear strangers. Their inhabitants are less helpful, and more lonely. The impersonal laws and rules that govern them seem emotionally deficient compared to the context-specific norms of smaller communities, which do not require formal contracts and armies of lawyers. But small is not always beautiful. Larger scale can make it easier to trust, easier to cooperate, and easier to survive than small bands and villages. Some nations without any ethnic or genetic homogeneity have elicited far more passionate commitment than apparently distinctive ethnic groups, and many empires have delivered long periods of trust and peace. Instead of romantically promoting smallness as a good in itself, what we need to understand is the delicate balance between scales that makes societies prosper.

Of these, the most elementary unit is arguably not the family, but rather the conversation. Social psychology has shown that there is a rough upper limit of four to the ability to take part equally in a conversation. Once groups grow larger, they tend to break apart, one practical reason why in large Victorian families children had to be 'seen and not heard'. Next, there is the scale of intimate connections. A remarkable amount of research has confirmed that for most people this is around a dozen. When researchers ask people to list the friends and relatives whose death would be a major blow, or the intimates with whom they communicate regularly (such as once a month), they typically come up with a list of around eleven or twelve, which is also, not coincidentally, the number of apostles and the membership of juries, inner cabinets, company boards and many sports teams. This may be the primordial unit of social bonding, the scale within which rich understanding and high levels of intensionality are possible.

A layer up from this, we come to the scale of recognition and understanding: the scale of group within which we can have reasonably detailed knowledge about how people relate to each other. There is intriguing evidence that in many animals brain size, or rather the size of the neocortex, correlates quite closely with the size of groups. Put another way, the typical group cannot grow beyond the capacity of brains to understand the different dimensions of relationships within the group. In the words of Robin Dunbar, 'given that primate social life is characterised by the ability of the animals to recognise relationships between third parties – Jim's relationship with John as well as John's relationship with me – there is a real sense in which the social complexity of a group rises exponentially as its physical size increases . . . the evolutionary pressure selecting for large brain size and superintelligence in primates did seem to have something to do with the need to weld large groups together'. From the evidence of brain size, evolutionary psychologists predicted that the typical size of human groups should be about 150, and this is indeed the typical village size in early settlements in the Near East. The Fundamentalist Hutterites say that once a community grows beyond 150 people it becomes increasingly difficult to control its members by peer pressure. Armies typically use a similar size for fighting units, and experiments asking people to use their circles of friends to help in social research found that in American cities the average number of friends was 135. Similar figures are sometimes cited in describing the numbers of major decision-makers in small nations or medium-sized cities of a few million, village-scale numbers that may explain why they are better able to coordinate their affairs than big nations and cities.

Above this there are other scales. One is the scale of memory. People can remember up to 1,500–2,000 names typically. This is roughly what the head teacher of a large school needs to be able to do, and it suggests the uppermost limit for the proprietor of a firm to retain a personal connection with their employees.[7] Another is the scale of neighbourhood, which in dense cities appears to be around 8–10,000, since these are the numbers needed to sustain common institutions like schools and libraries. None of these scales of attachment is intrinsically more primary than any other. Instead, we probably need to be able to take part in all of them to live a rounded life.

Connexity makes it possible for these memberships to be far more dispersed than in the past. There are few intrinsic reasons why any of these scales should be geographically close. Our dozen intimates may be spread across the world, talked to on the phone. The names we remember may come from very different cultures, or from fictional soap operas as well as reality. Yet even in the most technologically advanced societies there is still a role for connections based on place. Proximity matters because humans are unavoidably physical: our well-being depends on the quality of the immediate environment, its safety, the cleanness of its air. It matters because so much communication is non-verbal, and face to face communications have an intensity that no technologies can match.

So geography creates one limit to scale and to ever more extensive connections. The other comes from what could be called the economics of attachment. All attachments and memberships take time, and time is scarce. We cannot be members of an infinite number of groups in the same way because attachments require not just 'quality time' but also quantities of time, to learn about the people involved, their motivations and idiosyncrasies. Most people retain connections to their family and schoolfriends for this reason, and this is also why, even though the apparent value of networks rises exponentially according to the numbers connected, in practice most people repeatedly use the same few telephone numbers to keep a small circle of friends and relatives in touch.

However large the scale of the social order, all orders rest on much smaller compartments. This may seem an obvious point, but in the industrial age it was widely believed that progress would bring a transition from small, parochial units into the altogether grander scales of big business, big government and big nations. Isolated communities would be tied together in an economy based on a limitless division of labour. Specialised organisations would take advantage of ever larger economies of scale to displace small shops, small crafts and small manufacturers. A wholly rational set of rules would prevail over the particular and the specific, and the benefits of this would be so transparent that self-interest would hold the social order together. Big would be beautiful, and popular. The spread of networks could be seen in this light too, replacing the intensive orders of the family and community with the extensive orders of a global village, governed by transparent rules.

Such was one projected future for humanity, but in the post-industrial era much of this apparently remorseless logic falls down. While bigness may lead to lower costs, it also means remoteness, and remoteness means less understanding, less reciprocity and less richly modulated information. Given that the aspiration for intimacy and understanding remains undimmed, it is not surprising that the pendulum has swung back to an interest in smaller compartments. Smaller units may be better at demonstrating symmetry and reciprocity, giving it emotional colour rather than just embodying it in abstract rules. They may understand our peculiarities and make us feel at home.

The return to smallness in many Western societies has been encouraged by declining trust in big institutions, such as manufacturers, governments and trade unions, and the corresponding rise in trust in personal relationships, such as those with siblings, spouses, work colleagues and friends.[8] Rankings of trustworthiness consistently show that those institutions which maintain a face-to-face relationship with consumers – such as local doctors, teachers or pharmacists – have continued to be trusted more than ones that are dealt with only at one remove. Another telling sign is that consumers are more willing to return to a company that has made a mistake but then rectified it, than to one that has not made a mistake in the first place: the act of admitting an error confirms the authenticity of the relationship more than the efficient delivery of a service.[9] Other symptoms of the return to smallness include the revival of regional identities, dialects and minority languages, and the fragmentation of religions into smaller evangelical communities, with experience taking over from the sacrament and texts as their core.

These changes signal a shift in the form of social order away from the stratifications of class and occupation towards a more cellular structure that is held together by communication. In a stratified society what matters is your position on a vertical hierarchy which is recognised by everyone else. In a cellular order what matters is your membership of a number of different cells – a profession, sport, religion, family network, political party – and their relationship to the larger society. Indeed, it is one of the paradoxes of connexity that the more things interconnect, the more people want to be members of self-contained compartments. Even the largest institutions have to respond; big companies try to respond to their employees' wishes by turning themselves into smaller cells with clear identities and autonomy, and balancing formal hierarchies with the informal sociability of coffee rooms and weekends away. Big cities try to remake their neighbourhoods, with local festivals, boundaries and signposts, and self-governing parishes to tap into local pride. Governments and big service firms offer a named individual as the point of contact for outsiders, to give the appearance of being a friend or colleague rather than an impersonal bureaucracy.

Seeing personal links as the foundation of social order can

be surprisingly illuminating. Recent research on the networks within which people live has shown that who you know, and how you know them, turns out to be every bit as important as what you know. Ronald Burt, for example, has shown that within firms the most successful people are often the ones who straddle a series of separate networks. The manager who knows people in marketing, research and finance can act as a broker between them, seeing opportunities earlier than others. In a sense, their financial capital and human capital can be amplified because of their position on social networks. These ties that bind people together can take many different shapes. If you only know people who do not know each other, your network is like the spokes of a wheel, but without a rim, with you at the centre. If you live in a close-knit community then every point on your network is joined to every other point. The most valuable networks in a cellular society turn out to be the ones that are reasonably extensive. In a seminal study published in the 1970s, the American sociologist Mark Granovetter pointed out that what people need most to find a new job are 'weak ties', ties which are not particularly strong or emotional but which range widely. The value of these ties is that we usually have them with people who move in different circles from us, and who can therefore open up opportunities that we would miss if we were stuck with our own immediate community. Recent research has confirmed that a very high proportion of job seekers find jobs through personal contacts, and that people with relatively few weak ties, such as working-class women and some ethnic minorities, suffer as a result. One study which showed that church membership was the best predictor of getting a job in the American inner cities was originally interpreted as a sign of the value of religion; in fact, it is simply that churches provided more chances to mix with people from different social backgrounds. We prosper, in other words, when we are members of many clubs, and when we cultivate links to many different cells. Family and community remain valuable to our well-being. But in a cellular society we also need links that connect beyond them.

*

Aristotle described man as a *zoon politikon*, political animal, but for most religious and philosophical traditions it is man's nature as a social animal, who easily makes connections with family, friends, associations and clubs, that is paramount, and it is in this sphere that people find their true nature. People are being drawn again into this space that lies between the coercive power of the state on the one hand, and friends and family on the other, a space that is both private and also public and outward-looking. It may be hard to pin down exactly what is meant by civil society, the civic, the voluntary, the associational, and it may be hard to define such activities with statistics, because the informal club of a group of friends merges imperceptibly into the formal association, and because it is the nature of associations that they grow up and die away, energised by a passing enthusiasm and then left to drift inertly downwards. But intermediate institutions of this kind seem to speak to fundamental human needs for sociability and belonging.

The Old Testament warns that 'it is not good for man to be alone', and we know that people become depressed, sick and confused if they are denied human contact for too long. We know, too, that civic organisations teach people how to co-operate and how to set their own goals with a moral integrity that is impossible either in government, which is necessarily coercive, or in instrumental business. It is for these reasons that associations have at various times been held up as a model for society as a whole, an alternative to state bureaucracies and rapacious private companies, and in the 1990s the world has been passing through another of those phases.

The immediate reasons are evident. The collapse of the Soviet Union revealed just how weakened its old civic structures had become because of the state's distrust of anything independent which stood between it and the citizen (in East Germany one writer described the result as a 'niche society', in which people huddled away in a niche of trusted friends and collaborators, almost the opposite of a confident, outward-looking civic sphere). This dwindling faith in the omnipotence and omniscience of the state coincided with a dawning awareness in the West that markets cannot breed economic cohesion on their own without a base of mutual trust and willingness to cooperate. The high noon of neo-liberalism rekindled earlier fears[10] that acquisitive market forces would corrode the mentalities on which markets depend. Individualistic consumerism would undermine the work ethic, just as the pursuit of self-interest would make people less likely to obey laws if they could get away with it. The implication was that capitalism as an economic order had neglected the social order on which it invisibly rested.

Pessimists warned of an irreversible disconnection from civic life. The cells in which we live would become disembodied ones, tying the individual to a screen, a video game or a television programme rather than to other living human beings. Robert Puttnam has argued on the basis of American evidence that engagement in civic life is in secular decline, partly because television viewing has psychically disconnected people from their neighbourhoods and absorbed the free time that would otherwise be devoted to local associations.[11]

Similar arguments have been made in Germany, where it has been estimated that no one attends 50 per cent of funerals, and in Britain, where one study found that 50 per cent of two-TV-set households were watching the same channel on both sets at any one time. In East Asia the much prized cohesion of families and communities is rapidly showing signs of strain as younger generations become more prone to divorce and less willing to carry out obligations to their parents. Within households worldwide the advance of the microwave and the instant meal, the computer and video in the child's room, has made families more cellular and less of a unit. Even friendships may be becoming more instrumental.

These claims of a dwindling capacity to make relationships and social trust are very difficult to measure. Membership figures for voluntary associations are always skewed towards older rather than newer ones: the fact of falling membership among older churches and older organisations like the scouts or political parties proves little. The absorption of time by television is at least matched by the new availability of time amongst the retired and the unemployed,[12] and there is no sign of a long-term decline in time spent helping others. A study of civic involvement in the UK by Peter Hall showed that it had remained buoyant over many decades, and if anything was rising, partly because of government encouragement and partly because of the rise of university education and white-collar jobs which tend to be associated with greater civic engagement. There is also other evidence that would lead one to expect more, rather than less engagement. As Abraham Maslow's famous hierarchy of needs predicted, once the needs for sustenance have been met, and once people have tired of the pleasures of consumerism, they turn to less tangible questions of well-being and quality of life.

Autonomy becomes a paramount value, but so does authenticity, the search for products and ways of life that have integrity, embodying clear values: the bicycle, perhaps, instead of the car, simple clarity instead of clutter. Few of these goals can be achieved alone, and relatively few can be achieved through passive consumption. Instead these shifting values make the association a more congenial home than the impersonal and instrumental nation or corporation. They encourage a social order based on lifecraft rather than lifestyle – activities rather than just consumption, and the steady rise in the number of self-help health groups, self-education, burgeoning sports and amateur music clubs that engage people in 'organising around enthusiasms'.

Nor is it right to jump too quickly to the conclusion that Western societies are becoming more selfish. In Christian and Kantian ethics, helping behaviour which is also pleasurable or useful for the helper is morally suspect, but the rise of a culture of autonomy means that people now engage in associational life more for self-fulfilment and pleasure rather than a religious motive or duty. Employers encourage volunteering because it makes people more employable, cultivating their skills, their capacity to work with others and to solve problems. Self-help health groups, or self-build projects, draw on many different motives, including selfish ones. Intriguingly, in one study of sources of joy carried out by Michael Argyle of Oxford University, volunteering even came out above apparently more selfish activities like sports and music. In the same vein, Robert Wuthnow's survey of compassion in the USA in the early 1990s showed that the people most likely to value 'being able to do what you want' were also often the ones most active in care for others, since care might be convivial and therapeutic for them as well as for the beneficiary.

The most valuable recent concept for understanding societies' capacities to regenerate themselves, and their citizens' abilities to form reciprocal relationships with others, is social capital. The idea that there might be a social, as well as a human and financial, capital was first put forward by Jane Jacobs in *The Death and Life of Great American Cities*[13] before being theorised in more detail by James Coleman.[14] It suggested that societies' capacity to organise themselves rested on a quantum that could be invested in, or frittered away. Social capital is, admittedly, a peculiar kind of asset, in that an individual cannot possess or exchange it and in that it is replenished by use. But its explanatory value lies in casting light on the reasons why in some societies people find it easy to create associations and common projects, and to do so without the costly services of lawyers and auditors, whereas elsewhere society remains a war of all against all.

Usually social capital is defined as a form of trust, which is the 'expectation that arises within a community of regular honest and cooperative behaviour, based on commonly shared norms, on the part of other members of that community'.[15] As Robert Puttnam put it, 'the greater the level of trust within a community the greater the likelihood of cooperation. And cooperation itself breeds trust.' If trust can be promoted, it sets in motion a virtuous circle which encourages both economic growth and social cooperation.

There is much that is appealing in this explanation of social cohesion in terms of people's capacity to create reciprocal relationships with others, whether in business or civic life. It is corroborated by a great deal of research into the dynamics of cooperative and competitive behaviours that has shown that people do best when they are cautious reciprocators: that is to say when they are predisposed to trust and cooperate, but will retaliate against people who take advantage of them. Some societies clearly make it hard to learn the virtues of reciprocation. Where clan or national identities are very strong, reciprocity is tightly bound; dealings with strangers are more likely to involve violence and deceit. As a general rule societies that give many chances for people to learn how to cooperate will be more trusting. Schools that encourage teamwork; economic systems that encourage enterprise and common ventures; democracies that reward those who are able to organise parties and campaigns with strangers – all of these strengthen the bonds of trust, and the habits of reciprocity.

But the idea of social capital leaves out some of the most important questions to be asked of any social order. Trust is not always an unalloyed good, and many forms of trust are literally anti-social in that they constitute conspiracies against other people or against moral principles. Organised crime is one extreme example, cartels (or trusts as they used to be called in America) are another, and groups like the Freemasons are a third. Healthy societies depend on mistrust as well as trust, and one of the virtues of connexity is that it tends to weaken the power of such closed cells that are always resistant to transparency and accountability. Some of the advocates of trust, like the influential writer Francis Fukuyama, sometimes appear almost morally blind. Association is taken to be a good in itself, whatever its end point. Yet trust is not a virtue. It is at best one possible means to ends which are good.

All social orders have some of the properties of a game, one which has rules, winners and losers, and goes on long after each participant has died. The best games are fair ones, where everyone enters with an even chance: this is why people end up rejecting social orders that apply different rules to different players. But one of our problems in creating a healthy social order is that there are radically different ideas about what kind of competition we are engaged in. James Carse puts the difference well in his book *Finite and Infinite Games*. The first approach, he writes, is the warrior mentality, which sees the role of the game as to win a victory, and to crush one's foes. The game is finite, the rules are fixed, and great energies are spent on contests within these rules. The litigation of societies like the USA is a good example. The martial, military and male cultures of many traditional societies are also predicated on seeing the world as a zero-sum game.

In the infinite game by contrast the rules are continually evolving, or rather coevolving. In the finite game the goal is to win, once and for all, whereas in the infinite game the goal is to keep the game going. The irony of the finite game is that it brings to an end what it claims to cherish – the fact of competition. It favours monopoly, oligopoly, one-party rule and dictatorship. The infinite game by contrast favours many competitors, whether these are firms or parties or voluntary organisations, because 'when your opponent is on the ropes you stand back to let him recover . . . many of the Asian martial arts such as bushido, aikido, judo, sumo are disciplines to be perfected and only incidentally contests to be won'.[16]

In nature, within each species contests for supremacy are usually non-lethal, because it is in the interests of each animal to retain a group around it. But sometimes in the Western social orders these ideas of continuing competition have been lost to an idea of supremacy, of winner takes all, that ultimately corrodes the social order because fewer gain from its persistence. The major wars, particularly of this century, were disastrous because those waging them had lost any sense of limits. In business, the culture of hostile takeover bids, using the language of conquest and annihilation, can be equally destructive.

Here we come to the heart of the matter. The idea of an

order in Western culture has been warped by the meanings imposed by conquerors. For them an order was a permanent victory, an edifice that sat on top of the conquered, not a continuing and reciprocal game. This is why deep in our culture there is great resistance to the idea of order, even though common sense tells us that it is impossible to live without one. But the kinds of order we need now are very different from those of the conquerors. They are less permanent, less fixed, less brittle and more open to change. They are reciprocal, not hierarchical, open, not secretive. Their use, in other words, is that they make things predictable, but in ways that can evolve and adapt.

7

ECOLOGIES OF MIND

*The goals and values we now have are appropriate to a
species blindly struggling along with other species in the
stream of life. They are appropriate to passengers not to
navigators.*

Mihalyi Csikszentmihalyi[1]

Behind the question of social order lies an even more basic
one: whether human nature is inherently good or bad, malleable or fixed.

A narrow reading of evolutionary psychology implies that
human nature leaves little scope for shaping. People are
inescapably driven to reproduce their genes. Institutions have
to be shaped around natures rather than the other way
around. Others take the traditional conservative view that
human nature is intrinsically malign, prone to disorder and
rebellion, and therefore needs to be held in check by powerful
authoritarian institutions.

For the liberal tradition, by contrast, our nature is a bless-
ing not a curse. The self is sovereign, separate, immaculate,
pure, always able to make its choices consciously and rationally. Clifford Geertz, the great anthropologist, summed up
such a self as 'the bounded, unique, more or less integrated,
motivation and cognitive universe, a dynamic centre of
awareness, emotion, judgement and action'.[2] Precisely
because it is sovereign, such a self can, and should, make and
remake itself at will. No other institution, and certainly not
the state, should be able to recast individual mentalities to fit

some higher purpose. Even to talk about mentalities as good or bad, appropriate or inappropriate, offends against a liberal sensibility.

This scepticism is well-grounded. The bold attempts of recent history to create new mentalities have largely failed. The Bolshevik programmes to produce a selfless Soviet Man, like those of the Maoist cultural revolution, foundered in disaster. None achieved their promise of an irreversible mental shift.[3] Indeed it is arguable that the communist believers in cultural determinism did even more damage than the Nazi believers in genetic determinism (and not just to people: Lysenko's theories, which drew on Lamarck's claims that experience shapes inheritance, had disastrous effects on Soviet agriculture).

Yet two hundred years ago, liberals habitually talked of the importance of shaping character. Then it was common for politicians and philosophers to discuss the psychological effects of institutions, and to make this a matter of political concern. Thomas Jefferson for example warned that manufacturing would corrode civic virtues, creating an unhealthy dependency on distant economies. Others distrusted big industries that would accumulate concentrations of power that were bound to be abused. Unless people's capacities were built up, they would be vulnerable to the new economic powers of an industrial age. Proud citizens would end up as manipulated pawns.

Few modern liberals feel able to talk in these terms. From the free market right to the liberal left there is a consensus that the best that a society can do is to guarantee a framework of laws that gives people choices about whether to be good or bad, active or passive. Going any further invariably means trampling on someone's worldview. As likely as not it means imposing the values of an older generation on a younger one, or the morals of powerful institutions on to the powerless, as when far stricter moral principles are imposed on poor single mothers than on the idle rich.

But no state or society can honestly remain neutral about the mentalities it produces. Simply in order to function societies depend on trust and the willingness to cooperate, or to obey laws. If governments spend vast sums of money on welfare, they have to be concerned if the dependency thus created undermines the character of the recipient.[4] If they encourage adults to explore every avenue of their potential, or just to have fun, they have to be worried if one consequence is that children are left unattended. In practice every political or economic order not only produces people, but also does this more or less purposefully, and more or less well. Families prepare their children for careers, or to be parents, or carers. Schools cultivate adherence to the national flag, to moral principles or the love of knowledge. Employers try to suit their employees to their corporate cultures, to make them docile or loyal. Trade unions cultivate a spirit of solidarity. Advertisers promote a mentality in which consumption is the route to happiness. Policies that are shaped by the assumption of consumer sovereignty in turn make people act more like calculating consumers.

For all of these reasons it is naive to pretend that mentalities are beyond the bounds of legitimate government. But when governments try to shape mentalities they have to do so with more care than other institutions, because their powers are so much greater. The temptation to overreach can be irresistible. If they try too hard to impose a way of thinking, people rebel, and young people naturally test the limits of restraints on moral behaviour. But if they try too little, the society may end up without the mentalities it needs, and so has to fill the space with more rules, and more coercion. This is why the power of governments always needs to be balanced by other forces like professional ethics, consumer pressure or public opinion.

Tax collection is a good example of the importance of mentalities and cultures, and the subtle symmetry that any healthy society rests on. All systems of tax collection necessarily give a fair amount of discretion to the collectors. Such systems can only work if the collectors do not exploit their discretion to take bribes, and if there is some basis of mutual trust between collectors and those being collected from. Otherwise more policers and auditors are needed, not just to police the public but also to police the tax collectors. Health care is a parallel, but very different, example. Because doctors know so much more than their patients, even today, about the treatments on offer, we use professional ethics such as the Hippocratic oath to ensure that they do not abuse the power this gives them, while also depending on patients' self-restraint not to waste doctors' time. The same is true of political systems which give vast power to presidents and ministers on the assumption that they will use it wisely and not abuse it to serve their own self-interest, while also giving the final say to electors who must take their duties seriously if power is not to be given to knaves and fools.

These symmetries rise in importance in an era when other people's mentalities affect us more than ever before. Strangers are more likely to be walking along our streets, and so it matters if they are liable to be violent, or to drop litter or be abusive. We are affected by what unknown foreigners put into the sea, or into the air, by how much they use common resources, whether they make violent or pornographic material available to our children and neighbours, whether they are warlike or pacific. All of the effects of connexity in extending the capacities of human action give us a legitimate interest in other people's mentalities and require of us a heightened responsibility to others in respect of our own mentalities. As a result, we should not be surprised if others call us to account for how we think and feel and behave, or if they call to account the societies of which we are a part.

Most of us are familiar with the idea of physical ecologies, where change in one part of the system affects another. There may be chains of food, symbiotic relationships between plants and insects, dependence on the weather or the movements of a river. Our own behaviour in hunting a particular species, or polluting the air, may have complex ramifications for the ecology. Much the same kinds of consideration apply to mentalities, and human societies can be understood as complex mental ecologies. In order to function well the typical modern society needs to generate the right number of people who will enjoy caring for the sick, patiently teaching children, or taking financial risks. If it generates a reluctance to lead, it stagnates. If it generates too great a will to drive the society forward it may be disfigured by the clashes of egos. More generally, for societies to function harmoniously despite greater powers and increased reciprocal dependence, they need people who are able to understand their effects on others, to perceive the nature of complex systems, and to empathise and communicate with strangers.

Institutions can support mentalities, or destroy them. Successful institutions often broadcast ways of thinking when their employees leave and go to work elsewhere. Pioneering universities, hospitals and firms with a clear sense of mission all have this effect. Bad ones radiate bitterness and cynicism.

Childhood is the starting-point for understanding mentalities, and our ability to make connections with others. None of us is truly, like Shakespeare's Coriolanus, 'author of himself' and known to no other kin. Instead, for almost everyone, the first connection is with their mother, and after that with close family. Even in the most apparently mobile and individualistic societies the kinship link remains powerful: so for example the willingness to help or make sacrifices is higher for kin than non-kin, murder rates by step-parents are far higher than for parents, and levels of health can be traced to the proximity of support networks which come mainly from the family.

Yet the meaning of the parental connection remains elusive. For Freud parental control was largely explicable as a way of containing the drives of instinct, developing a superego of moral control. More recent research has suggested that parenting is less a matter of imposing alien concepts and more one of cultivating qualities that are already there, prosocial dispositions that have evolved over many millennia. This is why there is a happy fit between the expression of these dispositions and other signs of well-being. James Q. Wilson writes that 'developmental psychologists have drawn a portrait of children who are most likely to help or comfort others and share things: they are sociable, competent, assertive and sympathetic. They do not crave approval and they are not fatalist. They are typically raised by parents who combine nurturing love and consistent discipline and who themselves help others and share things.'[5]

Children are innately sociable, and this sociability is 'the vital embryo in which a capacity for sympathy and an inclination to generosity can be found'. As these capacities and inclinations evolve, children pass through reasonably clear stages of development; from seeking to control the moods of others for their own pleasure, they mature to a point where the emotional state of others affects their own well-being, to such an extent that as adults they even physically imitate the feelings of those closest to them during experiences of joy, sadness or stress.

For the school of thinking and practice that has grown up around the work of John Bowlby, attachment is the key both to contented lives and to a successful society. It is only from security that we feel able to reach out and make connections to others. Its source is simple. Children form secure attachments with parents (and sometimes with others) to protect them from harm. The biological significance of attachment is equal to that of feeding and mating. By being close to someone, by having a relationship in which we know that someone will come to our aid if there is a problem, we can gradually extend our own autonomy, reasonably safe from predators. All that we need is to feel confident enough that the person concerned is available and responsive.

Without secure attachments children grow up to be distrustful and paranoid, or excessively sociable. They are more likely to be angry and resentful, less capable of empathy. With them they are more likely to form successful relationships later in life. Children with secure attachments see themselves as people 'able to cope but also worthy of help', whereas if their parents are unresponsive and threaten to abandon them, the image is of the self as unworthy and unlovable. Patterns of attachment usually form between the ages of six and twelve months, when behaviour like smiling and crying focuses on the mother, and they consolidate in the following two years. Thereafter children steadily become more autonomous, and any constraints that keep them too dependent stunt children's development. Good parents strike a delicate balance. As the work of Diana Baumrind on parenting styles has shown, while aloof, cold, authoritarian styles lead children to withdraw into passivity, laxness in rules leads to their having inadequate capacities to control themselves, whereas a combination of warmth and close control seems to optimise the capacity for self-control.[6] The key is that strong attachments within families tend to make it easier for people to be generous and connected outside them.

Our attachment to people and places contributes to our physical as well as our psychological well-being. The outer ring of life-maintaining systems provided by secure attachments corresponds to the 'inner ring' of physiological systems that maintain the blood pressure, feeding and warmth, and there is some evidence that if the outer ring is deficient, then greater pressure is placed on the inner ring, and people are more likely to suffer physically, with physical symptoms of their disconnection.

There are huge complexities around the concept of attachment and the abundant research conducted to test it, which has to negotiate such issues as the child's temperament (which may make it easier or harder for parents to feel sympathetic), differences between cultures and different methods of measurement. But in a wide range of studies attachments do act as a reasonably good predictor of future behaviour.

The significance of theories of attachment is that they illuminate how we should think about the mentalities appropriate for a more connected world. Two implications stand out. First, that the mythical idea of the self-sufficient individual is not helpful in understanding what makes people truly strong. Second, that help in the right circumstances does not encourage dependence but rather autonomy.

What these theories do not prove is the superiority of any particular form of family. Instead, secure attachments can be made in almost any kind of family, which is just as well since families are as varied as any human institution. Some cultures, for example, see nepotistic favouritism for distant cousins as normal while others frown on it. The methods used to raise children vary widely, and detailed studies ranging from the Kung San, to kibbutzes where children sleep in special infant houses, to Japanese mothers who sleep with their babies, have shown relatively little differential effect on the well-being of the children.

We should also be careful not to mythologise the parental relationship. Attachment involves trust, but also power, and often that power is abused by parents, far more than earlier generations imagined. Nor is it necessary for a child's primary attachment to be with a parent, or with a mother. It can be with someone else, especially in societies where there is a permanent childcarer who is not a parent. More distant members of the family can also be important. Research on grandparents by Arthur Kornhaber and Kenneth Woodward in *Grandparents/Grandchildren* showed that children without grandparents suffered a sense of 'loss, deprivation, abandonment' and were more likely to be bitter or cynical about old people in general.[7] Children with grandparents could more easily imagine themselves as old. If the grandparents had died recently, they still seemed to remain present psychologically.

But here too what matters is the quality of the relationship. Simply having a grandparent or parent present is not enough. When grandparents look after children solely in order to earn money, they often prove worse carers. Unless the relationship is freely and happily chosen it will be flawed. The same is true of mothers. In societies that place a high value on jobs and careers, researchers have found that full-time mothers often subconsciously resent their exclusion from the world of paid work, and suffer from worse well-being and less capacity to provide a secure attachment than mothers who are balancing a job and looking after the children.

Such subtle issues concerning the qualities of relationships have become more important because the traditional impulse to create families has weakened. Today the decision to have children has become bound up with the individual search for authentic intimate relations that are missing elsewhere in life. Becoming a parent means forging a more secure attachment for the parent as well as for the child. Ulrich Beck has suggested that 'the child is the source of the last remaining, irrevocable, unexchangeable primary relationship . . . with the increasing fragility of the relationships between sexes the child acquires a monopoly on practical companionship'.[8] This choice is also one that is more conscious than ever before because parents can now know much more about the impact of their own choices – passing down the generations the bad habits or genes of their own parents and grandparents.

Yet the rediscovery of parenting as an intimate relationship may also have weakened the role of the wider society. Becoming a parent has come to be seen as a private choice, like the purchase of a consumer durable. If parents have children for their own fulfilment, there seems to be less justification for society to subsidise them, through tax reliefs and benefits, free childcare or schooling. Indeed it is not hard to imagine a future where child-rearing becomes wholly privatised. The problem with this view, however, is that how children are raised impacts so directly on everyone else, not just narrowly in terms of the costs later borne in law enforcement, remedial education or unemployment, but also because badly brought up children affect the very feel of a society, making it less trusting, less committed, less reliable. Being a parent is classic example of a relationship and an activity that appears personal, intimate and individual, yet is anything but.

The relationship between families and society is often described through an architectural metaphor. The family is a foundation stone, the rock on which society is built. For this reason it should not be tampered with: it should be left intact, shored up where possible, and never interfered with by the state except in so far as the law keeps it protected by making it harder for parents to divorce. But the very idea of a bedrock is a misleading one, since it implies that society is a static edifice. We can distinguish healthy families from unhealthy ones by their qualities of love and care, but it is wrong to infer qualities from forms, and families have been far too malleable to be bedrock. Families can be single or multiple, two generations or four, engage in infanticide or polygamy, sexual abuse or circumcision, primogeniture or division. They can include servants or only consumer durables, be characterised by love or neglect, infidelity or wife-beating. Strong families can often coexist with widespread adultery. Moreover when economic conditions change, families soon change too. Periods of rapid change tend to pull them apart, as fathers make long journeys to new places of work, unemployment heightens stress, and new opportunities draw women into work and careers. Every time a migrant group enters a new society it soon sees its familiar norms wash away, and its arranged marriages dissolve when the next generation smells freedom.

When life-expectancy goes up, then so does divorce. If welfare is given to people more generously where there is no father, then women respond to the incentives by being more likely to choose to bring children up on their own. If states choose to fund the old, then, not surprisingly, the extended family weakens.

The relationship between parents and children is in some respects a primary one, certainly from the perspective of each person's life. But from the perspective of the system as a whole, the lines of causation work both ways, from the society to the family as well as vice-versa. That is why it is legitimate for societies to make assessments about what are healthy and unhealthy qualities of family life, and about whether families are promoting prosocial or antisocial mentalities. Indeed it is precisely as an alternative to the mythologisation of the family that we need to recognise its role as the place where basic morals are developed – responsibility, sociability and sympathy. The very mark of a healthy social order is that the feedback messages should be appropriate – that good parenting should be rewarded, and bad parenting penalised (something that oddly becomes harder if the family is mythologised).

The focus in all of the sensible approaches to families is on their qualities, not just on their forms. Families with two parents are, other things being equal, likely to provide more care and love for their children. But then families with three adults may be even more supportive, and families with two parents who resent their situation may make the worst parents of all.

Precisely because of the limits of the family, all societies have depended on other institutions to cultivate the mentalities they need. Industrialising societies needed very different mentalities from the ones that flourished in a close-knit village: an interest in change and innovation, and a more open sense of self. Through schools they typically tried to nurture citizens who would know how to do factory jobs, how to deal with strangers, how to owe allegiance to the nation. Through the factory and office the residue of agrarian habits was knocked out of people.

Industrial-age education systems became fairly proficient at producing the basic mentalities needed to operate in an industrial world: punctuality, self-restraint, and the capacities to obey orders, to do repetitive tasks, to master basic numeracy and literacy. All over the world new nations built systems of education, with some common elements and a common culture. Few went so far as Plato in giving guardianship to the state instead of to parents, but most recognised that parenting could only be one pillar supporting the new mentalities, and conversely that schools are not even primarily places that teach the things described in curricula.

However, we are now a stage on from the industrial world that so many school systems were designed for. While schools are still organised on the model of factories, processing children through standardised exams, in the economy the factory model is in decline. Many machine-like jobs

119

are better performed by machines, and growing numbers of jobs require people to take initiative, to be creative and inventive. Even most daily interaction with machines is in truth interaction with other people. A more intensively social model of labour is coming into sight, where learning and work are no longer clearly separated and docile obedience is not enough.[9]

Schools are coming under pressure to cultivate the mentalities that a post-industrial economy requires. So alongside the classic curriculum elements of knowing how to count and how to read, the message from the labour market is that equal weight should be placed on learning how to deal with other people, how to read their emotions, their motivations and cares. In more diverse, and globally connected societies, it is that much more important for school-leavers to be sensitive to other cultures and values. The pressures of daily life point in the same direction, at a time when few school-leavers are well prepared to start a family, to travel, or to know how to look after an elderly relative. Alongside analytic intelligence, we now need schools to harness what Howard Gardner described as interpersonal and intrapersonal intelligence, the capacities to empathise and communicate on the one hand, and the capacity to know yourself on the other. Without them, children are unlikely to turn into good workers or spouses, parents or citizens.

It might have surprised earlier generations of educationalists that these softer qualities should become so prominent, or that the capacities to form attachments should be taken as seriously as the ability to answer exam questions. But many might have been able to guess from their own experience that the ability to act socially and behave morally has a remarkable fit with how well children do in education and in later life. One report for the US National Centre for Clinical Infant Programs, for example, found that the seven most critical qualities that children needed in order to do well at school included: confidence, curiosity, the wish to have an impact, self-control, relatedness, the capacity to communicate and cooperativeness. Most in other words, turned out to be social skills, skills of managing connections. There is also abundant evidence that to succeed in any domain children need inner strength, the discipline to marshal their energies towards their goals. So, for example, the capacity to delay gratification turns out to be a better predictor of success than IQ.

Once inside a school, however, much can go wrong. It is an irony of most school systems that whereas in their early years at school most children believe themselves able to tell a story, sing a song or paint a painting, by the time they leave few have that confidence any more. The same is sometimes true of their moral capacities: at an early age they have an instinctive grasp of right and wrong, but by the time they leave many teenagers have retreated into an inarticulate relativism.

The reasons are the same: lack of practice and lack of clarity. Aristotle said that people can only be educated into a life of virtue through active participation in laws and mores, just as people can only be educated in music through making music. But some of the tools of moral education have worked in an opposite direction. The influential Values Clarification Movement in the 1970s, for example, left it up to individuals whether they should accept anyone else's moral claims. A good relationship, it was argued, is just one that is good for you. This ethos fitted the expressive individualist ethos of its times. But, like the art teaching and music teaching that let anything go and passed no judgements, it did children few favours. For, like a good parent, the best environments are those that give clear guidance, warm support and clarity of values, since it is only with this foundation that children gain the self-discipline and self-control to act in a moral way. Everyone has within them some moral and social understandings, but without the combination of inner discipline and external discipline these remain formless.

To provide that form, children need to be given consistent messages. One of the best studies of the external side of how morality is learnt was carried out by Francis Ianni. In research covering 300 different communities in the USA he found that the best predictor of conduct was the extent to which the people and institutions in a child's life shared a common set of standards and so sent a consistent set of messages for the child to draw on and experiment with.[10]

Given such a background of consistent messages, experiment then allows children to develop a sophisticated moral ear. As with music, that can only come from practice. The Italian phrase *impara l'arte, e mettila da parte* (if you learn how something is done, you forget that you know it) captures the idea perfectly. It is through helping others, taking responsibility, and making decisions that the citizen is formed, not through classes explaining what is right and wrong, or how laws are made. Healthy mentalities are learnt through methods precisely opposite to the infantilising models of the classic hierarchical school where the child is little more than a passive recipient of received knowledge. Indeed, all experience confirms that values do not form just through being taught, but rather arise from compelling experiences that transform our sense of self and enable us to transcend it. So even if the curriculum of the future involves much more interaction with technologies, it will also need to leave time for a very different kind of learning that is less pedagogical and more practical, involving the school in the life of its community, in real decisions and real organisations, so as to cultivate the appropriate mentalities, and those qualities of character which Amitai Etzioni memorably called the 'psychological muscle that moral conduct requires'.[11]

Learning of this kind should not stop at the school. We saw in an earlier chapter how often people feel themselves to be inadequate to their social tasks, such as being a parent, a lover or a friend, and one of the reasons is that they are rarely prepared for an environment in which there are fewer fixed rules and points of certainty. Without much guidance, most people experiment blindly, unable to draw easily on the experiences of a previous generation, but equally uncertain where else to turn. The result is endemic, predictable failure, and a growing need for services to reduce conflict, to mediate and to teach people how to manage their own relationships.

In the Middle Ages it was assumed that the well-being of people's bodies was their own responsibility, while the state of their souls was a matter of public concern. Today these positions are reversed; we have public policies for the health of bodies, but only private tools to improve the condition of our souls. Now we may be witnessing a further twist, since while we increasingly acknowledge greater personal responsibility for physical health, people's mental capacities are becoming a matter of obvious public interest.

If we can reshape our institutions to cultivate stronger people, the benefits should be obvious. If people are treated as adults who are allowed to risk, to fail, or to take responsibility, they will respond by rising to their treatment. If they are treated only as children they will behave as children. In a modern liberal society we see ecologies of mind as somehow outside the realm of politics and of conscious choice. The choosing individual is sovereign. But in densely populated societies this is not a sustainable perspective. We depend on the minds of others, on their being healthy and well-intentioned. For the same reason every institution should be open to judgements about the mentalities they tend to create, whether they leave those who come into contact with them stronger or weaker, more able to bear responsibilities or less so, ethically fluent or ethically stunted. And if they drain, suppress or destroy the human spirit then it is legitimate to ask them to make up the cost they impose on everyone else.

But the ultimate promise of cultivating stronger people is simply this: that the state and law can be lighter, while the individual can grow both outwards through more confident connections and attachments, and inwards to a better integration of life, work and the spirit.

8

MORAL FLUENCY

A MORE CONNECTED world should be a more moral one, or at least more sophisticated about morals. We should be able to learn the insights of other ethical systems, from Buddhism or humanism, native American mysticism or Confucianism, and the limits of the simple precepts of faith and family that have often passed for morality in our own society. In the past the widening of connections has served as an engine of moral progress, awakening world opinion to slavery, serfdom and child labour, and then to racial and sexual oppression, and most recently to environmental destruction and the abuse of animals.

Yet for most people in the West the idea of moral progress now seems like a picturesque but ultimately futile goal. They are certain that morals are in decline, that standards of behaviour have deteriorated, that people (usually other people) are less responsible and that selfishness has taken over from altruism. By a margin of 63 to 28 per cent, for example, Americans in one recent poll reported their belief that people are becoming less interested in helping one another and that the delicate balance between individualism and altruism is tipping the wrong way.[1] Similar conclusions have been reached by the public in most other Western countries.

These statistics can be taken with a pinch of salt. They may not mean that people are behaving less morally. The statistics for crime, charitable donations, divorce, child abuse, to take just a few examples, all have contradictory implications, with higher charitable donations as well as more crimes, more care

124

for animals as well as more divorce and (possibly) child abuse.

But it is foolish to dismiss public anxieties too readily. As I will argue, there are grounds for worrying about the moral implications of connexity, as well as grounds for optimism. Without a clear moral compass, there is a real danger that a more connected world could end up confused, shrill, mutually suspicious and devoid of any common reference points or standards of judgement.

To understand the morality that will help us live in a more connected world, we first need to understand our inheritance. Morality originally meant customs (from the Latin root, *mos*), but it has also come to mean rationally deduced ethical principles. Generally, we use the word to refer to the shared rules that govern how we live together, some of them encapsulated in laws, others sustained by custom. But moral actions also have special qualities that do not apply to all of the rules we share: they reflect an imperative, a sense of must or should; they are general and symmetrical in that we justify our moral actions with reference to general rules; and they express a commitment, rather than just being means to ends. This definition broadly accords with how most people understand moral questions; they combine emotion and thought, drives and reflection.

What, then, are the sources of morality and why do people act morally? Two and a half thousand years of ethics have failed to resolve the question. According to the tradition of the Sophists, Hobbes, Machiavelli and St Augustine, people are essentially selfish, behave altruistically only to make themselves feel better, and need external authority to make them do the right thing. For the tradition of Plato, Rousseau and Kropotkin, people are essentially benevolent, and society is usually the source of evil.

This argument still rumbles on. But framed in this way it is largely futile, because there are at least three distinct, and often contradictory, sources for the moral behaviour of any real individual. We are influenced by the dispositions that are embedded in our genes, and that make us sociable and sympathetic as well as sometimes violent and promiscuous. We are influenced by tradition, which over time has sculpted rules to fit the conditions of life (so that Muslims refuse to eat pork, Hindus refuse to eat beef, and Americans refuse to eat cats and dogs). And we are influenced by reason, which gives us the capacity to deduce moral choices from abstract principles.

Sometimes these three sources point in the same direction. When they do, moral issues are simple, as they generally are with questions of murder, theft or fraud. But on many different fronts they speak in conflicting voices. Should life be sacred? How free should people be to pursue their own sexual fantasies, so long as they don't harm others? What responsibilities should a firm have to its employees? When should political leaders be allowed to lie? Because the sources of morality are different, there can never be final answers to these questions. Instead they are argued about and campaigned over until common judgements are made, and laws are passed by democratically elected parliaments and congresses. This is the sense in which today we live in a moral republic, with no absolute authorities and no divine rights, but rather a continuous conversation.

The more serious moral pessimists do not argue that humans are naturally evil, but rather that the sources of moral behaviour are now drying up. We may still have underlying dispositions to be moral (just as we have dispositions to be selfish, and sometimes violent), but neither tradition nor reason can be relied on to provide a moral steer. Reason has become the enemy of morality because science has become detached from any concern for its ends, immersed instead in abstractions and uncertainties. Traditions have lost the capacity to make claims on people because in multicultural societies they no longer have any special status. For the pessimists, the most important source of traditional morality, religion, has lost its voice. Religious rules once guided people on how to live and what to avoid. The moral voice of God, family and ancestors provided a ready counter to excess individualism. In different ways and at different times they spoke with a loud voice that kept people in check, and forced them to attend to the needs of others.

One of their voices was fear, and for pessimists about human nature fear is the only reliable foundation of morality. As Rudolf Otto wrote in his classic account of religion,[2] the feeling of terror came before the feeling of the sacred: fear at the sight of an overwhelming superiority of power, and the fear that comes from knowing that exit is not an option, whether that meant exit from the family, from the religion or from the community. That voice of fear, and the voice of awe, have fallen silent.

So has the idea of morality as external restraint. Seven of the ten commandments are prohibitions, and all traditional moral systems take the form of obligations that have to be met, and actions that have to be avoided. Reason by contrast is necessarily a weaker basis for morality, and in any case liberalism commonly paints internal or external restraints as wrong. Today we automatically side with Anna Karenina, the archetypal and tragic figure who chose to ignore social restraints, discovering her true nature by rejecting the nature society imposed on her. But if we are left without external restraints we inevitably become more vulnerable to temptations and pleasures that pull us away from necessary sacrifices, care about the distant future, or considering others before ourselves. And so we get another version of the old story of decline, with the present just another stage in the inevitable cycles through which civilisations pass; with our own cycle long past its days of virtue, and locked instead into a culture of licence, where the pursuit of excitement and sensation, aided by ever more exotic technologies and pharmaceuticals, dominates everyday life.[3]

Every age is prone to look back on a recently lost golden era, when there was order, a clear sense of right and wrong, respect and deference. It is easy to forget the poverty, murder and casual violence that were rife even in the recent past. But contemporary fears of moral decline are not entirely fanciful. Even if we reject a morality based solely on fear or religion, we cannot deny that some of the structural effects of a more connected world do indeed weaken moral rules. Where there are fewer repeated relationships and exchanges, we have less reason to behave in a moral way, and where our connections are more extensive, we lose the live contexts for understanding moral languages, and are left mouthing the words but failing to understand their meanings. The active presence of the mass media, and the fragmented media of the Internet and CD-ROMs, make it all the more likely that people will receive conflicting moral signals. Some may be prompted to think harder about their actions, but others end up just confused about whether, for example, children should be told how to behave, whether it is fair to keep an animal as a pet or whether it is smart to be a con-man.

The golden mean is the principle that we should treat others as we would wish to be treated ourselves. It is one of the most accessible ideas of moral philosophy. This idea of reciprocity is crystal-clear in a closed society. The fact that everyone has to deal with everyone else repeatedly reinforces it, even makes it second nature. But in larger groups, where it is easier to leave and to be mobile, these pressures weaken. If relationships are less likely to be repeated, they are less likely to be reciprocal (as Marcel Mauss explained, gift relationships depend on the expectation of future gifts; in the transient relationships of the city square or the World Wide Web there are fewer grounds for confidence, and every friend may turn into a stranger).[4] If it is easier to exit a relationship (with a lover, a child or an employer) there is less reason to have to negotiate a fair and just accommodation. If it is simpler to exchange things in readily commensurable quantities, like money, then relatively less energy may be spent on exchanging things that require layers of mutual understanding and intensionality, such as love. Even the basic dispositions to care for children are muddled when relationships can be easily exited, when there is serial monogamy and one parent may have several families.

All societies and institutions are in some respects balances between drives and restraints. More porous societies find it harder to organise restraints, since the restraints can be ignored or circumvented. This may be benign, because it limits the abuse of arbitrary power and violence. But it also carries a high cost, because social pathologies have more scope for spreading, whether they take the form of drug addiction, parents without commitment to children, and parasitic behaviour by firms, individuals or governments.

If the links between everyday actions and effects are becoming looser and more distant, then it must be more tempting to deny responsibility. If we buy a hardwood piece of furniture, should we really feel guilty about the effect this has on global warming? If we vote for tax cuts, should we feel guilty if a rise in homelessness follows when there are so many other variables at work? We know that when people's sense of responsibility is diminished they behave in less moral ways. Stanley Milgram's famous experiments on torture showed just how readily people were prepared to inflict extreme pain on others if they believed themselves to be following orders from an authority figure, and this sort of disconnection is made much easier for users of modern technologies, like the missile-launcher who sees only an electronic screen, or the investor who sees only a share price twitching rather than a factory being closed. Together these seem to add up to a strong case that the underlying structures of modern life are biased against moral behaviour. They make for less intimate, less grounded, less committed relationships.

The idea that the modern world has detached people from authentic moral choices is not new, although it takes new forms amidst information technologies that replace human consciousness and calculation with machine intelligence. Most of the leading philosophers of the modern age have written about estrangement, the feeling of living in an alien world. Romantic poets and novelists lamented the loss of the authenticity, warmth and mutual support of traditional societies. More relationships seemed likely to mean worse relationships, less reliable and trusting, emotionally impoverished. Martin Heidegger wrote about our 'thrownness', dumped in an alien world, Karl Marx of the alienation of the worker from the things he or she produced, Emile Durkheim of the anomie of societies losing their bearings, whether as a result of growth or recession, and many contemporary green

129

thinkers have written of the loss that results from no longer living amidst nature and the seasons. Each is describing a disconnection from the roots of life, from family and community, from a sense of place and belonging, and the replacement of an authentic, virtuous way of life with ways that are superficial, meaningless. Each is suggesting that this disconnection weakens the bonds that make for moral, committed and responsible behaviour.

The most articulate recent advocate of this view is the philosopher Alasdair MacIntyre. He argues that moral behaviour thrives only in what he calls 'practices'. These are everyday communities that define their own standards of excellence and their own goals. They might include monastic orders, a profession like teaching, a private firm committed to excellence in design, or a team of scientists. The moral principles they develop become subtle and complex, suited to a particular way of life. Today, he warns, our practices have atrophied. We use the same moral language as our ancestors but the words have lost their resonance. Vocations have been replaced by careers, religious institutions by leisure facilities, and a culture concerned with goals has been replaced by a consumer culture concerned only with means.[5]

MacIntyre concludes that moral decay is unavoidable, and that since its causes can no more be disinvented than the nuclear weapon or the semiconductor, it is only possible to recreate the conditions for virtuous living in an isolated cult, or in small communities that deliberately shun the outside world. In other words it may only be possible to act morally outside society rather than in it. Alternatively it may only be possible to recreate moral living within a dictatorship, an autocracy of the virtuous who are prepared to override the wishes of their moral inferiors.

It is all too easy for moral unease to lapse into authoritarianism. If the forces working to weaken moral behaviour are so strong, then perhaps it is incumbent on governments to 'shore up' the traditional family, instil absolute moral principles in schools, and punish more severely anyone who commits crimes. Programmes of 'remoralisation' have once again become fashionable, drawing on the analogy that in the nineteenth century the combined work of churches, charities and governments sharply tightened up the standards of behaviour that had gone astray in the industrial revolution. Certainly societies have 'remoralised' themselves in the past, especially when there is a shared sense of crisis about the effects of moral decline. But, as currently constituted, governments are not well placed to lead. In part this is because they lack the knowledge to understand what effects their actions will have. As in economic life, they can usually only set in place frameworks; they cannot command and control. Nor are the major religions well placed to exercise moral leadership, since they have been sadly unable to keep up with the pace of moral argument over the position of women, the environment or homosexuality, as well as being pitifully inadequate in devising new forms of altruism and social responsibility.

However, the more serious flaw of the call for remoralisation is that it is reactionary, in the literal meaning of the word, and consequently doomed to fail. It calls on power to be mobilised against the grain of change, and ignores those new forces that might help to promote moral behaviour. This weakness is a decisive one, because new structural forces are doing every bit as much to enhance morality within connexity as to destroy it. It is these that give grounds for hope instead of despair, and cast doubt on the cruder forecasts of an imminent moral apocalypse.

Relationships are a good starting-point, since personal relationships with family and friends are the crucible of moral understanding. Contrary to the prevailing wisdom, the scope for people to make lasting relationships is greater than ever before. There may be many more divorces than in the past, but the typical successful marriage will now last for forty or fifty years. Typical parents will see their children grow well into middle age. The typical friend made in adolescence will remain a potential companion for sixty or seventy years. With a backdrop of stability in most of the basics of life, it is also a good deal easier for people to direct their energies to moral purposes – such as caring for an old relative or volunteering – than in an era of war and grinding poverty. We may be endangered by new insecurities, insecurities that could dampen morality, but most of these remain on the margins of life. Moreover, because our expected lifespan is so much longer than before, the personal incentives for morality are strikingly higher. If you are likely to die at twenty-five you have less reason not to cut corners, to cheat and lie. You are also more likely to be violent: evidence from the USA shows that a propensity to use violence or to commit murders corre-lates closely with a brief life expectancy (even if one excludes the murder statistics) for the simple reason that it is more rational to take risks to get the things you need. Conversely, if you expect to live until ninety, you cannot afford to make too many enemies.

The second ground for optimism is that more communica-tion widens the scope of moral argument, and brings many more people into its orbit. Morality changes from being a given, part of a culture, to something moulded, engaged with, and argued with. Unthinking conformity is difficult in a sea of conflicting messages. For traditionalists this is precisely the problem: morality must be accepted in a leap of faith or sub-mission. But in an open society moral ideas that are argued with and internalised through reason may be stronger than ones that are simply swallowed whole, and may just as easily be rejected whole.

Within larger societies there is literally more space for moral disagreement. It is more likely that people with a griev-ance or anxiety will use a moral language to get others' atten-tion, as they have more to gain from seeking allies. It is more likely in a highly communicative world that people will learn moral fluency, feeling the need to justify their desires and complaints in universal moral language, and to take part in moral arguments that were once the preserve of a small minority of adepts, such as those over animals, the rights of strangers, future generations, or unborn children.

The third reason for optimism is that a connected world is not without moral restraints. The force of shame may be more potent than before in a media-saturated society, particularly for the powerful who in the past were relatively insulated from the free flow of information about their moral transgressions. If a powerful man rapes a girl, or robs another, or abuses a servant, this action is more likely to enter the public moral domain than in the past. Our moral standards for politicians and business leaders would have shocked previous generations not for their laxness but for their toughness. Intrusive media may be unsettling and even sadistic, but they are undoubtedly a curb on personal misdemeanours by the rich and famous (although oddly, in public policy debates, shame is usually recommended as a deterrent for poor young men who are probably least likely to be affected by it).

These three factors – the deepening of relationships that is balancing their disruption, the widening of moral language and community, and the broadening of shame – all mitigate the potential threats of connexity. As powerful structural forces that work against the thinning of relationships, they are what make the moral language and argument so much more alive at the beginning of the twenty-first century than at the beginning of the twentieth, as societies grapple with the ethics of everything from military and reproductive technologies to medical decisions over matters of life and death.

But what of the nature of morality itself? The relationship between what ought to be and what is frames our view of the scope for morality, and the extent to which we think of it in terms of policing or of education. G.E. Moore confidently called the equation of 'is' and 'ought' the naturalistic fallacy, a confusion of the descriptive and normative, but one of the great intellectual achievements of the late twentieth century has been to rediscover the extent to which morality may indeed be inscribed in our nature. It is not an external imposition by an angry deity. Instead we have moral dispositions at least in part because in the formation of human beings it conferred an evolutionary advantage for creatures to have sympathy, a sense of equity, and certain kinds of altruism. We are programmed to think morally, just as we are programmed to seek sexual partners, to eat, and to defend ourselves from attack.

Precisely how this programming works is open to question. Its investigation combines ethics, neuroscience and developmental psychology, and remains at an early stage. But what we know suggests that human moral thinking, rather than being solely comprehensible as part of the reasoning of the neocortex, may originate in the limbic region, as do more selfish instinctual drives. It is deep within us, and as such cannot be legislated away, although like all predispositions it can be either suppressed or encouraged.[6] If this is true, it would explain why the idea of ought, the idea that underlies all moral systems, is universal. As James Q. Wilson wrote, 'You cannot discuss morality with someone who is devoid of any moral sense. The fact that you can discuss morality with practically anyone suggests to me that the word "ought" has an intuitively obvious meaning and that people are in the great majority of instances equipped with some moral sense.'[7] Moral sentiments can find very different expressions, but their ultimate sources, whether translated through reason or tradition, are common. Perhaps this is why we find psychopaths so fascinating, in that their capacity to be intelligent and calculating and yet devoid of any moral sense makes them the very opposite of what we think of as human.

A common nature helps to explain why moral argument has survived many attempts at displacement and the repeated denial by successive generations of philosophers that morality is anything other than an artificial construct. Marx described it as an effect of power, Freud as a product of social repression. Post-modernism and relativism in different ways either deny its reality or so personalise morality that it loses any universal characteristics. But despite their influence moral questions continually return, and are always experienced as something more than rational.

The persistence of moral concerns is matched by the persistence of disputes about morality. We are built with a grammar for thinking about morality, and not a fixed code. We learn moral reasoning in the same way that we learn languages, drawing on our instinctive grasp of moral ideas, making sense of patterns, but coming to millions of different conclusions.

As is the case with languages, moral rules are extremely complex, and sensitive to context. They cannot meaningfully be summed up in a handful of ready guidelines, or for that matter ten commandments. As one researcher put it, 'to hope to condense the subtle moral expertise encoded by a biologically realistic neural network into a tractable set of summary principles or moral rules is in all probability a quite hopeless task. In this respect moral expertise looks set to follow the pattern of expertise in general. Long volumes fail dismally to capture the knowledge of the expert chess player. The knowledge of the successful moral agent is probably no less complex.'[8]

That morality draws on genetics and on subtle capacities to learn is the basic cause for optimism that even without a religious foundation societies can become more rather than less morally fluent if they give their citizens opportunities for moral thought and action. Forecasts of a moral Tower of Babel, in which the citizens of a teeming world are utterly unable to understand each other's moral precepts, are almost certainly wrong. However this idea of moral learning does cast light on why each generation often feels that its moral heritage is flawed. Just as human bodies have inherited appendices and weak backs that now cause us problems, so have we inherited inappropriate moral ideas. Judaism and Islam have inherited rules on eating that were designed for the hot Middle East before refrigeration. The ruling elites of some of the older countries have inherited rules of chivalry and warfare that made some sense for medieval knights but have no bearing on the automated battlefields of the post-modern era. The idea of marriage for life changes its meaning in an age of ever-rising longevity, when the longest period of marriage is likely to come after children have left home. The ideal of the sanctity of life becomes an amoral idea if it blocks euthanasia and the capacity to have a fulfilled death.

Everyone may have a different list of obsolete precepts, but the important point is that every age has to engage in moral arguments to translate its instincts and intuitions into laws and rules that govern life. Even if moral dispositions are, as it were, hard-wired into our makeup, it does not follow that morality, the way in which we interpret these dispositions, is so fixed. A healthy view of morality instead sees it as a combination of rules and capacities, or fluency. To emphasise only rules, as if morals could be taught like geography or maths, is naive. It makes morality too brittle to survive the stresses and strains of everyday life. But to see morality only as a capacity, according to which each individual can tailor their own morals, is equally dangerous, since it denies the social foundations of morality.

I mentioned earlier the three main sources of morality: tradition, reason and disposition. Moral fluency means being able to meld these three sources into a coherent whole. But how should this be done? In Western philosophy reason has been the most prestigious source of moral principles. Its most valuable idea is, perhaps, the notion that we live in communities in which each person should be able to choose the life they lead and to negotiate the space they need in order to live, and in which their liberties are bound up with their relationships with others. Characterised in this way, the moral tradition is far richer than its translations into the political forms of rights and liberties. It assumes that each person can give reasons for their actions, and distinguish between good and bad reasons, again in a public domain. It assumes that people must be free to pursue their goals and take responsibility for their actions, that they must be sovereign over the things that shape their own existence.

The idea of people living in a web of relationships that govern their freedoms and responsibilities, a web in which they try to live by agreement with others, was expressed most beautifully and profoundly by Immanuel Kant, and is summed up in the idea of the categorical imperative: that humans should be treated as ends and never only as means. This idea sees each person as equal, and as a unique and irreplaceable part of the shared moral order. For some, this implies the possibility and desirability of a world governed by rules that guarantee our freedom from other people's purposes. The liberal view of a rule-based world mirrors the traditionalists' belief that morality is just a matter of learning rules. It suggests a legalistic world which is oddly desiccated, as if our negotiations with others were like those in business or law, concerned only with interests. Yet in practice other emotions are always present, as is the third source of morality, our own nature and dispositions.

Owen Flanagan recently wrote that any useful moral theory has to be realistic about human nature. 'Make sure,' he wrote, 'when constructing a moral theory or projecting a moral idea that the character, decision processing and behaviour prescribed are possible, or are perceived to be possible, for creatures like us.'[9] We feel affection and love, sympathy and pity, and we find it hard not to do so. All of these emotions often run counter to reason, and to the apparently rational rules with which the world might be run. They encourage nepotism as opposed to appointment on merit, mercy as against justice, sentimentality as against clarity of judgement. But they have an unquestionable place in the moral realm, and it is from these that we can derive the fairly consistent view across the ages of what constitute virtues – wisdom, prudence, charity – all of which make sense only in a social setting. These virtues can run counter to sympathy, but any moral society requires the cultivation of virtuous outlooks so that sympathy does not lead to immoral choices, so that people act on an impartial verdict even if it runs against their own interests, and so that courage allows them to ignore the pressures of a crowd.

Seeing morality in terms of virtuous outlooks has some surprising implications. If we think it good that people are convivial and generous, and that this brings out the best in them, it is wrong to oppose the use of alcohol or drugs in settings that bring out these virtuous characteristics, just as it is wrong to support their use in settings that make people aggressive, depressed or selfish. Similarly, if hard work makes people stressed, mean to their friends and family, then we should oppose it. These distinctions are not easily summed up in rules, but they are usually understood by anyone who is sufficiently morally fluent, able to make subtle judgements about the complexities of human life.

There is also one other emotional source of morality which is not easily captured by formal rules, but nevertheless helps us make sense of connexity. This is piety. In traditional societies piety refers to the honours bestowed on ancestors and tradition. Rituals respect the sacredness of things, but piety also has a wider meaning and appeal. It is one aspect of our greater awareness of the world as a single entity: the ability to photograph the earth, or the immensity of space, induces it. As Roger Scruton writes, 'Piety means deep-down recognition of our frailty and dependence, the acknowledgement that the burden we inherit cannot be sustained unaided, the disposition to give thanks for our existence and reverence to the world on which we depend, and the sense of the unfathomable mystery which surrounds our coming to be and our passing away. All these feelings come together in our humility before the works of nature and this humility is the fertile soil in which the seeds of morality are planted.'[10]

Science has contributed to this piety, through showing both the immensity of the universe and the limits of our own role. Lynn Margulis, for example, put it well when she wrote of our discovery that 'humanity plays a relatively small part in the great phenomenon of life that transports and transforms the earth. We accelerate but do not dominate the metabolism of the Earth.' But although piety is congruent with scientific knowledge, it is not amenable to reason, since it marks the point where certain kinds of reasoning become silent.

In a rational culture these feelings are often suppressed. We tend to look for decision rules, laws that make things explicit and clear, whereas emotions, and in particular the sentiment of piety, are rarely sharp in this way. But piety is what plants in us a sense of responsibility towards the future, towards others, and towards the world beyond us.

*

Each of these sources of morality can be traced to an evolutionary origin, but their origin matters less than the fact that these sources are universal. They allow us to come to some common judgements about whether actions are more or less sympathetic, fair or pious, and they even allow the possibility of making judgements about the moral level of societies.

As one measure we might start by looking at an everyday moral capacity, such as empathy. The golden rule requires us to imagine what others are feeling. When the word 'empathy' was originally introduced into English it meant feeling into the experience of another, although today it has a narrower meaning of feeling with another; sensitive people literally mimic the physiological changes that their loved ones go through. Empathy thus requires a capacity for intensionality, the ability to read and interpret how people interact with each other. It develops within the family, and all cultures value the capacity of mothers and fathers to empathise with their children. It can be cultivated or suppressed, and it provides the basis for judgements, which is why John Stuart Mill called empathic anger the 'guardian of justice' – when we see a wrong and want it righted. From it flow many of the elemental moral ideas: love, virtue, compassion and sympathy, and what Iris Murdoch described as 'attention'; entering into someone else's felt and lived experience with the 'patient eye of love'.[11]

These are not abstract concepts. They can be encouraged and can grow in a benign social order just as they can wither away in times of fear and insecurity. They can in principle even be measured, and at some future time societies might evolve that put as much energy into measuring their empathic capacities as contemporary societies put into measuring the quality of the air or the supply of money.

Empathy is a first step towards a more challenging moral goal: the transcendence of the separate ego. One of the surprises of twentieth-century sociology and anthropology is that they have revealed consistent notions of morality and moral development that can be found across many different cultures. All see this development in terms of becoming freed from instinctual selfishness and drives, and then from excessive individuality, so that individuals can blend their personal autonomy with the needs of ever larger groups until ultimately, in Henry Sidgwick's words, they take the 'point of view of the universe'. Within Western cultures these ideas of moral development have been set out in Abraham Maslow's hierarchy of needs, Peter Singer's account of the deeper satisfaction to be gained from the ethical life, Lawrence Kohlberg's theory of 'moral development', George Vaillant's 'hierarchy of defences', and Jane Loevinger's theory of 'ego development'.

The techniques of yoga, Buddhist meditation and Zen are based around similar developmental paths. All describe a progress that entails using methods for mental discipline and self-discipline to control the mind and direct its energies towards virtuous beliefs and behaviour. Their aim is to help people to lose the child's sense of being all alone, of being the only one to experience feelings, until ultimately their sense of self dissolves. Crucially, too, they acknowledge that moral development involves tension and dissonance. By passing through doubts and criticism of the moral precepts we have learnt, we move upwards to a higher plane of understanding, rather than sticking, like most adults, with one or two all-purpose justifications such as tradition, relativism, hedonism or subjectivism.

All moral maturity involves coming to terms with complexity: the sheer number of different appropriate responses there are to the variety of human situations. Yet, it is significant that none of the many theories of moral development sees it in terms of ever-expanding freedom. Indeed the limitless expansion of freedom looks rather more like psychic entropy than development.

Moral maturity should translate into being wiser, better able to make judgements. Yet in governments and businesses the careful evaluation of circumstances is all too often replaced by quantitative decision rules. In welfare systems it is easier to have replicable points systems for deciding who deserves what, than it is to leave judgements to front-line staff. In the environmental field it has proven easier to measure physical effects and risks than it has been to open up debates about the rightness of interfering with life. Institutions find it less troubling to guide themselves with the aid of techniques like audits, benefit-cost techniques or valuations, than to make overt judgements, and they are helped in this respect by philosophers who deny the possibility of making judgements on the grounds that experience is superior to judgement, or that forms of knowledge are so diverse that none can make judgements about any other.

But the danger of substituting techniques for open judgements is that instead of being argued about and justified, judgements go underground, hidden in techniques. People opt for the lines of least resistance rather than the right lines: journalists hide behind codes of conduct, managers behind formal rules, and so we end up with a less morally fluent society.

The alternative of wider access to moral reasoning is not an easy option, but nor is it utopian. When Protagoras promised that on the very first day his disciples would go home better men than they came, Socrates replied that virtue could not be taught. He was right in one sense. The difference between right and wrong cannot be taught like algebra or history, any more than punishment inculcates virtues. Instead, experience shows that virtue and judgement are less likely to be taught than caught from people who have them already, and who warrant respect. In the same way punishment only contributes to moral development when it is understood, and seen as an expression of the judgements of people who warrant respect. Otherwise it is just seen as bad luck, something to be avoided by being smarter, rather than by desisting from the crime.

Earning such respect is the first step towards moral teaching. But once that connection has been made it is possible to teach and encourage moral reasoning. For parents and relatives this may mean being prepared to argue and discuss with children, reflecting on actions rather than simply accepting or denouncing them, and thinking through their consequences (rather as the young Benjamin Franklin, who wrote a pamphlet on the meaninglessness of vice and virtue, had to famously learn about its implications when two of his friends refused to pay him money they owed).[12] For schools it means teaching reasoning so that children become familiar with expounding arguments, listening to others, and gaining the confidence to make judgements and stick with them, even against the majority. For institutions in the adult world it means habitually thinking through, and justifying decisions that are made, and never letting people delegate their moral responsibility upwards or downwards.

It has become fashionable to believe that in a turbulent sea of conflicting messages, data and ideas, no certainties are possible. There are only meanings that feed off other meanings, and truths that are temporary. Moral reasoning is not something general, but rather something that exists within social niches, rather as Benjamin Lee Whorf suggested that different environments produce wholly different languages, with distinctive and mutually incomprehensible views of the world.[13] So one kind of moral behaviour may fit a small cult, another a large firm, a third the functions of a university. Their fitness can be judged only by the extent to which they enable that niche to persist.

But if morality is ultimately social, and the unit of society is now as much the world as the nation or community, then there are no genuine niches in this sense. The world is tending to become a single society and a single ecology, even though it contains compartments in which radically different ways of living may prevail. However much we may want to dig deep into our own culture, into a sense of nation or race or family, the needs of the whole – its survival, maintaining a climate, oceans, food, and peace – require an overarching moral framework that provides the universal umbrella for particular ways of life.

Contrary to the claims of philosophers like Alasdair MacIntyre, connexity makes the universal potential of morality practical for the first time, just as it brings to the fore some specific moral principles, rather than simply multiplying them in a relativistic soup. So the injunction against actions that might endanger the future of the species (such as the development of new organisms which could mutate into incurable viruses) is a new one that would have meant little a century ago. So would be a veto against the overuse of non-renewable resources, or against careless destruction of the cultural or biological heritage. A whole raft of self-limiting principles have become central simply because of the weight and density of our impact on the planet.

Some old principles also gain a new force, such as the paramount importance of truth-telling in a world where we depend much more on second-hand information,[14] or the importance of responsibility, a word that captures perfectly the social dimension of morality, since it refers both to accountability to others – the assumption that people can explain their actions and justify them to those around them – and to a personal sense of obligation. Similarly, ancient ideas of stewardship over things which cannot speak for themselves, and of trusteeship over children, natural environments, or power, gain new meanings in a closely connected world.

How hopeful should we be that these, or any other moral principles, might be more than dreamy aspirations? It is only in this century that morality has broken free from its religious anchorings. Before then, moral argument was dominated by people who believed in higher forces which gave us our sense of right and wrong. The liberation from God has meant that for much of this century our sense of ethics has been floating rudderless, as philosophers debated the abstruse meanings of words or viewed moral reasoning as retrograde. It is arguably only now that morality is again coming to the fore, as an alternative not only to the traditional ways of thinking, in which right and wrong were fixed points, but also to ideological ways of thinking that subordinated moral principles to political goals.

It is only now that we can reconnect morality to its original role as a guide to the well-being and survival of the individual and of the group. In his book *Reasons and Persons*, Derek Parfitt concludes that ethics is the 'youngest and least advanced of the sciences' and that 'we cannot yet predict whether, as in mathematics, we will all reach agreement. Since we cannot know how ethics will develop, it is not irrational to have high hopes.'[15]

9

AFTER THE MACHINE

THE MENTALITIES AND moralities that I have been describing are those that enable people to organise themselves, not alone on a desert island, but within environments that are made up of other people. Sophisticated moral reasoning makes it possible to see the self as part of larger systems, whether social, economic or ecological.

Over the last few years, thinking about how systems work, and how things organise themselves in complex and sometimes chaotic ways, has spread across many different disciplines, as the intellectual corollary of a more connected world. These ideas have brought with them a related set of notions about the unpredictability of the world and the limits of knowledge that follow from the collapse of the boundaries between the observer and the observed. Together they seem to signal a paradigm shift in the sciences, and not only the natural ones, since the same ideas have been used to map the apparently chaotic paths of commodity prices in economics or the spread of crimes in sociology.

Some of the leading thinkers on complexity, such as Stuart Kauffman, have taken a step further, arguing that there is immanent in the world a drive towards organisation and complexity and away from simplicity, a propensity towards integration rather than separation.[1] This is the subliminal message of the current interest in self-organising systems, and of the popularity of such examples as shoals of fish turning and weaving in perfect formation without any obvious leader. These images fit the ethos of a democratic era that has grown up beyond dependence on tradition and authority. Not only do they, literally, make sense of the world, they also offer a distinct sense of the position of humans within it, the recognition that life is mainly a property of the larger ecology, and only briefly an individual one.

Ideas of this kind suggest a novel answer to the question about the tension between freedom and interdependence, and show why there may be no need for any contradiction or tension. Within a self-organising system each element can be both free and dependent on all the others. Within the context of human history, both freedom and interdependence may, in the current terminology, be 'coevolving' (as flowers and bumblebees did over many millennia), so that any expansion of freedom makes it possible to develop new types of interdependence, and vice-versa. Neither causes the other, but both evolve in tandem or rather, a more accurate metaphor, like two improvising dancers responding to each other's new steps.

There are good reasons for thinking about the modern world as shaped by its nature as a system. In a connected world many more things interact and shape each other, and many more domains take on the properties of a complex system. This is why connexity has posed such a profound intellectual challenge: most of the concepts used to understand societies are still pre-systemic, such as the individual's rights relative to the state, or the sovereignty of the consumer.

The tradition that has done most to rectify this first took shape nearly fifty years ago when Ludwig von Bertalanffy laid some of the foundations of a new way of understanding the world in his General Systems Theory.[2] In it he described the properties of open systems that depend on the external environment for their sustenance. Most human systems are of this kind. The body draws on the sun, on water, air and food. Governments depend on the taxes they can raise from their society, businesses on consumer spending, voluntary organisations on their ability to tap commitment. His approach replaced the classical distinction between the parts and the whole with that between system and environment, and showed a way of linking the cybernetics of Norbert Wiener to the information theory of Claude Shannon, and the computing ideas of J. Von Neumann and Alan Turing. All could be reinterpreted as ways of thinking about how systems operate, with flows of commands and information feedback to guide them. Many of the basic ideas remain valid. For example, Bertalanffy described the properties of homeostasis (the ability to maintain a steady state) which we see in thermostats or currency exchange rates; entropy, the property whereby systems run down, like a hot oven cooling down to room temperature; and how systems draw new energy from their environment, like plants using the sun's energy through photosynthesis. He showed how systems need specialisation and differentiation to cope with complex functions, and why they need what W.R. Ashby called 'requisite variety' – sufficient complexity to match that of their external environment.[3]

In their simpler forms, many of these ideas have filtered into public understanding. Jay Forrester demonstrated with computer models of cities how small changes in one place could lead to vast and unpredictable changes in others, and led a generation later to the legions of Sim City players. Positive feedback, one of the basic concepts of systems thinking, was the main subject of the Club of Rome report on *The Limits to Growth* which showed how food, pollution and population were being driven by positive feedbacks, and were consequently not sustainable. Negative feedbacks have become familiar through economics: rising demand for a resource like oil raises its price which then dampens demand.

To understand any system it is essential to understand how both of these feedback forces are working, and whether they are in balance. The environmentalists who warned of imminent shortages of resources, for example, tended to underestimate some of the negative feedback forces – such as public opinion, politics, consumer choices and the development of substitutes – which prevented their more apocalyptic forecasts from being realised. Economists have tended to underestimate positive feedbacks, such as the herd mentalities that push markets up during booms and bubbles, or the cumulative effects of new knowledge.

Few schoolchildren learn how to think systemically. In history or the sciences the priority is given to learning about linear causes: which decision caused which war, which chemical reaction produces a particular compound. Most disciplines also prefer to ignore knowledge outside their boundaries, so that doctors like to play down the effects of social status on health, just as economists disregard the effects of cultures on growth. Even governments, which one might expect to have to think across domains, are rarely well prepared for thinking systemically about the cross-cutting relationships between employment and health, or demographics and crime. In thinking about a national economy it is easier to ignore the fact that it rests on a base of domestic work (which usually takes up more time than paid work), or on flows of matter and energy. But clear systems thinking is one of the basic literacies of the modern world, not least because it offers unexpected insights that are not amenable to common sense. So, for example, systems thinking reveals that when anti-drug regimes become harsher they drive up prices and tend to strengthen organised crime, or that when welfare systems become more generous they can promote the very behaviour they are designed to alleviate. It shows why heavy spending on road infrastructures can lead to more congestion, or why higher spending on weapons can make a country less secure. Some of these tools can be taught. Computers make it easy to model systems and learn through modelling them. Children can simulate the workings of a city and learn how a decision affecting one part can alter the viability of the whole. They can come to understand the effects of time-lags, or how some links are reinforcing while others are dampening, or how predators and prey are interlinked. They can learn to collect information about the environment around them, to distinguish the regular patterns from randomness and noise. They can learn to understand the importance of 'coarse graining' – the appropriate level of detail at which a system can be understood (since it is easy both to summon too much detail and get lost, and to rise to too high a level of abstraction and lose sight of the key determinants). Like any method these ones need to be used with care. Some children using computer simulations have come to accept the built-in assumptions as fact: in one example from Sim City, that higher taxes always lead to riots. But so long as childrens' critical faculties are kept sharp, making them play at God, toying with systems, seeing what works and what leads to disaster, provides a vital understanding of the world.

This set of intellectual tools is particularly valuable for fields like politics and business. Most political theory has been developed to understand closed systems, and the relations between individuals, communities and the state in idealised societies that have no borders and no relationships with others. Utopia means literally no place, and utopias rarely have to worry about their links to other societies.[4] Most of our words for thinking about larger social units are based on the nation-state in the form that it took in the second half of the nineteenth century. Discussions about 'the economy' or 'society' usually take it for granted that these words apply only to those things that happen to take place within the boundaries of a nation. Since modern politics was built on the notion of sovereignty within borders this is understandable: the state was, at least in principle, all-powerful within a territorial unit, unlike the medieval power that radiated from the monarch through layers of allegiance with diminishing degrees of commitment.

In business too, it is assumed that managers are all-powerful within the boundaries of the firm, while the external environment is simply taken as a given. The job of business is only to respond to the signals that come from consumers or competitors, not to be concerned about the health of the larger system.

This legacy has left us with misleading metaphorical frames: whether we want to or not we end up seeing the world, the nation or the institution as if it were bounded, like a house, or perhaps like a farm with a fence around it. We end up talking about what is inside and what is outside, what belongs and what does not, rather than about the larger system.

Systems thinking escapes from these constraints. It also helps us to break free from the dominant idea that has shaped thinking about governments and societies over the last century, the idea of the machine. The ubiquity of the machine-metaphor was the legacy that the military bequeathed to governments and then to manufacturing, through the influence of military factories like Springfield, and a chain of ideas that can be traced through from Frederick the Great to Frederick Taylor. Well oiled, efficient and measurable, the ideal machine had a clear purpose or function which it carried out perfectly. Everything could in principle be conceived as a closed system, consisting of cogs and wheels, instructions and commands, with a boss or government at the top, pulling the requisite levers and engineering the desired effects. Each element would interact harmoniously with every other, in a perfection of interdependence that left no room for freedom.

This was the image that Fritz Lang captured so well in his film *Metropolis* – that fact followed fiction in the designs of a generation of architects and planners. As an image of society it encouraged fears that the world was being taken over by one-dimensional 'organisation man', as well as justifying predictions that the mentalities and structures of both the capitalist West and the communist East would converge around an alienating form of large-scale bureaucracy. It reached its apotheosis in the early ideas of cybernetics, which suggested that societies could indeed be run like a smart machine given a sufficient number of feedback loops.

These machine images have had a profound influence on how we think. They shaped everything from psychoanalysis to revolution: both imagined a world made up of pressures and constraints, and occasional moments of release. They gave a modern shape to the assumption that someone or something must always be in charge, with a hand on the tiller, directing the machine (this was why the psychoanalysts invented the idea of the superego, as the internal policeman of wayward instincts). They influenced ideas of organisation to such an extent that many organisations were built deliberately as machines, and so long as their environments remained stable, these machine bureaucracies proved extremely effective in marshalling resources and energies to particular ends.

But the environment for machine-like things has gone into decline. If ideas of self-organisation are now more prevalent it is at least in part because the conditions for machine-like organisations no longer hold. Fewer systems can be kept closed. Nations, and even selves, no longer have clear boundaries. The multiplication of connections makes for greater uncertainty and speed of change, which requires adaptability rather than only efficiency. Within organisations, the rising number of flows of information over Internets and Intranets generates unpredictable new patterns and relationships which create new purposes, rather than accepting the primary purpose of the organisation as a given.

The simplest reason for the obsolescence of the machine ideal is the ubiquity of intelligence. In the ideal machine all of the intelligence goes into the design: once designed the machine runs automatically and has no need to redesign itself. Its ultimate benchmark is the perpetual motion machine that has no need for any further inputs. In intelligent systems, by contrast, everything can be redesigned and every structure is temporary. Each element of the system is capable of thinking rather than only doing. Each element can be connected differently to the world outside.

The machine model assumed that communication is costly and must therefore be limited to the transmission of commands downwards and feedback upwards. Only those in charge of the machine need to be bothered about external relationships. The model is fixed, designed for a purpose, and intended to be changed only if the purpose changes. This was true of many factory assembly lines, as it is of the household washing machine or television. None of these is built to communicate horizontally, or to change itself. If something goes wrong, a specialist is needed to put it right. But unless the designer can foresee every eventuality it is always more efficient for a system to be able to repair itself (like the human body) or even to redesign itself, rather than remaining in one particular form.

Organisations operating in open systems work more efficiently if they can respond to change and reshape themselves to exploit it. The useful metaphors that guide their design are more likely to be biological ones, concerned with adaptation, and existence far from equilibrium, rather than mechanical ones. The structures they need to develop are more likely to be parallel than linear, where decisions are taken in a cascade of interdependence, with each element simultaneously reacting to the others rather than to a single line of command. This is what happens in a crowd watching a sports match, or at a neighbourhood meeting.

In retrospect, we can see that even in its prime, the metaphor of the machine never fitted the most revolutionary social changes. Although generations of social engineers left their mark on everything from contraception to town planning, many of the most far-reaching long-term shifts were not those mandated from above, but rather those that evolved organically from below. The spread of the car, for example, was never ordained, but happened cumulatively because a succession of innovations met the public desire for mobility, catalysed the growth of a cluster of support functions and in time reached a level of usability and cost that made cars accessible to a mass market. The early forecasters who assumed that the world could only support a few million cars because of the shortage of chauffeurs could not imagine that ordinary people would learn to drive such dangerous metal boxes at high speed, nor that thousands of drivers would so readily learn to share the roads reasonably harmoniously. Having fired the imagination, and fostered the relevant skills, the influence of the car then fanned out in a series of waves that shaped everything from the layout of towns to shopping, and from the quality of the air to the social mores of drinking alcohol. Many of these steps involved planning, but the whole process could never have been planned or even conceived in advance.

The same is true of the rising power of women during the course of the twentieth century. This was helped by the spread of electricity and labour-saving devices, by men's falling working hours, and by a democratic culture of rights and freedoms. But it can only be understood as a long-term, cumulative process whereby change was reinforced at the smallest scale, in kitchens and bedrooms, interview rooms and offices, with technology responding to culture and politics to economics, rather than as the effect of a single decision, a law or an institution. In neither of these cases did society change like a machine. Instead it changed through the cumulative interaction of millions of little steps that were occasionally shunted forward by milestones like the achievement of women's suffrage, the invention of the contraceptive pill or the building of the Interstate Highway Network.

Examples of this kind show why it is more helpful to understand human societies as parallel processors rather than serial ones. They consist of many different elements interacting, rather than a hierarchy of decisions that start at the top and work their way down. Even in the most ruthless monarchy, the sovereign was never wholly sovereign. But the parallel character of societies becomes far more marked when information flows cheaply and easily. The car spread as fast as it did because of the messages and data that flowed from consumer markets to engineers, from manufacturers to planners. Women's power grew because small victories in the struggle for power with men could be spread rapidly via magazines or the telephone.

Today this ease of mutual adaptation has become a cardinal principle for effective organisations, and the justification for encouraging knowledge and even gossip to flow freely. With richer information flows it is no longer necessary to centralise knowledge and strategic intelligence. Businesses can be reorganised as federations of sometimes competing, sometimes cooperating units. Franchising models in government and business can separate operational from strategic roles in place of the integrated department. The scientific community can develop knowledge through the rapid feedback offered by conferences, academic journals and electronic networks, rather than depending on a single authority or a single committee to arbitrate.

This adoption of more horizontal forms of control and communication is not universal. Communications technology has also made viable stricter central control than was ever possible in the past, notably through real-time control over factories, flows of money, or over the physical position of objects. Some organisations have markedly tightened their vertical structures: armies for instance are probably more centralised in their control structures than ever before, necessarily given the power of nuclear weapons. Yet a century ago even parts of the German army resembled the decentralised, self-motivating units that are now favoured in business. Political leaders dependent on television to reach a mass audience have usually centralised control over images and policies, taking it away from the distributed intelligence of local parties. Firms responsible for dangerous chemicals and facing global liabilities naturally tighten their control over technical standards because they cannot afford decentralised responsibility.

But as a rule the availability of more bandwidth, more communicational tools and more opportunities for horizontal communication tends to favour what I have called weak power structures, structures based on the economical, light sharing of information rather than the hierarchical strong power of mechanical systems where information flows up and down, and where most of the organisation's energy is used to maintain internal control. Weak power structures have tended to be the norm in associations and voluntary organisations which lack either the authority of law or physical force. But all institutions have some of the properties of weak power structures. Societies and economies often look more like flotillas of many different boats rather than single entities. Firms can be seen as based not on their capital (their equivalent to territory) or their internal hierarchies, but rather on their webs of relationships to shareholders, suppliers and customers, and on their systems for distributed production, accounting, research and sales. Politics can look less like a competition between blocs to get hold of a static pool of power, and more like an information system attempting with varying degrees of success to aggregate millions of preferences, to devise common solutions and to mobilise changes in public behaviour such as harder work, better parenting, or greater willingness to obey laws.

Having illuminated how things connect, and how systems interact with their environments, the pioneers of systems thinking took a second step. They moved beyond input-output models, and the mapping of connections, towards understanding how systems organise themselves, making 'order out of noise' in Heinz von Foerster's resonant phrase.[5] The mystery of life, and of all societies, is why there should be order when the pressures towards chaos and entropy seem so strong, and in a range of fields from subatomic particles to stock markets, cells to weather systems, researchers have spent the best part of thirty years seeking to understand how patterns and orders are created out of apparent chaos. Rather than analysing how things respond to their environment, the focus turns to how they maintain their own internal order. Rather than seeing competition as the natural order of things, attention turns to how things produce order by cooperating: how, to take one of the most famous examples, eukaryote cells evolved from the symbiosis of previously separate cells rather than from the ruthless competition usually associated with Darwinian evolution.

Geese provide a good metaphor of self-organisation and the cooperative instincts on which it depends. When geese fly in a V formation the flapping of each goose's wings creates an uplift for the bird that follows it, so that the whole V gains some 70 per cent more flying range than if each bird flew alone. When a goose falls out of formation it suddenly feels the draught and resistance of flying alone. The role of being lead flyer is shared: when one tires another takes its place. When a goose is sick, wounded or shot down, two others drop out of the formation and follow it down to protect it.[6] This strategy offers several things at once: it is a model of freedom within a shared structure, of strength through cooperation, and of leadership that is more like being a servant than a boss. It symbolises an ideal of self-organisation where the interests of the part and the whole are indistinguishable.

There is an intrinsic appeal in such ideas of cooperative self-organisation which lie at the heart of modern green politics and of some strands of communitarianism. In themselves these arguments in favour of a self-governing society are not new, but have rather updated nineteenth-century utopian and anarchist ideas with a scientific language which draws authority from the close intellectual fit with the evolution of computers towards neural networks and connectionist machines based on parallel processing, and the ubiquity of distributed intelligence.

Connexity makes it easier than ever before to imagine a self-organising society, as opposed to a society made up of separate self-organising groups. The nineteenth-century utopians imagined separated communes based on the land, which would only occasionally have to deal with the outside world. As the counterpart to the destructive turbulence of industrial cities, they could only conceive of a static society. Today we would imagine instead a myriad of units communicating with each other, but engaged in many different activities from farming to knowledge, care to services, and coordinating their activities in the light of the activities of everyone else. Such a society would no longer try to cultivate habits of obedience, or respect for power. Instead it would place a high ethical premium on truth (since misleading information would blunt the systems' capacity to adapt) and on responsibility (since distributed intelligence must also mean distributed responsibility, culpability and worry). It would embody at each scale the principles of reciprocity that are the basis of modern social orders.

The philosophical idea that best expresses this ideal of a self-organising society is autopoïesis, or self-creation, one of the most potent themes in contemporary systems thinking. The Chilean scientists Humberto Maturana and Francisco Varela gave autopoïesis a modern form.[7] They argued that rather than thinking of systems in relation to an external environment we should see them as autonomous, circular and self-referential, primarily concerned with their own organisation and identity. The human brain for example should be conceived not as a receiver and processor of information but as a means of creating stable meanings, just as the cell's primary purpose is to sustain itself rather than to adapt to an external environment. Taken to an extreme the idea is solipsistic or idealistic: from the perspective of the system there is no environment, and no outside, only an inside that must be produced and reproduced.

This complex and counter-intuitive idea is richly suggestive. It has been taken up by philosophers and poets, and has had a wide influence in the natural sciences. Part of its appeal (although one that its inventors would shrink from) is the implication that the idea of autopoïesis may show how it is possible for a part, the individual human being, to internalise the needs of the whole (the society or biosphere), so rendering redundant the conflict between freedom and interdependence. If we think of freedom not as the possession of a separate individual, living in one lifespan, but rather as the exercise of consciousness by larger wholes – the group, the society, the species, the biosphere – then some of the tension is resolved.

This may seem an extremely abstract goal, but it is precisely what most religions have deliberately striven for. It is what every group or collective attempts to achieve. Where perhaps we differ today is that in a culture of autonomy it is not possible to produce this fusion of individual and system through domination: the subordination of individuality. There is no institution with the monopoly of powers that once enabled churches and nobles to achieve such supremacy. Instead, today that integration of self into a larger whole has to be chosen, understood, thought through, so that with sufficient maturity, sufficiently evolved mentalities, individuals can freely choose behaviour patterns that assist in the adaptation and survival of the system of which they are a part.

The idea of autopoïesis is suggestive of how a society might organise itself, adapting and evolving, without the need for hierarchies and belief systems that stand above people, enforcing continuity and responsibility. Like all utopian ideas, this one has a magnetic pull. If each human life makes the transition from dependence through independence to interdependence, then it is intuitively appealing that societies should make the same transition, evolving into a common framework within which each element can take responsibility for itself and for the whole.

The vision of a self-organising society takes to a logical conclusion the central ideas of democracy: popular rule and self-government. But like all ideas it has limits. These limits are worth spelling out in some detail because they help to define why even the most democratic societies still need leaders who stand above and beyond the communities and interest groups that make them up.

The first reason is given by one of the starting principles of systems theory which states that complex systems, like a society, rest on subsystems that are necessarily less complex. Institutions like a firm, or the family, reduce the complexity around them to simpler goals and rules of thumb, and the whole achieves greater complexity precisely because it can produce simpler subsystems.

We can understand this point if we think of our own selves. In order to function effectively we use simple guidelines for making decisions: emotions and tastes provide these for most people, and clever people without adequately developed emotions can be unable to make the simplest decisions because rationally there is no way to judge why one option is better than another. Success as a person depends on keeping complexity at bay. We use rules of thumb to guess who we can trust or how to behave in an unexpected situation. If we were ever to truly match the complexity of our environment, to understand in detail the feelings of everybody we came across, we would be more likely to collapse into madness than to achieve the beatific wisdom of autopoïesis. For similar reasons, genuine telepathy might feel more like hell than heaven.

For the subsystem simplicity is a virtue. But if a system consists only of such simplifying subsystems, then it may be harder for the whole to adapt. Although in a complex system each subsystem can observe itself and its environment, whatever it sees is marked by its own unique perspective. There is no longer an Archimedean point from which everything can be contained in an all-embracing vision,[8] no perfect citizen, or philosopher-king, who can internalise all of the complexities of their society and view it in the round. Instead everything has to be translated and simplified until it can be absorbed. So, for example, economic systems can only understand the environment by translating it into the form of prices and discount rates, or commercial opportunities. The media can only come to grips with a movement like feminism by translating it into a series of political issues (such as abortion), and can only grasp public moods by turning them into opinion polls.

In general, it takes less effort to deal with things through simple rules than complex ones. For an institution it is easier to concentrate on a handful of simply measurable goals, with easy feedback, such as profitability or cash in the case of a company, exam results in the case of a school, or votes in the case of a political party. But if a society finds that as it becomes more complex its subsystems are becoming stronger and its integrative systems, like religion, morality or politics, are becoming weaker, then this is a cause for worry, since it suggests that problems or challenges that cut across domains will be left unsolved, and that no one, and no institution, will take responsibility for the whole system. This is why, even in the most egalitarian society, there is still a need for some hierarchy and authority, for someone to see things from the perspective of the whole.

The second set of limits to self-organisation become apparent as soon as we recognise that everything is in some sense an open system. In a world of self-governing small communities who deals with the invaders, or for that matter the inner invaders, the parasites that feed off a system without giving back? We usually think of parasites as like diseases that feed off the body's healthy cells, and more recently we have become familiar with computer viruses that attach themselves to programs and use the host program's functions to replicate themselves. But parasitism is also a social phenomenon, because all social systems, particularly ones resting on reciprocity, are vulnerable to being abused. So parents make sacrifices for their child, with a tacit assumption that their child will make sacrifices for their children in turn. States finance children's education on the assumption that those children, when adults, will subsequently pay taxes to finance the education of others. Citizens watch out for each other's homes, rather than robbing them when their backs are turned. People help strangers in need because of the tacit assumption that those strangers would help them if their roles were reversed.

Networks of trust of this kind are always vulnerable to parasites. In the land of the trustworthy the con-man can become king. Criminals are parasites who feed off the legitimate economy; fraudulent preachers feed off the accumulated capital of a dominant religion. Capitalists who extract a natural resource and then leave behind them a devastated social and natural environment are as much parasites as the teacher who exploits a child's trust to sexually abuse them. The larger the system, and the less subject either to centralised control or decentralised strengths, the easier it is for parasites to prosper.

Because this threat is so universal, most societies have devised intricate ways to prevent parasitism, and in particular the form of parasitism in which people take advantage of the community to do the work needed to pass on their own genes. Some have rigorous mechanisms to test the capacity of parents to bring up children so that others will not be forced to do it for them. Others have used the expectations of chastity in unmarried women, complex dowry systems, and requirements for bridegrooms to demonstrate their wealth, as a means of stopping free-riders. Modern governments have framed restrictions on welfare to discourage mothers and, more often, fathers from taking advantage of the state to pay for their children's upbringing.

Complex interconnections generally favour parasitic behaviour. Computer viruses spread more easily when computers are networked, because it is so hard to program them all against all possible viruses. Diseases spread, and evolve, far faster in cities than in rural areas. Social ills spread faster too, because more atomised societies are less resilient: this was the point made by Ibn Khaldun when he showed how the atomised populations of cities were more prone to exploitation by governments than the tightly knit peoples of the deserts. But densely populated cities are also vulnerable to parasitism because it is much harder to mark out the lines between cause and effect than in a close-knit community. So for example, the clever modern thief doesn't rob peasants of their meagre savings but instead tries to siphon off a tiny percentage of the huge trades of a big company in the hope that it will not notice. Other modern parasites might include the current generations who run down natural resources or build up debts, both public and private, and pass them on to future generations; the individuals who abuse their own health when health care is socialised, safe in the knowledge that others will pick up the bill; or the polluters who pass on discomfort and ill-health to others, safe in the knowledge that others will pay the price.

Throughout history the danger of parasitic behaviour has been one of the reasons for having power and authority to punish those who take without giving, or attach themselves to the labour of others without working themselves.

The technical analysis of networks provides a third set of insights into the limits of self-organisation. At first glance all of the effects of making networks bigger are positive. Increasing the number of nodes on a network means that each increases in value. This effect runs contrary to conventional economics. Whereas the presence of more cars tends to mean that your car is worth less because the roads are more crowded, having more people with telephones makes yours more valuable, because you can use it to call more of your friends. The same is true of languages. English is more valuable than Esperanto because more people understand it.

Widely shared social norms and etiquettes are more useful than ones that nobody else recognises.

By adding an extra node to a network you can also reduce the overall length of connections needed: by turning a node into another hub connected by spokes, the overall value of the network can rise even while its physical extent declines. But these positive effects are matched by less obvious negative ones. Adding new routes to networks should speed them up, yet, as the German operations researcher Dietrich Braess found, it can also slow them down. Systems analysis has also shown that excessive connectivity and excessive speed of reactions can reduce the adaptability of the system as a whole. In one mathematical study of networks Stuart Kauffman showed that while too few connections may mean that there is insufficient change and adaptation, beyond a certain level too much connectivity decreases adaptability: 'large networks with thousands of members', he wrote, 'adapted best with less than ten connections per member'.[9] Too many connections mean that too much time and energy is spent on them. Conformity spreads too fast and dampens innovations. It becomes necessary to disconnect (sometimes literally) to get anything done as the system clutters up with chatter and noise.

In his classic study of order and chaos, the Belgian bio-chemist Ilya Prigogine made a similar point, showing how if changes in one small area were too quickly communicated across a system as a whole they would tend to be dampened out.[10] Only with some insulation from the larger system could they evolve to the level of complexity needed for them to then change the system as a whole. This is intuitively applicable to human societies. Usually when a dissenting idea emerges the reaction of most people is to dismiss it. Since it lacks sufficient supporting evidence or theoretical sophistication it is vulner-able to being humiliated out of existence. Only if it can develop at one remove from such negative reactions will it gain sufficient depth and complexity to survive. Subcultures, cults, political groups and academic disciplines all perform this function. They provide safe compartments. But some of the effects of connexity make their boundaries more porous, and thus perversely make it harder for the system to develop new strains and new ideas that may be essential for its long-term survival.

Self-organising systems may be good for economic life, or for cultures, but if the threat posed to the system as a whole is too big, then we legitimately look for a steering mechanism or guardian to avert it. It may be a king, a state, a party, a church, a charismatic leader or an international organisation, but when that moment comes we want them to have the authority to act.

Such threats are common. It used to appear that ours was the first century to threaten its environment and thus its future. The nuclear weapon and the effects of industrial civilisation made for a radically new situation in which civilisation had suddenly become more fragile and brittle, whereas in the past human societies were able to live in perpetual harmony with their environments. But today this view is untenable. We now have far more knowledge about how bad human societies have been in the past at steering themselves away from disaster, and how often they pursued self-destructive paths until their civilisations collapsed. Sumerian civilisation declined, for example, when wheat crops failed because excessive irrigation had made the land saline. Mayan civilisation began to disappear in a few decades after 760 because of indiscriminate irrigation. The Anasazi civilisation in the south-west of the USA seems to have disappeared for the same reason.

The limit to the more naive accounts of self-organisation is simply this: complex adaptive systems need some hierarchy of organisation because challenges, like those from parasites or from environmental collapse, may be beyond the capacity of subsystems to respond. The role for higher authorities is not to engineer the system, or to monopolise power and knowledge, but rather to perform the roles that the lower elements are unable to perform: watching out for threats, averting disasters, resisting parasites and taking responsibility for the future.

10

ADULT POLITICS

IN DEMOCRATIC SOCIETIES we give the job of steering to politicians. We choose our steerers and throw them out if they go astray. This tradition of democratic steerage has ancient roots. In all of the Indo-European languages there is a root word which means the people brought together for deliberation. In Greek the word is *demos*, which meant both the people and, more specifically, the people gathered together to debate and decide. In German the parallel word is the *thing*, or *dinc*, which remains in use today in the name of the Icelandic parliament – the Allthing. In Latin the *res publica* (literally the 'public thing') was not the republic but rather that which is known by everyone and is deliberated in public.

Democratic politics has thrived because it achieves things that are beyond the capacity of markets and voluntary associations. The first is agreement about society's ultimate goals – what we mean by well-being, and how we are to achieve it. There may be fierce arguments about what these goals should be, but politics is the only mechanism we have for resolving them and translating them into common rules and spending priorities.

The second role of politics is moral: upholding virtue and a common sense of right and wrong, by passing laws, honouring some people and dishonouring others. Again, it is through politics that modern societies ultimately work out their moral stance with regard to issues like welfare dependency, date rape, *in vitro* fertilisation, domestic violence or insider dealing. This moral role is unlikely to disappear. With the flood of

164

complex moral choices being thrown up by advances in genetic knowledge, which may give parents the power to select, either positively or negatively, for the intelligence, looks and life-chances of their children, politics is likely to be drawn ever more into a world of fluid ethical choices. The third role of politics is recognition. It is through politics that societies recognise their own minorities, interests and histories, just as it is through politics that they often suppress them.

Finally there is the task of ensuring the survival of the group, the city or the nation. This is where politics takes on the role of that which was once performed by chieftains and kings. Government means literally steerage (from the Latin word for 'helmsman', *gubernator*). If a society faces an imminent crisis, an invasion, plague or recession, its citizens look to politicians to define a way out. In previous eras royalty, organised religions and castes played this role, as steerers of first or last resort. But today no other institutions want to take it on, certainly not the big global firms that sometimes look, misleadingly, like an alternative to politics.

At its best politics plays these roles, which help to connect societies into some shape and coherence, in many different keys. It sometimes works as negotiation, distinguishing differences which are resolvable from those that are not: for example differences over spending priorities are usually more easily negotiated than differences over abortion laws. Sometimes it works as a stretcher of people's horizons. Sometimes it brokers new settlements between mutually suspicious social groups.

Politics can be divisive, atavistic, vengeful and deceitful. But at its best it performs roles that no other institution can discharge either adequately or consistently. Religious bodies can define moral rules, judges can push the boundaries of reform, and businesses can create virtual polities within them. Single-issue pressure groups can mobilise public opinion and the media can serve as informal forums for debate. But nothing other than the political process can determine collective judgements: the decisions which fix trade-offs, directions and rules, whether to declare wars, to punish people or to raise taxes.

The tragedy is that politics is now ill-equipped to perform the roles which it alone is destined to play. The noble view of politics as wise, far-sighted, honest about trade-offs, has few adherents. Politics is more likely to seem venal, myopic, a squalid balancing of narrow immediate interests. If politicians make promises they tend to be broken. If politicians claim to uphold ideals they are liable to be betrayed, and the characteristic language of politics is now seen to be the superficial twenty-second soundbite, or the secretive deal. During the course of the twentieth century, the pendulum has swung all the way from a view of politics as the vehicle of the highest human hopes – those for utopia, equality and the full realisation of human potential – to one that sees it as flawed and prone to failure. Even the most democratic Western electorates might agree with the Chinese saying that 'democratic leaders squat in the outhouse but seldom produce anything'.

Paradoxically, although more countries engage in democratic politics than ever before ours is a profoundly antipolitical age. To a younger generation life is elsewhere – in a dynamic global economy, communications systems, a world of science that is continually generating new knowledge and technologies, and in the moral champions at one remove from power, defending the environment or human rights. Modern heroes achieve their popularity precisely by keeping their distance from government, and only very rare exceptions (such as Nelson Mandela) have been able to retain their integrity while also dealing in the day-to-day realities of power. Politics has come to seem like a backwater, a bad career choice. If you want to achieve change, better do it through direct action, or a sharply focused pressure group, than through general-purpose political parties. If you want to exercise power, then run an agency, or a business.

Over the last few decades there have been successful moves to narrow the role of politics. Central banks have been given independence to manage monetary policy. Judgements of trade have been delegated to apolitical international organisations. The judiciary have carved out a bigger role in scrutinising government, and in shaping people's rights. Many influential figures in international business would like to see politics wither away, leaving the market to provide for people's welfare, and leaving the corporate boardroom, not the parliament or assembly, as the main decision-making forum for a connected world. But despite the efforts to squeeze politics out, it always seems to find a way back in. Businesses find that they need politicians to shape the terms of competition. They need them, too, to legitimate their decisions, particularly the unpopular ones. They need politicians to persuade taxpayers to invest in education or transport systems, to keep the streets safe or to open up foreign markets. For some of the same reasons politics has never been successfully excluded from diplomacy despite the best efforts of generations of diplomats to rationalise international affairs with legalistic rules to determine when other states have broken rules whose breach warrants punishment.

Even the family can no longer be easily insulated from politics. In societies with smaller households, people are more likely to depend on the state to provide them with the means of life. That implicates governments in making judgements about the relative worth of family arrangements, if only because their own policies shape family life, making implicit assessments of the entitlements of single parents, or the obligations of parents to children and children to older parents. In these and many other instances politics is present both because people use it as an expression of their emotions and interests, and because societies have a functional need for negotiation, and for a steerer, an adaptive mechanism.

All of these are reasons why we have to be concerned about the state of politics, its health or otherwise. Yet in theory democratic politics regulates itself, in ways that run directly parallel with how markets operate. The very essence of democracy is that it is competitive; no one has a monopoly of power, a divine right to rule. Instead, competition between ideas is fought out in a public sphere where, other things being equal, the valid or truthful will prevail over the false, the effective policy over the bad one. The same competitive principle applies to political office, as elections test out the relative virtues of parties, presidential candidates and manifestos. In principle, these internal structures of the political system ensure that there are benign outcomes. Indeed, James Madison argued in defence of free speech that, regardless of whether a particular programme is misconceived, or a particular politician lies, the overall effect of a system based on competition between ideas and arguments is to move the society towards better rather than worse outcomes.

The theory is compelling. Competition between ideas and policy proposals should weed out the ill-conceived ideas, and those that will only benefit a minority. Yet it is not hard to see how this system can become distorted. It depends, like efficient markets, on the relative ease of access of new competitors. It depends on how readily new ideas and arguments can gain access to the public sphere. Often, in practice, the symbiotic interests of political incumbents and powerful forces in society serve to exclude new ideas; political power rewards its favourite groups, which in turn reward political power, creating mutually reinforcing loops. Marginal ideas are kept on the margins, and ideas that threaten those in power are treated with scorn or ignored. In many Western societies the farming and arms industries have been particularly good at organising the loops between them and politics, channelling funds to politicians who channel back state subsidies and contracts.

Some of these distortions in the political marketplace also reflect the extent to which democratic governments borrowed direct from monarchies and empires. Today's centralised bureaucracies, general taxation, secrecy laws and rational management principles can all be traced back to the era of absolute monarchy (as can many of the buildings and even the titles used by governments today). Even the USA, with its powerful states and balance of powers, is by past standards a massively centralised system. Monarchies presumed to govern for people, not with them, to give them information only when they felt it appropriate, and to ask their opinions as a matter of courtesy rather than right. The assumptions that passed from monarchy to the elected leaders of democracy took it for granted that the public is essentially passive, and that there is an unavoidable asymmetry between the knowledge and judgement of the governors and the ignorance and confusion of the governed.

The environment that shaped politics in this form has now radically changed, bringing with it innumerable signs of a worsening clash between the culture of democracy, which is essentially a culture of self-government, and its forms which delegate authority to small elites. Indeed, politics has been experiencing nothing less than a climatic shift. With widespread access to global media, databases and multiple opinions, today's politicians have lost their edge. When as much as half of the population has a university degree, and most of the rest feel perfectly able to form their own judgements, the esteem, the mystique and the trust that once surrounded the best politicians have melted away. Instead, although politics retains its monopoly powers, the public on which it depends for money and legitimacy has become ever more disconnected from it; the relationship with politics has become thin. Today's citizens are rarely directly engaged in the political process. They vote in elections only occasionally, and have little direct contact with politicians. Nor have governments been good at managing their interface with citizens. The professionalisation of politics, the use of advertisements and billboards instead of public meetings, market research techniques instead of consultation: all have widened the distance between public and decision-makers.

Time has played its part too. Many valuable activities require large investments of time. Good relationships and happy families are obvious examples. Democracy too depends on people being prepared to invest the time to find out about issues, attend meetings, or sit on committees. But today we have a sense of unprecedented pressure on time. In part this is because working hours have started to rise again in most Western societies after a century of decline. In part it is because most families now have two earners, not one, so far more people are juggling childcare and jobs. In part it is because the value of time has risen. In terms of its productivity, the typical hour is now worth twenty-five times as much as it was in the mid-nineteenth century, and so we are far more impatient of time-consuming activities: short slogans and soundbites are preferred to the three-hour speeches of a Lincoln or Gladstone, swift decisions preferred over lengthy committee meetings. Many sectors have adapted to this new pattern of time, by accelerating the provision of everything from food to entertainment, and encouraging the replacement of slow sports like golf and cricket with more intensive sports like aerobics.

But politics by contrast remains relatively unmodernised, and so this squeeze on time draws energy out of it, leaving it only as a place for those with surplus time – usually the old and the young – or for people with political careers in mind. Most political mechanisms remain inefficient in their use of time, and because the political professionals have little interest in sharing their power with others there has been relatively little use of modern technologies – like committees meeting by e-mail, MPs voting from afar, and virtual parties.[1] Nor does politics offer citizens much choice. Electors can choose between a handful of packaged party programmes, but they cannot pick and choose elements from different ones, and in any event the programmes are often vague and confusing, and abandoned once the party comes to power. Where other organisations focus on their core tasks, and offer a direct link between choices and outcomes, the political system perpetually shifts its focus. It frequently has blurred vision, and jumps to short-term rather than long-term priorities. It attempts to deal with anything and everything – from regulating family life to framing the world trading system.

This lack of focus – which makes governments such poor problem-solvers – is also an effect of inappropriate scale. Most organisations, whether firms like Shell and Siemens or non-party political organisations like Greenpeace, can adjust their shape and scale to their market or function, but politics remains trapped in the national scale, the scale at which historically it grew up. So although in practice governance works by sharing tools in ever more complex structures – especially in Europe – politicians have to behave as if issues are resolvable on a national level. Lyndon Johnson once said that all politics is local, but today the opposite is the case: all politics is becoming global.

Perhaps the most profound problem is that although politics can be defined in terms of the formal constitutions of elections, legislatures, executives and judiciary, it is increasingly shaped in practice by what could be called the informal constitution of media, opinion polls, e-mail and computer conferences. The *res publica*, or public realm, is no longer primarily organised in parliaments and party conventions. Instead it has moved over into the radio and television studios, the newspaper columns, and single-issue pressure groups, all of which together constitute more effective channels of communication between citizens and governors than the formal democratic institutions.

The growing significance of this informal constitution has some virtues. It may make it easier for new ideas to be taken seriously. It brings more scrutiny to bear on politics. But, in practice it often locks the media and politics into an intimate embrace that excludes the public, with the media usually less accountable, less willing to take responsibility for their actions, less open and less democratic than the politicians they claim to oversee.

The net result is that politics is no longer able to perform its central tasks well. It cannot clearly define societies' true sources of well-being, and help in their achievement; it cannot articulate a sense of virtue and translate this into laws and behaviour; it is poor at providing recognition to new minorities and interest groups; and it cannot act to further the long-term survival of the societies it is meant to serve. Most of the political forms that took shape in the last century, the elections, political parties, manifestos, opinion polls and public meetings, now look obsolete and stuck. Politics has been left peculiarly at odds with the culture of a connected world that favours interactivity, reciprocity and openness.

*

Much of the unease with politics has been caused by the failure of political institutions to keep up with their societies. But there is also another factor involved: our suspicion of power in all its forms. The twentieth century brought more outright abuses of power than any other, because for the first time industrial technology was harnessed to the paranoia and megalomania of figures like Stalin and Hitler, Richard Nixon and Mao Zedong. We have learned that the same communication technologies that can be used for direct democracy can also enhance the reach of the already powerful.

In Western culture the profound ambivalence about power means that is has been seen as the polar opposite of freedom and fulfilment, and of love. Carl Jung was typical when he wrote that 'where love reigns there is no will to power; and where the will to power is paramount, love is lacking'.[2] Wagner's Ring Cycle is a long meditation on the incompatibility of power and love, and even Machiavelli drew a distinction between the realm of power and the domain of the soul. In each of these perspectives power is the enemy of life and nature. Etymologically, the roots of the word 'power' lie in the Latin *potere* and the Greek *posis* from which the word despot derives. This etymology embodies the idea that agency, the capacity to do things, is associated naturally with hierarchy and bossing around. Even God in this worldview is *dominus* in the church, top in a pyramid of rule over people and things. So the primary idea we have about power, and thus of politics, is one of domination: power over rather than with, a male rather than a female principle, which contrasts the active with the passive, hard over soft, force over lack of force. Not surprisingly this view leads many to conclude that power is something to be resisted, not embraced.

Suspicion of power has also been a response to its association with growth. For most of recent history, political organisations have seen their role as one of building and creating, energising material things. The best symbol of this power is the army of workers going to build new homes and new power stations, or the parade of tanks. In economic life the primary focus of politics has been to achieve growth and accumulation as symbolised by skyscrapers and motorways, through the rigorous application of principles of productivity, efficiency and output, of rational mind over irrational nature. The kinds of power that are primarily concerned with transforming inputs into tangible outputs make efficiency primary over other concerns, such as purpose.[3] Politics may, in principle, be the way in which we collectively deliberate over ends, but often it has been subordinated to the pursuit of means. So even though there is little evidence that, after a certain level of income, economic growth contributes to well-being, politicians still compete to deliver bigger quantities of steel or ships, GDP or disposable income. Instead of the pre-monarchical ideal of power as a burden to be carried, or as a step on a hierarchy which leads up to the gods, we have the idea of power as the means to a limitless supply of material things.

Against those asserting power in all its forms, there has been an equally persistent tradition of opposition to power. Where politics is concerned with managing power, these traditions are anti-political denials of the need for power. Anarchism and utopian communism promised the elimination of power by finding its sources in private property. Feminism took the arguments a step further by finding the sources in patriarchy. Philosophers like Michel Foucault set themselves up as pure dissenters against power in any of its subtle forms, and saw their task as being to unmask it. All favoured a society based on cooperation, without leaders, and without power over people. Strangely, they showed much less interest in understanding how people have experienced powerless structures. Structures that deny power often simply generate new kinds: in place of structure there is the power exercised by charisma, or bullying (since power that is not meant to exist does not need to be held back by formal constraints). Equally, fear of power easily turns into fear of difference, and an acceptance of conformism and mediocrity. Communes without overt power can survive for many decades, but no one has found a way of radiating their ethos more widely through a society.

We need order and power, but we also resent them. As a result we are left with the syndrome of disobedient dependence, like disaffected teenagers, who take money each week from their parents while pretending to be free-living bohemians, business leaders who will break any rules to win public subsidies, or grumbling assembly-line workers who would never dream of setting up in business on their own.

The tension between the fact that some people and institutions can compel us, punish us and take our money, and our aspirations to be freestanding, sovereign and inviolable, produces much of the ambivalence of modern politics. It means that we both acknowledge our need for order and stability, for the authority of someone to police the streets, and yet also reject it. Kipling wrote of 'making mock of uniforms that guard you while you sleep', and Freud wrote that the masses want someone to play the role of father, but also someone to rage against. Modern citizens seem simultaneously to resent and depend upon power, and to resent that dependence.

There is perhaps one other reason for this ambivalence. In the Western democracies the majority of the population were brought into fuller participation in decision-making at precisely the moment that power began to drift away from the national states into which they had been coopted. The final extension of the franchise in Britain, for example, took place one year before the 1929 crash when the public was told by its representatives, the Labour cabinet, to follow the commands of global capital and stick to the gold standard, even at the cost of high unemployment. The spread of democracy in Europe after 1945 coincided with the realisation that nation-states had to pool their military and economic powers. Democratisation in Eastern Europe or Latin America was followed rapidly by the news that international financial institutions were imposing new restrictions. Hence, perhaps, the subliminal sense of betrayal and loss.

But the larger story is one of people becoming stuck in a polarity of independence and dependence, but without making the transition to a third stage of interdependence. So politics remains infantile rather than adult, as the public pretend to believe and the politicians pretend to listen.

What can be done? It is not too hard to imagine what a more adult politics would look like. For at least two decades politicians have been fond of talking the language of 'empowerment', which means distributing packages of power to citizens so as to replace dependence with the means for people to be independent. Many countries have experimented with decentralising power, and the responsibility which comes with it, to regions, cities and neighbourhoods. Within the public sector, it has become popular to give users more opportunities to choose what services they receive, or to allow local residents to organise their own refuse collection or policing. A more adult way of doing politics also involves changing how we organise representation. Representation separates citizens from decisions by concentrating power amongst a relatively small group of professionals. As a model of democracy, it was fitted for an uneducated electorate, and for an era when travel and communication were difficult. Its effect through the electoral system is to bundle decisions together, usually leaving citizens only binary choices between two different parties and programmes. Worse, it leaves legislatures oddly *un*representative, skewed towards men, towards professions like the law and teaching, and towards the relatively rich. All of these features undermine the authority of representatives and make them less able to take responsible decisions. The simple answer is to return to some of the qualities of the original democracy of ancient Athens which was direct, unmediated by professional representatives. With sophisticated communications technologies there is no longer a need for decisions to be monopolised by parliaments made up of professionals meeting in distant cities, and over the last century there has been a steady rise in the use of the main tools of direct democracy, like referendums initiated by citizens themselves (as in Switzerland, Italy and some states of the USA).

More use of referendums acts as a check on the political

class. But their limitation is that they can produce ill-thought-through results. The great weakness of a truly push-button democracy, in which the population as a whole would vote on every major issue, is that few citizens would have much knowledge about the choices they are making. Without time for deliberation, the danger is that decisions would be taken on the basis of knee-jerk reactions, rather than wisdom. To encourage greater deliberation, other methods are needed. One answer is the use of juries made up of representative groups of citizens to advise on complex issues. We are familiar with the idea that justice should be dispensed by a randomly selected group of citizens. Extending this principle to political decisions brings several clear advantages. In the first place it only makes demands on the time of a very small number of people, who can stand in for the rest of the public. The jury also has the advantage of giving those involved plenty of time to come to terms with complex facts and arguments; it makes them better able to resist powerful rhetoric or special pleading. In Germany, Spain and the USA juries have been used to advise on planning decisions or major policy reforms, and have shown that ordinary citizens can deliberate just as competently as politicians, and with a better chance of genuinely representing the mood of the electorate as a whole. A range of other methods can achieve some of the same effects. Deliberative polls that bring several hundred randomly selected people to consider an issue are one example, as are the 'consensus conferences' used in Denmark to advise on difficult scientific issues, such as the ethics of biotechnology.[4]

A similar compromise between representation and full direct democracy would be to replace today's elected second chambers with assemblies chosen by lot, which would genuinely represent the makeup of the population, with a balance of rich and poor, men and women, different races and beliefs.

These various methods for reinvigorating democracy, and connecting it better to more educated and more assertive citizens, all have a common theme. They are ways of extending the political conversation beyond the political professionals, and creating richer flows of communication than the occasional choice between two or three options.

Democratic politics has undeniably been threatened by the rise of global markets and media. But we should hope that it is going to be reborn rather than buried. After all it is through the expansion of politics that most modern freedoms have been won. It is through politics that most people achieved the basics of life, even in the most capitalistic economies, since politics helped them to translate the power of the vote into an economic power. Above all it is through politics that our societies steer themselves, making themselves more than the sum of their parts, and there are times when any polity has to make demands of its citizens that are unwelcome: fighting wars, raising taxes, making sacrifices for future generations. Yet the legacy of several centuries of struggle against authority is an odd synergy whereby authorities shrink away from their authority, defining it in narrower terms and denying their power, while we, the public, despise them in return for their inadequacy. One of the hardest lessons to be learnt from today's crisis of politics is that authority is indispensable, but producing it is never easy. We know that it requires clarity of purpose, honesty, and leaders who embody widely shared virtues. We know that it requires success, because successes provide the authority for future decisions. And we know that it requires leaders who are seen to be there out of a sense of duty, so that there is a distance between their authority and the power they exercise. But the old sources of authority, like tradition and deference, have dried up, and the authority of newly elected leaders sometimes seems to have a half-life of months, not years.

The importance, and elusiveness, of authority has often been brought home to radical movements when they make the transition from opposition to power. Having spent decades undermining authority, they then find when they need it that it is no longer there to be used or mobilised. Governments of the left found this in the 1930s as they tried to maintain discipline between warring factions, and more recently the green movement has discovered that even if it can persuade politicians that its arguments are right, they may lack the authority to force people to change their ways of life. Milan Kundera once compared the devilish laughter of dissent, satire and cynicism and the angelic, childlike laughter of belief, and presented them as permanent poles in the human condition. But a culture that favours laughing and disrespect, which is a necessary stage in any process of maturation, a step between dependence and independence, can become stuck so that it is impossible to move on to decisions and actions. This, indeed, is the legacy of a political system that infantilises its citizens. It means that however apparently empowered they become, they remain in a condition of dependence, outsiders rather than insiders. However much they appear to be sovereign, in practice their governors grant to themselves many of the same privileges that monarchs had before them.

Animal ethology teaches that when the group is secure the individual feels safer taking risks, but when insecurity rises the individual pulls closer to the group and its embrace. Often politics takes this form. So during periods of prosperity and peace, politics is used more to enhance freedoms and the opportunities to take risks, while during periods of danger it reverts to its protective function. But at its best politics should amount to more than an oscillation between freedom and protection, dependence and independence. It should also leave room for responsibility to be shared.

I I

Is Government Coming to an End?

THROUGHOUT HISTORY BRAVE people have left their homelands to create new, stateless orders where there would be no need for power. The people who colonised Iceland a millennium ago and created the world's first parliament, and the pioneers who settled in America to build a 'city on the hill', are only two of the most prominent examples. Neither attempt succeeded. Both ended up with governments exercising extensive powers and raising high taxes.

The main reason was that only governments could guarantee security from being robbed or invaded. But what if today, against a background of peace in much of the world, government is no longer so essential? What if the spread of connections and markets across the boundaries of states means that other institutions can provide things better than governments, leaving government as an evolutionary dead end, with power and legitimacy passing either upwards to global corporations, with their own mini-welfare states and cities, or downwards to smaller communities governing themselves. In either case, the idea of government at the pinnacle of society becomes obsolete, condemned to go the way of the divine right of kings or the medieval church.

There is an important grain of truth in this argument. Many of the forces that shaped the modern state have disappeared. The most important of these was the pressure of continual war. For the idea of a national state, defined by its physical boundaries, took shape in a Europe ravaged by apparently endless wars, often fought for obscure reasons of dynastic advantage. The competition meant misery for most of their subjects but it left behind a harder, toughened form of state, which was expected to have many capabilities and many rights. Napoleon's empire, although in one respect a mark of the end of the old monarchical system, was also its apotheosis, exemplifying the potential of the state to be not only a phenomenal war machine but also a maker of laws, schools, new industries, and new rights.

It seems very odd for us now, but at the time it was not perverse for Hegel to see freedom and interdependence finding their perfect expression in the state. The 'history of the world is nothing but the development of the idea of freedom', he wrote, arguing that freedom can be attained only within a state to which people voluntarily submit, and within a nation that enables the individual to 'have a definite place in the world – to be something'.

States provided that sense of belonging, and expressed it through the idea of collective power and massed force. This was the image of the socialist clenched fist, and of the *fasces*, the elm or birch rods tied together that became the source of the word fascist. The *fasces* can be found in many settings, from Australia, where the *nururya*, or bundle of sticks or spears, is one of the sacred objects of the Arunta, assembled at the heart of the village, to the Speaker's stand in the US House of Representatives, to the former home of the government of London in County Hall. The image perfectly captures the idea of a collective power that is hard to bend or break.

Yet the military role which gave birth to the modern state has steadily become less important. Few of the most advanced states now defend themselves. Most achieve military security by cooperating with others, and compulsory military service for young men, the symbol of the nation's collective strength and will, is being phased out. Whereas in the past the wealthiest nation-states all sought to increase the territory under their sway, today none do (although the jury is still out on the territorial ambitions of China). Empire is seen as a burden, a waste of resources and morally undesirable. When states combine to guarantee their defence, they do so as much through information, the mutual surveillance offered by satellite systems, and inspections of weapons sites, as through the use of massed force.

This takes us, then, to the other way that states have defined themselves. Instead of military power, during the second half of the twentieth century most modern states directed their energies to maximising economic advantage and assisting the economic welfare of their citizens. The league tables of nations now take into account not the size of their armies, nor of the territories under their control, but rather the relative power of their economies: the competitiveness of their industries, the scale of their assets, the relative incomes of their citizens.

The legitimacy of modern states rests on their success in delivering material benefits, and by any historical standards many governments have been hugely successful over the last century or so, acting as the major force in connecting together millions of citizens, regions and towns. In most countries governments provided the great infrastructures, introduced radio and television, electricity and water. They forged legal systems, universal education, and public health – all taken for granted now. The tools that were invented, and then widely copied – the central bureaucracy, public professionals, mass taxation, national insurance systems, public corporations – were successes, and the few societies where government stood more on the sidelines, notably Britain and the USA, are exceptions that only confirm the rule. Even in them, successive challenges, from cholera to unemployment, terrorism to pollution, elicited effective responses from government.

But in the long view, the economic role of national governments is being superceded just as surely as the military one. Governments that defined their virility in economic terms find that they can no longer meaningfully set the value of their own currency, or raise growth paths, or solve chronic problems like unemployment. They can neither plan their economy nor guide it with any great precision.

The problems faced by modern governments can be best analysed by looking at the two tools that were the heart of the

181

classic state: taxation and command. Both of these tools reflected governments' military origins, and their continuing symbolic and practical importance confirms that today's governments are still linear descendants of the militarised, fiercely competitive nations of the eighteenth and nineteenth centuries, which assumed that the role of the public was to serve the state rather than vice-versa.

Taxation underpins all governments. Without taxes they cannot function. In democracies taxation is controlled by popular will, but our contemporary view of tax is inevitably influenced by the fact that tax was at the economic heart of earlier despotic and feudal regimes, and of all colonialisms. For most of human history tax has been wholly involuntary. All pre-modern states acted as predators on their populations, and their histories are full of the tax revolts which gave us such folk heroes as Lady Godiva, John Ball and William Tell. All of the great revolutions begin as tax revolts. The American War of Independence was sparked by the battle over customs and contraband. In France it was tax that brought to a head the great class conflicts of the 1789 Revolution, with the popular sacking of customs posts, the burning of tax registers, and the declaration by the third estate that all existing taxes were null and void.

Whenever governments tax they cannot help but look despotic, and the tax relationship is one of the only coercive relationships the typical citizen has with the state. Add to that the fact that the state's demands have steadily escalated, whether to finance war in the eighteenth century, internal peace in the nineteenth, or the demands of an ageing population in the twentieth, and it is not hard to see why disillusion with government has always focused on tax, and why tax revolt has been such a common theme in the politics of the West: from Proposition 13 in California, and the anti-tax parties of countries as varied as Canada and Norway, to the battles against the poll-tax in Britain.

But the public ambivalence about tax also reflects the fact that it is still levied in ways that deny popular sovereignty. Traditionally, taxes were largely raised for specific ends:

above all, warfare. In the eighteenth century, war and the costs of war debts accounted for 85 per cent of state spending in Britain. The connection between tax and spending was evident to all. Tax was what power did to the powerless. But with the rise of democracy and the growth in the size and complexity of the state, the context has changed, first because citizens can vote against tax-raising parties and second because of the centralisation of tax collection and disbursement. This centralisation is one of the most striking symptoms of governmental hubris. In most countries most taxes are pooled into the national state, which means that anything up to 70 per cent of the national wealth goes into what looks like a black hole where it is very unclear how taxpayers' money is being used. While citizens are free to know and to choose in other areas of life, when it comes to tax and spending they have no choice beyond occasional elections between packaged promises. Moreover much of the state's spending is effectively controlled by client groups – farmers, pensioners, industries dependent on subsidies – which cramp its room for manoeuvre.

The second tool that reflects governments' origins as militarised states is command. It is virtually a definition of government that it can issue decrees and pass laws, and much of the bureaucracy of modern government is a command structure, a means of passing orders down from the head offices in the capital cities to police officers or teachers in towns and villages. In the communist world the state became literally a system of commands, and because the state could never garner accurate information it was a chronically inefficient system. In recent years the state's role as commander has come under sustained attack. As we shall see, other ways of achieving goals, the use of incentives, encouragement and contracts, have proven more successful than command and control. At the same time self-confident citizens no longer accept being on the receiving end of commands. They prefer to view the state as a servant, or at the very least as a partner.

The net result of the problems governments have experienced with taxation and command is a common unease. The *polis* seems to be inherently in tension with the facts of connectedness. The *polis* is always at root about territory and jurisdiction, where the new connections and communities cross over. The *polis* is geographical whereas the risks to health, life, and security are not. The *polis* is sclerotic in an environment which requires the capacity to change rapidly. As a consequence political power has neither the tools nor the authority to achieve the goals set for it by the public. The tools no longer work because mobile people and assets are harder to tax, or to command, and authority is deficient because a culture of scepticism assumes the worst before the best.

Hence the idea that big government may be just a passing phase, and that the phenomena of connexity are the primary reason for its imminent demise. The argument goes like this. Interdependence and freedom render government irrelevant – interdependence because the systems are too big and complex for governments to manage, freedom because citizens no longer want a protector, a taxer or a lawmaker, and can purchase for themselves security, insurance, health and education in transnational systems of exchange. Governments therefore face a slow drift to obscurity. In the end they may become like constitutional monarchs; they will be paid lip-service to retain a sense of continuity, but will be largely irrelevant to life. In the ecological competition of institutions to secure a niche and wrest resources to maintain themselves, governments will be defeated by others, just as big armies were made obsolete by smart weapons, or big steel mills by mini-mills.

The power of this argument is that it combines the 'is' of contemporary trends with the 'ought' of greater self-reliance. It is attractive because the story it tells is implicitly one in which people take on a wider set of moral and personal responsibilities. And it is an inclusive argument because so many different political traditions have imagined the end of the state in one form or another. In the nineteenth century every radical imagined that sooner or later the world would evolve into a series of self-governing communities (Marx and Engels wrote of the 'withering away of the state' that would leave it only with the task of the 'administration of things'). The Guild Socialists imagined that a shrunken state would leave power in the hands of self-governing guilds. More recently the neoliberals have again imagined a nightwatchman state returned to a few basic functions, including the maintenance of law and order and the value of money.

All imagine the future as a steady state in which a benign blueprint is realised. There is no view that the society may have to adapt, that there may be internal and external threats, or that the forms of government may have to continue evolving. There is no sense that government may have a role of steering. Instead progress is imagined as the steady approximation to a fixed ideal. But setting aside that deficiency, how strong is the case for governmental obsolescence? In order to be convincing, the argument that government is made obsolete by the facts of connexity needs to prove that both the supply of and demand for government are in decline, and that there is no longer a comparative advantage for a nation or region in the strategic role of government as an adaptive mechanism.

As we have seen, in the past the prime task of governments was external security: protection from invasion and conquest. This was the main good that governments supplied, and they did so with armies and weapons, funded out of taxation. Although the armies and weapons remain, the threat of war has virtually disappeared in Western Europe, North America and East Asia. In each of these areas governments have pooled their sovereignty to guarantee security, with the help of complex new systems of mutual surveillance (such as the inspectors of nuclear weapons sites, or the monitoring satellites that can pick out an individual soldier on the ground). None of these measures would have been imaginable in the age when national sovereignty was understood in terms of protecting national boundaries. Yet all represent not an erosion of government, but rather a hugely successful extension of national government's competence, and one that could well extend further. So the capacity of governments to supply peace has arguably risen substantially.

Government's other traditional role has been to promote internal order: to supply peace on the streets. This may have diminished by some measures, certainly in gang-ridden American cities, and there may be new threats from domestic terrorists of the kind who have gassed and bombed Tokyo or Oklahoma. Crime has tended to drift upwards (although demographic factors and smarter policing have pushed it down in some countries). But by any criteria a typical modern government has vastly more power to maintain domestic order than its predecessors. With exceptions like the USA, levels of violence are minimal by any historical standard. Modern police forces can use the paraphernalia of closed circuit cameras and DNA testing, and access to records which can chart the use of telephones and credit cards. Indeed, so great has been the expansion of the tools and capacities of governments that laws have been desperately running to keep up with them.

What of the economy? Government may be less able to shape the economic weather – although this was probably never possible. Governments cannot independently supply rising growth rates or low inflation, and national economies have become ever less like closed systems. But the postwar history of growth – under the umbrellas of Bretton Woods and the European Union, and the Pax Americana in Asia – is not a story of declining capacity to supply economic prosperity. It is much better understood, rather like external security, as an example of how by working in concert, and thus extending their capacities to provide an ordered environment for business, governments have been able to achieve more than their predecessors. Modern regulatory institutions – the

World Trade Organisation or the European Union – are in this sense simply new tools for managing a complex system. They are based on the sovereignty and legitimacy of national governments rather than competing with them.

Welfare is a more complex example. In order to supply it, governments need to be able to raise taxes and to manage systems of more specialist provision – care, cures, housing for the homeless. Here too there is little evidence of declining capacity to supply. The resistance to paying taxes on the part of electorates has coincided with ever greater technical capacities to provide sophisticated services, like care for the elderly, as well as more efficient mechanisms for raising tax. Value-added tax, for example, is significantly easier to collect than earlier sales taxes, and, surprisingly, self-assessment of tax leads to higher tax returns than assessment by a government bureaucracy. There are also more developed professions for delivering care and welfare, and more sophisticated techniques for targeting benefits. The problem for policy-makers is not so much the efficacy of welfare – although there is no shortage of doubts about the power of welfare programmes to cut poverty – but rather that the public has lost faith that money is being spent wisely.

It would be misleading to exaggerate the capacities of national governments to supply things. Their strength relative to transnational firms has probably diminished. Firms with unique access to technologies can strike a hard bargain with national governments. Western governments have had to learn painfully that they are now supplicants for investment by companies from countries like South Korea that were impoverished only forty years ago. But what we have is not business anarchy, and certainly not the dystopian vision offered by writers like Marge Piercy in her remarkable book *Body of Glass*, in which transnational firms have literally displaced government. It is rather a new interdependence of global business on the one hand and a variety of public institutions for regulating the systems of education, infrastructure and popular consent on the other.

*

What then of the demand for government? If there is a declining demand for its outputs then it matters little if it still has the technical capacity to deliver. Today, some would claim, there is a critical mass of citizens, perhaps a majority, who no longer want or need government to provide them with the essentials of life, who can obtain for themselves the things that governments used to provide. Connexity helps them: so for example a citizen in a small German town can use their computer to buy an insurance policy from an American firm rather than relying on the welfare system first put into place by Bismarck.

Clearly this argument does not apply to physical security. Very few can defend themselves against aggressors, or dial up a global security force to help them when they are mugged on the street (although the number of gated estates, with privately-run security services, has steadily risen). Instead the argument focuses primarily on welfare and services, claiming that the conditions that supported mass demand for generous government provision have now disappeared.

In the past, collective provision of welfare by governments depended on there being a reasonably equal distribution of income and of economic risks. This made it unattractive for people to try to insure themselves against risks. Now, so it is argued, a range of factors are undermining this sense of common destiny. These include widening disparities in pay and employability, in health, and in family structure. If sufficient numbers are either able to provide for their own insurance, or sense that it is against their interest to pool their fate with others, then they will remove their political support from governments wanting to redistribute resources or find ways to avoid paying taxes. Alternatively, if the major risks are concentrated on a minority of the population – as might be the case with gays vulnerable to AIDS – then it may be in the interests of the selfish majority to reduce support for them. Looking ahead, the wider availability of knowledge about genetic predispositions could be a powerful additional force against risk pooling, since it would highlight from a very early age who is likely to be a costly burden on the state. In either case the demand for government would become a minority one.

There is evidence to support both scenarios. The combination of more open markets and a greater weight for skills and human capital raised pay disparities in most societies during the 1970s and 1980s. The highly qualified could earn more than the average, and the most qualified, who could sell their services to global customers, could earn vastly more. For a time, national pay-bargaining systems obscured this, but the cumulative opening of global competition put ever greater pressure on these systems, widening the gulf between assembly or service workers having to compete with low-paid workers in Korea or China, and those with scarce skills. Most countries have seen growing earnings dispersion and inequality. It is no more possible to escape competitive pressures than it was in the eighteenth century when British textile workers lobbied for protection from unfair Indian imports.

But the facts are far less simple than the story suggests. In the first place it is no longer credible to assume that competition will only affect low-skill manufacturing jobs, thus raising the relative value of the elite knowledge workers. Although this was the case in the 1980s and 1990s, as the demand for highly skilled labour rose faster than supply, there are plenty of signs that the opposite is now happening. Rapidly rising numbers are going through university at precisely the same time as international competition is sweeping through many of the middle-class professions – management, consultancy, design, architecture, even teaching and lecturing. As a consequence they may be more likely to believe that they share risks with other social groups rather than being insulated from them.

The effects of technology point in the same direction. According to the conventional wisdom, advancing information technologies tend to push downwards on the wages of the less skilled, since they can be cheaply replaced with automated machines. But if economic theory is correct the direction of technological change should be the opposite: it should encourage business to replace the scarcest, not the most abundant, resource. There are more incentives for a big firm to replace expensive lawyers and accountants with expert systems than to replace a poorly paid garage attendant or a cleaner. Over the next few years several of the technologies evolving around neural networks and expert systems look likely to mature to such an extent that they will displace many currently secure elite jobs, just as in the last century some of the craft groups that escaped the first wave of mechanisation found themselves wiped out by later ones. The implications for the demand for government are obvious. Any pressures to widen the disparities of income and employment opportunities are matched by pressures to narrow them. These latter pressures make the experience of economic anxiety and insecurity more widespread, and so increase the demands on government to produce security.

The basic thesis that growing disparity is going to remove the political base for welfare is flawed. This is not to say that welfare will not be transformed by demographic forces, or changing moral views of desert. But the equation between globalisation and welfare collapse is at best unproven. Societies can be viable at very different levels of welfare spending and, if anything, the pressures on public spending from an ageing population point upwards rather than downwards, as we might have guessed this from the experience during the 1980s and 1990s, when government shares in GDP did not fall but stabilised through a decade or more of neo-conservative rule.

The demand for government is also a demand for stability and reliability. Here, too, there is little sign of demand shrinking. Life is more regulated than in the past in part because the public wants it to be. This is why governments now intervene to ensure that parents provide for their children, why they declare wars on drugs or paedophiles, why rules govern the negotiations between trade unions and private firms, why businesses have not only to abide by the basic norms of company law, but also to follow new clusters of environmental, employment and health-and-safety legislation, despite repeated promises of regulatory bonfires. Even in those industries that have apparently been deregulated, there are now many more formal rules in place than ever before, in part because whenever the rules are removed, a public outcry soon follows over anything from contaminated food to excessive profits.

So neither the supply of government nor its demand is in terminal decline. Some governments' powers have waxed while others have waned, and even globalisation, often cast as the cause of government impotence, has given governments powerful new tools and capacities to act. But there is still one other plank to the argument that government is in secular decline, and that is the simpler claim that there is no comparative advantage for any region in having an institution with the capacity to adapt to threats and opportunities. Even if in the past it was essential for communities to have an effective government to protect them, in a world of free trade and open networks there might be no benefit in having a pre-eminent institution. Just as Costa Rica shows that nations no longer need to have an army, so perhaps there is no longer a need for a nation to have a government.

This is not an easy thesis to test, although there are occasional utopian schemes to establish new, government-free, city states in uninhabited zones. But there is some evidence to judge the argument and that evidence shows that effective government still delivers extraordinary rewards, and in ways that go beyond the mobilisation of capital or technology. The fastest-growing states (such as those in East Asia) are not those with the weakest governments, but those with governments that have the strength to deliver the rule of law, effective education, guaranteed property rights and high savings. These are governments that have also often been good at scanning the future to map out effective strategies for their nations (not least by concentrating their energies on human capital rather than traditional economic management), that perceive themselves as central organising intelligences, and that devote their energies primarily not to service delivery but rather to strategy. They may be criticised for misreading trends, or for misallocating resources on the basis of their forecasts, but it is clearly not maladaptive for governments to take an active role in steering.

If the thesis of governmental irrelevance was correct, one would expect that in a borderless world competition would be between firms and individuals, regardless of sovereignties. Economic differences between nations would be explicable in terms of underlying factors such as knowledge, skill or raw materials. But this is not so. As a rule societies with substantial natural resources tend to be poorer rather than richer. Saudi Arabia is poorer than Korea. Hong Kong, like New York, crams millions into a small space with no great attractions, and produces enormous wealth. Nor do skills levels alone explain the disparities in wealth between different nations. Self-employed migrants from Haiti to the USA earn two-thirds as much as those from Western Germany, even though the discrepancy if they had remained in their home country would be 100:1, just as the Chinese in Hong Kong earn ten times as much as their cousins within China, even though the latter benefit from an extremely effective education system.

The reason is simple and obvious. The productive returns in some countries are so much greater than others because of the economic and social order their governments have produced. That order is not the sole property of government, or solely produced by it, but it can never be explained in isolation from government. Countries with governments that do not steal, and that ensure that contracts are respected, and plan wisely for the future, deliver huge benefits to their citizens.[1] The best produce an order which in turn generates wealth. This is not to say that governments cannot be parasitically corrupt, or liable to grandiose failures, but however connected the world, and however great the flows of things, technologies and information across their boundaries, governments are likely to survive on a scale far beyond the 'nightwatchman' state beloved of nineteenth-century liberals, and they will survive because they deliver.

The more important questions are not about whether governments will survive, but about what they will look like when their shape is no longer formed by the military role of holding on to a territory. Some of the answers are already taking shape as governments increasingly syndicate their powers over warfare or trade in collaboration with other governments. But to understand how government is likely to evolve within territories we need to examine what will happen when governments move beyond their traditional approaches to taxation, to command, and to the organisation of their own bureaucracies.

Tax provides a good starting point. Instead of taxes that are the prerogative of the national state and pooled in the national treasury, in the post-military state we should expect to see taxes becoming increasingly differentiated, and increasingly closely connected to their uses, so that citizens will pay a continuum of different types of charge, ranging from a charge for receipt of a particular service, through levies and premiums, to the classic tax. There are no clear dividing lines on this continuum, but rather a range of different ways for citizens to pay money to the state with varying degrees of pooling and earmarking, and with funds going to different levels of government. Some of these payments directly connect the charge to the individual service, such as a bus ride. Others directly connect a tax to a commonly used service, such as policing. Some offer no choices to the citizen, but others give citizens rights to vote, or to opt out. Many of these different ways of organising tax already exist, for example in the rights of school districts to raise bonds in the USA, the earmarking of environmental taxes to environmental goals (as in Sweden and the UK) or the referendums over local taxes that have been held in many countries. Going too far down this route could lead to chaos. But the trend is clear. Tax is ceasing to be a monopoly of national governments. Instead it is becoming more variegated, more complex and increasingly subject to popular choice.

The second example of change is the steady shift beyond

command and control. The attempts to take states away from military structures have a long history. Many of the eighteenth-century utilitarian reformers tried to bring reason to government, and devised a range of new methods that would eliminate arbitrary decisions and apply a precise calculus of means and ends to the state's capacities without depending on a military-style bureaucracy. They proposed introducing competition into government, separating purchase and provision, using incentives for payment, and the further professionalisation of groups like doctors, police and social workers to respond to problems that in another era might have been seen as the responsibility of the individual or the community. (Interestingly, almost every single reform proposed by neo-liberals in the 1970s–90s was prefigured by the utilitarians, the sole exception being the sale of public appointments.)

Many of these ideas have become commonplace. Governments now try to use incentives – such as tax incentives for savings or setting up businesses, rather than subsidies, so as to avoid bureaucrats having to make decisions. The day to day operation of public services increasingly uses market principles, leaving the state to set broad objectives and monitor results rather than run things itself. Another example of the evolution beyond command and control has been the rise of techniques for influencing cultures of behaviour through persuasion, education and role models: health campaigns on smoking or safe sex are examples, as are the attempts by government to persuade people to spend more time keeping an eye out for burglars. Some of these new approaches give shape to a more reciprocal relationship between the state and citizens by using contracts; so parents commit to helping their child with his or her homework, or giving up an unhealthy habit, in return for commitments from the state. Contracts which commit the unemployed to doing training or taking up a job are another example. The same reciprocal spirit can govern how states deal with large organised interests. In the Netherlands the government agreed covenants with different sectors of the economy to change their environmental behaviour, leaving it to them to decide how they would meet the specified targets.

Each of these tools embodies a very different mentality from that of taxation and command. Each implicitly sees government less as a closed system with a monopoly of power and more as an open system engaged in negotiation with other parties, a nexus of multiple connections rather than a bureaucratic monolith.

This takes us to the final character of the kinds of government that are emerging as the military origin of the nation state fades into the distance. Modern government grew up around bureaucracies divided according to function. Separate departments dealt with law, education, health, transport, internal security or foreign affairs. Around these departments professions clustered: teachers, doctors, police, tax inspectors. Through these professions the life of a family, or an area, was sliced up into separate issues, and problem families or problem areas found themselves having to deal with a battery of separate departments and agencies. This division of labour reflected the way armies were organised, with separate units for cavalry, infantry, artillery, and so on. It could be justified by the difficulty and cost of transmitting information. Keeping information within one profession or department avoided waste and confusion.

This model of government has been so successful that we take it for granted that it is the natural way to organise the state. Its weakness, however, is that it makes government bad at dealing with an individual's life as a whole, or for that matter the life of a neighbourhood. It makes government bad at seeing the connections between different things. This in turn has made it hard for governments to act preventively. Help in school, or help through the family might prevent a child from becoming a criminal, but this is beyond the capacity of the courts and police. Exercise and a good diet might prevent someone from becoming sick in later life, but encouraging these is not usually seen as the job of doctors and hospitals. Extra help with literacy at school might prevent someone from being unemployed ten years later. But governments are rarely able to make the link between the investment needed now and the potential benefits in the future.

It is now possible to imagine a very different model of government that could act more holistically, and that could anticipate problems rather than trying to cure them once they have happened. Much cheaper information and communication technologies are crucial since they make it possible for agencies and departments to share information and to assess much more rigorously the link between policies and outcomes. The risk factors that are liable to lead to problems later on, such as family conflict or illiteracy, can be mapped and dealt with. The new structures of government that are separating purchase from provision make it possible to use budgets in radically different ways, rather than carving them up between the great functional departments. So, for example, allocations of money can be linked to measurable outcomes, like a healthier population, rather than to clinical treatments making it possible for groups other than doctors to make a claim on health budgets. Instead of planning a programme of urban regeneration at the centre, funds can be made available for bidding, with the requirement that bids are jointly prepared by the main institutions, private, voluntary or public, in an area. Ministers can be given budgets to spend and problems to solve, rather than functional departments to preside over. These are all different ways in which government can act more holistically, making use of the intelligence spread throughout society rather than having to depend on its own knowledge. They imply, in the long-run, the very opposite of the military model since all the tiers of government might ultimately have to compete for the same funds, and be held to account for whether they achieve the results they promise. These new approaches no longer presume in favour of the public sector, implying instead a much more information-rich way of organising government in which it is no longer possible for states to jealously hoard knowledge and information for themselves.

This future may be some way off, although everything described in this chapter already exists somewhere. But what is beyond doubt is that the state's very success in delivering both external and internal security, has made it possible to move on. Much of the baggage of sovereignty and power that we have inherited from the days when the main role of government was to protect us from danger is now obsolete, and states are now making the uneasy transition from thinking of themselves as pyramids, with clear boundaries and clear lines of command, to something more like a flotilla where no one is in absolute command.

12

SELF-GOVERNMENT AND
COMMUNITY

THE EVOLUTION BEYOND a military ideal of government changes how we think about responsibility. It is not just that the state can become less of a master and more of a servant. It is rather that responsibility can be shared in a more reciprocal relationship between governments and citizens.

This question of responsibility is in part practical. Governments can rarely solve the most difficult problems on their own and if they exaggerate their abilities, they soon lose the public's trust. But the issue is also a moral one. Our ideal of moral development is one in which people are able to bear responsibilities, and to act in virtuous ways, and to accept the consequences of their actions. But a government which is too all-embracing, too powerful, or even too efficient, may so limit the scope for individual responsibility as to leave people dependent, child-like and passive. Indeed some politicians have gone so far as to suggest that there is a direct inverse correlation between the power of governments and the responsibility of their citizens. In practice, however, the issues are much more complex than this. Imagine, for example, applying it to physical security. Clearly if a government withdrew the police force, citizens would have to arm themselves and defend their homes. They would end up stronger and tougher, but not obviously either more virtuous or happier. Nor would it be in the general interest to have a population which devoted its time and energy to weapons and self-defence, since inevitably some of that energy would be directed at other citizens. In the same way, a government might withdraw welfare from an unemployed young man, but if it simply replaced inertia with clinical depression, or encouraged him to take up petty crime, this would hardly be in the public interest.

For it to be right for governments to encourage their citizens to take on more responsibilities, certain conditions need to be in place. Their citizens need the emotional and psychic capacities to carry the responsibility, they need to be able to access the requisite information or advice, and there needs to be a general benefit in cultivating this particular kind of responsibility. So it might be right to remove the restrictions stopping parents from starting their own schools, but wrong to assume that all schools can be self-governing. It might be right to encourage people to become self-employed, but wrong to deny the role of government as an employer of last resort for people who are prepared to work. It might be right to provide support for parents, but wrong to make it too easy for them to dump their children on to the responsibility of the state.

Cultivating responsibility requires governments to be sensitive to variety. What works in promoting responsibility amongst convicted criminals will depend very much on their characters (which is why standardised justice systems are so anachronistic), as will the appropriate sticks and carrots for getting someone who has been unemployed for several years back into work. Where responsibility is involved, the specifics matter. It is as morally wrong to impose responsibilities that are far beyond people's capacities, as it is to so cocoon people in paternal care that they lose all capacity to make judgements for themselves.

Our understanding of these subtle dimensions of the morality of government has been helped by communitarian ideas. Like all of the protean words of social thought, community is both impossible to define and undeniably useful. Its etymology derives from the Latin *communicare*, to share, the root too of communication. It refers to the sharing of place, belief and purpose, in a way that marries integration and differentiation (a community without differentiation and structure is just a crowd). It is generally used to refer to groups without state power, groups of relatively small scale (although it has become common to talk of the world community or the business community), and those with some shared values or beliefs.

The claim made by communitarian thinkers is that big governments and big economic institutions serve not only to disempower people, but also to make them less virtuous and less happy, because they corrode the bonds of trust and co-operation that exist at a smaller scale. Communitarianism focuses on people's attachments – to each other, to institutions and to government – rather than on more quantitative characteristics. It looks at the moral qualities of relationships, rather than emphasising the legal definitions of rights, or the economic aspects of governance.

Communitarianism has been much misunderstood, partly because beyond a few simple definitions communities have no general qualities. They have the same capacity for amoral, selfish and indifferent behaviour as individuals. They can be open or closed, generous or mean, prejudiced or tolerant. Some leave the argument there. They say that since communities can be oppressive, they have no virtue, rather as some people argue that since powerful states are oppressive, any policy which uses or enhances state power is morally suspect. But these arguments are of little help. Communities are facts of life, as are governments. The only interesting questions concern how they can be used, or shaped, to achieve benign ends.

In answering these questions the virtue of communitarian thinking is that it suggests practical ways of reversing the tendency of politics to disempower people by drawing responsibility away from them, reducing their power to a *post hoc* acceptance or rejection. To the extent that powers and responsibilities can be passed down to smaller scales, politics and government can be freed to concentrate on what they alone can do, the job of steering, of thinking strategically, while leaving citizens and communities to govern themselves. In any case, the potential dangers of community are much fewer than they were. Whereas in the past the great majority of people lived as members of only one community, the community of place, connexity widens people's horizons and makes it easier to form new communities, like the virtual communities of cyberspace, or the weak communities of shared interests or of fun. It reduces the dangers of being trapped.

What follows for how we should think about government is a series of new principles about the balance between big and small, the particular and the universal. When the modern nation-state grew up as a fighting machine, large scale was all important. Without the capacity to marshal a big enough army, or to find allies to do so, nations soon disappeared. It was inevitable perhaps that by the middle of the twentieth century the world's two predominant powers would also be those with the largest combination of population, economic assets and scientific knowledge. Throughout most of this century too, government and politics have been shaped by a faith in scale: the economies of scale offered by large parties, large-scale bureaucracies, and large armies of professionals. Social workers, social citizenship, social security and socialism were all manifestations of a belief in a large (usually national) unit of society that can be traced back to Auguste Comte and beyond. In the last quarter of a century, however, this cluster of ideas has fallen apart. Bigness has lost its lustre. The scale of effective organisation has shrunk – to that of the school, the neighbourhood, the group, which can provide a sense of belonging and engagement, but within the context of social orders of law and security that benefit from a larger scale.

This is where community comes in. It is not a synonym for the word 'society'. It may refer to neighbourhoods or workplaces, but to be meaningful it must imply membership in a human-scale collective: a scale at which it is possible to encounter people face to face. Confucius believed there to be a series of concentric circles of compassion around each person, with love devoted first to father, then family, then others, a very different goal from the Judaeo-Christian one of loving everyone as oneself. It is not necessary to go all the way along this line (and there are plenty of examples of compassion that defy the idea of concentric circles), but it is evident that the moral quality in relationships that involve proximity and repeated interactions is greater than in those that do not.

Proximate relationships also depend less on compulsion, and standardised rules. This takes us to the first of the major arguments of communitarianism, namely that one of the effects of the waning of the military character of the state is that it makes possible a different balance between compulsion and voluntarism. In the past there was a clear divide between the domain of states, which was about law and obligation, and the domain of community, which was seen as voluntary and chosen. This division was the reason why, for example, the Quakers chose not to repeat their experience of governing Pennsylvania. They concluded that this had been a category mistake: a society of friends could not carry out the coercive tasks of government.

But in a less formal state structure, less concerned with defence and command, there is a continuum between compulsion and voluntarism. Communities are ill-suited to formal, coercive functions, but these are a relatively small subset of the modern functions of government. While the hard functions of government, law and coercion, need clear links to traditional political authority, this is not so true of the provision of parks, or transport, or care for children. All of these can legitimately combine paid and unpaid work, formal and informal authority, and they are likely to be provided best if users freely devote time to improving them or shaping them to their distinctive needs.

Most of the new tools of government, those that engage with communities and citizens, emphasise voluntary engagement rather than compulsory compliance. The incentive, for example, leaves it to the individual whether to act in response to it. So does the use of information or persuasion to change behaviour (such as campaigns to encourage people to save more so as to become less of a burden on other taxpayers in old age). Similarly, the use of contracts with parents, patients or people involved in community policing schemes, helps to define a balance of responsibilities between the individual, their community and the state. All meet halfway the impulse to self-help and self-provision.

Giving communities more power – and more chances to fail – also has another, less obvious virtue. In *Community and Conflict*, a classic argument published forty years ago, James Coleman predicted that as local communities lost the power to make decisions, they would increasingly be shaped by externally imposed conflicts. The best way of mobilising them would be to threaten to build a road or place a toxic waste plant nearby. Disempowered communities would tend to become more parochial, divisive, and defined by their differences with the larger society. Re-empowering them, by contrast, makes it more likely that their energies will be devoted to positive goals rather than defensive ones.

How far should we go? Any geographical community could in principle be fully empowered to raise its own taxes, manage its own waste or police its own streets. Non-geographical communities could be allowed to organise their own social provision, their pensions or healthcare. But in most societies, to take these principles too far would clash with underlying ideas of social equity, since wealthy, well-organised communities would do so much better than poor ones without much experience of self-organisation. This is why the connections close at hand have to be balanced with wider connections and obligations, and the shared benefit in a larger social order. National and transnational governments legitimately retain powers to raise taxes and to redistribute resources, as well as powers to enforce common rules – such as prohibitions on discrimination – even when local communities want to reject them. The best models of community use the distributed intelligence of the society as a resource not so as to abrogate central responsibility, but rather so as to define a healthy balance between the whole and its parts.

*

Alongside small scale and the mixing of the voluntary and the compulsory, the idea of community also brings one other major change to the mentality of government. The modern states which grew up in parallel with rationalism constructed themselves on universal principles. The principle of law is that it applies evenly to every member of the *polis*. Votes are equally weighted for everyone regardless of capacity. Policies are framed to deal with functions or categories, not with persons. But in real life societies do not function in this way. They are mosaics of cultures, beliefs and behaviours, rather than universal principles, and they are made up of living breathing people rather than specified roles.

Philosophy provides a useful means of thinking about the contrast between the particular and the universal. Since the virtue of communities is that they don't only pursue self-interest but also produce altruism, we can focus on the point through the distinction between bounded and universal altruism.[1] Bounded or particularist altruism is the ethic of commitment to people who matter because of our connections to them. They may be related to us, or they may be members of the same group or religion. Universal or inclusive altruism, by contrast, disregards special interests and thinks impersonally. It determines the rights of people because of more objective criteria (such as disability, age or need), the morality of fairness and the rule of law.

Western culture has tended to disparage particularism. It may lead to nepotism, favouritism, even racism. Universalism by contrast has been favoured because it grows out of the capacity to reason – which creates demands for justifying actions, and for making these consistent. It grows too out of the experience of cooperation and reciprocity. Both of these causes tend to infuse rationalist cultures with moral arguments, as people appeal to general interests when they feel wronged. In such cultures, 'the primary form of moral argument is a request to imagine oneself in the situation of another person'.[2] Each type of altruism also has its own culture. Particularism is more emotional and expressive, universalism more cool and calculating, fitted to achievement-oriented cultures.

One view of history sees it as a steady expansion of particular loyalties, with the widening of community, the *civis* and the nation tending towards the universal, perhaps in the end underpinned by a world government. But people by their nature cannot be governed solely by universal, purely rational moral rules. Instead they need a balance between the particular moral relationships with family, work colleagues and neighbours on the one hand, and overarching universal rules on the other. When the particular is denied in public institutions that are close at hand, perverse outcomes result, and the state comes to seem blind or cruel. Schumacher made a similar point when he argued that we need both justice and mercy, even though they can sometimes point in opposite directions.

If we want a more morally fluent society then we cannot afford to disregard the particular, because morals that are lived through and fought over turn out to be more deeply held and understood than universal ones reached only through reflection or through teaching. By the same token a state based only on universal rules loses touch with its humanity, and its citizens lose touch with the effects of their actions. It is after all easier to avoid taxes than to take payment away from a poor eighty-year-old, easier to support a distant war than to hold a gun yourself.

Even within government's own operations this balance between the particular and the universal can be managed differently. The key is to recreate personal relationships. For example, a welfare system can impersonally deliver money to recipients according to standardised criteria: how many children there are, how disabled or how qualified the person is. But it may be much more effective to give front-line staff discretion to use given sums of money creatively. A personal welfare counsellor might then agree with the recipient to invest money in a new training course, or even perhaps a visit to a distant family member, if this is likely to be in their interest. Similarly, a probation officer might not just monitor an offender, but be given more discretion to tailor their punishment, with their own freedom of decision-making balanced by systems for appraising them according to the number of their clients who re-offend. In education, in place of teachers responsible for classes and disciplines, each pupil might have a learning mentor who would help them negotiate a wide range of educational opportunities both in school and after it. In each of these cases government would recreate itself as a web of personal relationships in which the front-line staff are no longer there just to deliver centrally defined products, but rather to use their discretion to consider particular circumstances, and even particular moral issues, within an overarching universal framework.

In thinking about any kind of government, form should follow function. The form of a centralised, hierarchical state followed the primary function of defence. The form of a multidepartmental bureaucratic state followed the function of standardised mass provision. When instead the primary function is to manage the well-being of very diverse individuals and communities, the appropriate form is a much leaner, more intelligent state, concerned with managing self-governing systems and their connections rather than intervening within them. This vision of states that slough off their origins as machines of war also suggests a very different model of leadership, which does not simply pull levers at the top, or command the nation in times of trouble. Instead it provides a clear ethos, values and narratives that make sense of a multiplicity of different communities and ways of life, and that suggest the generative rules from which people can make their own policies. Its role in other words is to steer when steering is necessary, but also to strengthen the capacity of citizens and communities to govern themselves.

The states we have inherited reflect their origins. The gentler ones ran society as harmonious machines, the more extreme ones ran them like armies: fascism with the use of uniforms, parades, and the glorification of violence, communism with the extension throughout civil life of command systems. All tried to protect the individual from the loneliness of big cities and industrial society by absorbing them into a much larger cohesive whole. By contrast, in the post-modern era states become more like servants of individuals and communities, there to deliver economic growth or personal well-being, not to impose their mass as a burden on their citizens. In *Measure for Measure* Shakespeare wrote that 'it is excellent to have a giant's strength, but it is tyrannous to use it like a giant'. Despite all suggestions to the contrary, states still have a giant's strength, but they are slowly learning that it is better not to use it like a giant.

13

LIVING ORGANISATIONS

EVERY ERA HAS ITS characteristic forms of organisation. We may like to think of ourselves as individuals with distinctive choices, tastes and idiosyncrasies, but most of our choices are highly organised, and even mass-produced. The paradox of an age which prides itself on its individualism is that so much of contemporary life takes place within organisations: these shape how people act, even how they think. Indeed it is hard to imagine a modern society except in terms of its organisations, which have replaced informal relationships with formal ones, agreements with contracts, shared assumptions with explicit rules.

Much of the modern world was framed by its new organisational rules, which rejected the old principles whereby monarchs and the church provided privileges and licences for things to happen, so that rank and status were paramount and freedoms flowed from power. Modern organisational law is very different. It sets the parameters within which organisations can operate more freely, and its founding aim was to take arbitrary caprice out of organisational life. Six organisational forms took shape in the nineteenth century and have dominated the Western world ever since. Each gave a particular group of stakeholders the dominant right to control revenues, and each defined a set of hierarchical relationships. The first new form was the joint-stock company, which gave power to investors. In Britain, incorporation by Royal Charter had been available for several centuries, but the new form reached maturity in the 1862 Companies Act, after which firms grew rapidly in size and scope. The second new form was the meritocratic bureaucracy of the Civil Service, which evolved out of the 1854 Northcote-Trevelyan report (with some of the same features that characterised Napoleonic government on the Continent, and the Mandarin bureaucracy in China). The third was the multipurpose local authority, merging the concerns expressed in separate pieces of legislation on matters such as public health, highways and education.[1]

The fourth was the mutual, which responded to the democratic urge for organisations that served the people rather than standing over them. Mutual organisations based on building societies and burial associations found legal expression in the friendly society and building society law of 1874, and then went the same way as their European counterparts by turning into bureaucratic institutions whose mutuality remained more as a memory than a defining principle. The fifth was the cooperative with egalitarian redistributive principles, which was formed by the Rochdale pioneers in 1844, became a national society in 1863, and soon inspired legislation on industrial and provident societies which provided a framework for organisations such as cooperatives, partnership firms and even universities (which are run by their faculties). Finally, the sixth was the trade union, which steadily gained legal recognition at the turn of the nineteenth and in the twentieth century, replacing the guilds as the best organisers of labour in mass industries.

These six have been the foundation stones for modern societies and economies. In retrospect, we can see that the historic shift into cities, away from rural relationships and informal kinship relationships, demanded an explosion of new forms to provide structure for people's lives. The old institutions had reached their limits. Some of the new ones were needed to raise far larger sums of capital to build factories or railways, some to give shape to the rational bureaucratic state, some to protect people from new kinds of exploitation. All spread like viruses as they found people in need of new forms.

By contrast the twentieth century has been much less innovative. In organisational terms it consolidated the innovations of the nineteenth century rather than replacing them. Most of the big changes involved subsidiaries of the nineteenth-century forms. The nationalised corporation and the municipal enterprise were subsidiaries of national and local government. More complex networks of company ownership and joint venture, of conglomerates and multinationals, were variations within the theme of the joint-stock company, rather than alternatives to it. The charitable company, which emerged as the trading arm of charities, made it possible for non-profit organisations to sell goods and services. But in each case, however much the internal structures changed, the basic lines of governance persisted.

It used to be taken for granted that the way organisations behaved would depend on their form. Firms would act to maximise profits. Public bodies would serve the public interest, universally and fairly, even if less efficiently. Charities would serve some higher purpose which might be religious. As a rule, organisations were understood in terms of their internal constitution: their architecture and structure of governance would shape how they acted.

This assumption in turn gave shape to the main line of ideological conflict in the twentieth century. The great battles between left and right often took the form of conflict over organisational forms. So nationalisation was pitted against the privately owned business, the planning state against the free market, the trade union against the bosses. This conflict gave many political arguments a neat simplicity: each ideological vision of the world simply multiplied the organisational forms it favoured. Utopia came to mean a world made up entirely either of public institutions in the socialist vision, or of private firms in the vision of neoliberals.

In truth, the world is and always has been far more complex. It is surprisingly rare for organisational forms to translate directly into behaviour. As far back as the 1930s, pioneers of the study of business found that firms responded more to managers than shareholders, and many businesses have arguably been more shaped by values than by the pursuit of profit. Government organisations have often been self-serving, or better at serving vested interests rather than engaging in the even-handed service of the public. Charities have often proved less responsive to their clients, and even less charitable, than apparently avaricious businesses.

We are now reaping the rewards of a slow revolution in the way we think about organisations. It still matters how an organisation is constituted, but we have learned that organisations, particularly amidst connexity, are better understood not by their forms but rather by two other characteristics: their ethos, that is, the guiding missions, stories and values that motivate them, and their interfaces – the ways in which they relate to other institutions.

Strictly speaking, ethos means the essential qualities of a people or group and, through the link with ethics, its highest qualities too. In the industrial era it was largely irrelevant to organisations, even though paternalistic employers like many of the Quaker firms in Britain and America instilled their organisations with inspiring values. But most organisations were glued together by functions. The division of labour ensured what Emile Durkheim called 'mechanical solidarity', just as wives and husbands were bound together by the household division of labour. It was enough for each person in an organisation to have a clearly specified task and a clearly specified line of command. Values and ethos might determine which orders were passed down the hierarchy, but it was not necessary for them to infuse each person's daily life.

The idea of the bureaucratic organisation was drawn directly from the military. The first factories were built by armies, and it was in military production that the principle of breaking each task into its component parts was first perfected. The very essence of an army, particularly before the advent of democracy, was that only the commanders could take part in decisions, only they needed to know the conditions of battle, and only they needed to know what broader purpose they contributed to.

In a democratic culture this ceases to be so. People expect

211

some engagement in the causes they give their life to, even if their engagement comes through the contract of work. They expect their emotions and motivations to be engaged. If the work is creative, or uncertain, or if it demands that they respond quickly to the needs of customers in ways that cannot be clearly specified, then it is essential that something beyond their narrowly defined function should bind them into the organisation. If communication is richer and more ubiquitous, then it is natural that it does more than pass down commands or pass up results, but rather communicates emotions and desires too.

This is what an ethos provides. It provides a link between the daily tools, the structures and architectures of an organisation and a higher goal. In the most successful organisations the ethos is crystal-clear, and cascades through the structure so that even on the front line individual workers understand precisely what mission they are part of. In a nation too, the greatest leaders provide such a clear sense of values and direction that each citizen can feel part of a 'we', with great and inspiring goals that bind them to millions of strangers in a common enterprise. In all of them the ethos brings simplicity to very complex systems without denying their complexity.

The corollary of the glue that holds institutions together is the quality of their outward connections. A powerful ethos defines all of the relationships with other people and institutions, drawing them under its spell, motivating or repelling. But greater connectedness also tends to bring more and more complex external relationships that have to be managed regardless of the actual form the organisation takes. So the firm comes to be defined by its links to suppliers, retailers, university laboratories or public contractors, and even locks them in through the ways in which it designs its communications systems. The non-profit organisation comes to be defined by its complex relationships to stakeholder groups, its various contracts with public agencies and its links to funders. Like the architecture that places the inner workings of the building on its exterior, what has happened to organisations is that their exterior character has become almost as determining as their internal ethos. Organisations are becoming like insects: their ethos, which is equivalent perhaps to a kind of cultural DNA, is held internally, but their structure is like the insect's exoskeleton, carried on the outside not the inside.

This is the case for firms both large and small, although in very different ways. Despite some expectations that they would decline, large firms have retained their relative weight in the economy, but they now exercise it more through the networks of relationships they have with smaller firms, connected by contracts and licences, than through ownership. They can increase their sway through strategic alliances, usually on specific products or markets, that do not preclude competition elsewhere. Small firms, by contrast, can now mimic larger firms by forming networks of collaboration with other small firms, just as large firms can mimic the flexibility of small firms by breaking themselves down into smaller, less bureaucratic, units. In both cases the key operating unit is no longer the business, but rather the business project which is organised in a network.[2]

Neither the ethos of organisations, nor their connections, are given by legal form. A private company may have an ethos devoted to reducing poverty or preserving traditional crafts. A public body may have an ethos devoted to knowledge, or to making money. Even a charity may be governed by an ethos that emphasises maximising market share in a field like housing, rather than propagating the gospels. Each may work through common ventures with other species of organisation.

This has important implications for politics and policy. If it matters less what form an organisation takes than what ecology it is part of, and what ethos gives it purpose, then it may be possible to influence it to behave in different ways. Rather than nationalising a firm, it can be regulated. Rather than directly providing a service, a local agency can manage a network of different organisations. Rather than working through tax incentives or rules, it may be better to seek to change the organisation's culture.

What lies behind these changes in organisational form? The main factor is that organisations are less defined by material things, less likely to produce material things, and less likely to use material metaphors to understand themselves. The nineteenth-century organisational forms generally had a kind of property at their core. The joint-stock company had its buildings and machines, the government its territory and official offices. The building society had its buildings, the cooperative its corner shops. Accounts measured physical things, but gave no value at all to the people who worked for the company, or to its ideas and its brands. Each stakeholder could make a claim on something tangible and physical, and treated these as real. In the twenty-first-century economy the most valuable things are rarely physical, and it is possible to create wealth almost out of nothing, or rather nothing more than ideas. Organisations are now enmeshed in a web of communications through to funders, suppliers, outlets and users. Some organisations can do without any centre. Virtual companies are being established without an office and in some cases without even a staff. Others have no easily definable property. Small software companies regularly emerge as if from nowhere to become corporate titans, just as traders now deal on world markets from remote cottages.

The weightlessness of the economy affects every sector. The electronics in the typical car now costs more than its steel. The average drink can weighs only a fraction of what it did twenty years ago – because of advances in materials science. The physical weight of output of the US economy is little more than it was a century ago but its value in real terms is twenty times higher. Microsoft exemplifies the new economy, with a market capitalisation of some $80-90bn and physical assets worth under $1bn. The difference is its know-how and brand value.

In this new economy even the idea of property has become suspect, since where information is concerned no clear divide can be made between what is owned and what is not. In practice, a combination of tradition, legal precedent and luck shapes who benefits from intellectual property and who does not: sometimes a tune, a phrase, an image may be owned, sometimes not. Often what the law protects is the form of knowledge, not the content, so that, for example, the structure of databases is owned, whereas the information in them is not. In practice, knowledge grows incrementally, just as cultures evolve by developing and hybridising the ideas of many people, yet in legal theory ownership is absolute and unshared. It is striking that none of the great advances of twentieth-century understanding, from the discovery of DNA and quantum physics, to the poetry of W.B. Yeats, depended for their existence on copyright protection, whereas such mundane inventions as tranquillisers and anti-ulcer drugs have been the most valuable patents of the postwar era.

The reason is that the rules governing an immaterial economy have been largely taken from a material one. Yet in a world of rapid flows of information, where it is easy to copy something, to send it across the world and to adapt it, material rules no longer fit. So, for example, on broadband communications networks the marginal cost of sending a signal may be literally zero, and the true cost of connecting another node may be less than zero, if it increases the value of the network to everyone already on it. Knowledge can actually gain in value by being used, unlike material things which are used up. The tendencies exactly mirror the effects of connexity on politics and government, since they are in effect favouring a pooling of sovereignty over knowledge, as know-how leaks, is appropriated and reshaped, rather than the absolute sovereignty of classic ownership vested in one individual.

The same point applies equally to organisational forms. Those organisations that have gone furthest in moulding their structure to the nature of information have proven far more successful than those that have stuck to older models. One of these successes is the Internet, the fastest-growing medium in human history. The Internet is not owned by anyone, but makes use of leased lines to interconnect different public and private networks. A handful of central computers manage much of the business of routing signals and organising addresses, but the system is a network of networks, with capacities spread widely. It is not coincidental that the main innovations on the Net have generally come not from the centre but from users and niche software companies around the edges: the World Wide Web, for instance, was invented by a computer scientist in Switzerland but the key technologies for using it were put together by a student in his early twenties.[3] From complexity and apparent chaos has emerged something like order, a useful system of knowledge and communication which grows at an exponential rate and which bears a distinctive ethos that favours openness, pooling of knowledge and reciprocity. Yet its performance has owed nothing to advertising or the assertion of corporate power; it has been the system's adaptability, the freedoms it gives users, that have given it its edge.

Another instructive model of an information-age organisation is Visa, in financial services. Instead of offering a credit card supported by the resources of one bank or a consortium of banks – like the failed experiments run by American banks in the 1960s – Visa operates a credit-card service which is owned by the large number of financial institutions (well over 20,000) which offer its cards and services. Visa itself is only a skeletal 'overseeing administrative organisation',[4] linking the operations of its members into a cohesive and efficient whole and maintaining, and communicating, its governing principles. By doing so, it has succeeded in growing to a scale where it carries over 7 billion transactions per annum, worth over $650 billion. This is, according to Visa's founding chief executive, Dee Hock, 'the largest single block of consumer purchasing power in the world economy'.[5]

What is interesting about both these new forms of organisation is the way in which they operate broad infrastructures incorporating diversity, competition and multiple lines of power. They are defined by their ethos and by their relationships, and by little else. It is no coincidence that the areas in which they have thrived are markets for information – markets in which the number of transactions, exchanges and communications handled would bemuse many more centrally directed organisations. But instead of being paralysed by this complexity, they have flourished with it. Consumers have been drawn to Visa by the ease of using the card anywhere in the world, and constant innovations, like cheap voice transmission, broaden the appeal of the Internet each year.

Both examples are more like biological organisms than machines. Dee Hock has argued that the development of more 'chaordic' organisations such as Visa would avoid the institutional sclerosis experienced by hierarchical, 'command-and-control' organisations. By distributing ownership and power, according to Hock, an organisation or infrastructure can embrace huge complexity, and like the human mind, evolve so as to withstand shocks and to constantly incorporate new ideas. Similar ideas have been proposed by Kevin Kelly, who champions evolutionary models for complex systems of information exchange and warns that our fixation on mechanical design is damaging and likely to retard innovations in many scientific and informational fields: 'a neo-biological technology is far more rewarding than a world of clocks, gears and predictable simplicity'.[6]

Many organisations are ill-suited to this type of organic structure: the form of their product or the nature of their markets make evolutionary, fragmented designs inappropriate. But the general lesson is that organisations can now be less heavily structured through internal architectures and more through interfaces. To grow it may be more efficient to spread like amoebae, or fungi, than like a building. To hold the whole together it may be more effective to use culture, or principles, than hierarchical authority. To fuel the organisation it may be better to use trust, both externally with customers, and internally with the main producers of value, rather than only commands or money.

Both the Internet and Visa deal with information. For organisations that deal with materials the lessons are somewhat different. Most of the organisations of the industrial age were inward-looking, in that they saw themselves as closed boxes, but they were open in terms of their use of physical resources and their emission of wastes and pollution. For organisations that have come to terms with connexity the imperatives push in exactly the opposite direction. For external relationships there is the same logic pushing towards more relationships, more joint ventures, more participation in networks and more openness about information. But in terms of what happens inside the organisation, awareness of how the enterprise affects others leads to a radically different approach to production.

One of the peculiarities of the capitalist system that has connected the world so successfully is that it managed to build into its structures a remarkable degree of myopia. The technical definition of economics defines it as the study of the allocation of scarce resources in the pursuit of ends. But most economists and most economic policy-makers ignore the second half of the sentence and take ends as a given. Businesses concern themselves almost entirely with the means: markets, profits, competition, rather than with the ultimate value of the product or service they provide.The result is an oddly disconnected economic system, in which workers are detached from the product they make, in which owners of capital are detached from the uses to which it is put, and managers are detached from the wider effects of their actions. The invisible hand is often blind and the typical modern economic organisation reverses Kant's categorical imperative: everything and everyone external becomes solely a means rather than an end. Businesses which cultivate awareness of their connection to other things turn these principles on their head. Instead of rapaciously seeing materials simply as things to be used, they seek to minimise resource use or waste, and to reduce the size of the firm's material impact on the wider world. Instead of imagining the production process as open, with an ill-defined heap of detritus at the end, attention turns to how the whole chain of production can be closed off, by reusing all materials and designing products like cars and computers, homes and food products, in such a way that nothing need be thrown away. An economy based on awareness of how it affects others is likely to be much more intolerant of waste. It will offer less rewards to growth and more to radical reductions in the use of materials and energy:[7] what Amory Lovins of the Rocky Mountain Institute calls 'negawatts' (savings in energy) rather than megawatts, and 'immaterials' (savings in matter) rather than materials.[8] To achieve such reductions it is often best to keep focused on the end and not the means. If the real end is to make people warmer, or more mobile, it may make more sense to redesign the whole system of production rather than just to produce a new product. So in the case of energy, attention turns to how homes can be better designed and insulated, rather than how a new power station can be financed. In the case of refuse, attention turns to refashioning the links between what happens within the home, the municipal systems of collection, the secondary materials processing industries and the potential new uses of recycled materials. System changes of this kind depend in turn on a much more open approach to analysing products than has been the norm in the past, with firms jealously guarding as much information as they can. It is only with an open and public analysis of the life-cycles of products, all the way from raw materials to their re-use and disposal, that it becomes possible to identify savings and new ways for the organisations involved at each stage of the cycle to co-operate in eliminating hazardous materials or re-using waste.

Some of the same principles are changing how we think about consumption, again by emphasising the connections between different parts of the economic system. Instead of seeing consumption as a passive activity, where we buy in ready-made packages of food, education or entertainment, there is a parallel trend towards what might be called lifecraft as opposed to lifestyle – an active engagement in making or changing things rather than only using them, that often implies using less, but better. Examples include actively separating waste into different streams so as to ease recycling, spending time cooking complicated meals, teaching children at home rather than relying on a standardised curriculum, do-it-yourself decoration. The industrial era's separation of work from home, which involved work for money and passive consumption, is being replaced by models of active consumption mainly because these contribute more to well-being, and more to our sense of being alive. Such strategies of self-limitation do not go against the grain of a capitalist economy, since waste minimisation, and more engaged patterns of consumption, can increase efficiency. But they do help to reconnect the means of economic life to meaningful ends.

The same need to reconnect economic decisions with ends and ethos changes how we think about ownership and responsibility. Modern capitalism has detached ownership from responsibility. Global capital markets work swiftly and without friction precisely because traders do not need to have any involvement in the end uses of the capital they trade. Property rights are the legal foundation of the system, but there is no need for owners to take responsibility for the effects of their assets, except in the limited instances of legal liability. Formal property rights are things to be collected and disposed of, regardless of any social context (the libertarian philosopher Robert Nozick for instance wrote of acquiring them like picking up seashells on the shore). The owner's function in a classic market system is simply to move their capital quickly enough to ensure that its returns are maximised.

The alternative is to see ownership as bringing responsibility with it: the responsibility of being a steward or trustee. To make this meaningful the owner needs some presence and proximity to the work of their assets, otherwise their sense of responsibility will remain theoretical rather than real. Equally, organisations that are framed by a shared ethos also need that ethos to be embodied in ownership. There are many ways of doing this, and thus of bringing power and responsibility closer together. The simplest is to pass ownership of capital to the people working in an enterprise, in reflection of the relative importance of human as opposed to financial capital.[9] Recent decades have brought a huge expansion of employee ownership, sometimes in response to crisis (as with the American airlines), sometimes as a reflection of the value of knowledge workers (as in companies like Scientific

Instruments and much of the American computer industry), and sometimes as a consequence of privatisation. Even when employee ownership is relatively marginal the mood and culture of organisations can change palpably. Mutual ownership can even be used when there are no assets at all. Some trade unions and personnel companies have been evolving into what might be termed 'employee mutuals', selling their members' labour time to employers but providing the supports in terms of pensions, training and health, that would usually be associated with the employment contract. One might also imagine shared ownership reconnecting ownership and responsibility for the communities affected by big industrial projects, giving neighbourhood associations property rights alongside big investors and employees. Traditional economists would argue that some of the same effects can be achieved by imposing legal restrictions on property rights so that decisions have to involve consultation, or openness of information. But wider ownership is the clearest and most unambiguous way of reframing the purpose of the enterprise, restoring the link between capital and its uses.[10]

Could some of the same principles be applied to money? We have become used to money that is wholly disconnected from goods and services, and we see its liquidity as its virtue. But monies can be designed in many different ways, and some of them can be used to establish a closer connection between buyers and sellers. They can, for example, be designed so that they can only be used to buy local goods, like the Buynes tokens that were minted in eighteenth-century Britain or the vouchers used in Wörgl in Austria in the 1930s, or the tens of thousands of local-exchange trading systems now in operation around the world to help communities provide services that are not viable in the formal monetary economy. At a simpler level, schools can organise networks for swapping time, so that parents can ring up a pool for someone to look after a child at short notice, and then repay the pool at a later date.[11] Systems of this kind are becoming technologically much more feasible with the advance of smart cards and cheap networking. The same technologies that are driving the development of integrated monies, like the Euro, are also making it possible for money to once again become more differentiated. There are already markets operating for quasi-monies like air miles, and it is entirely possible that companies will create their own credit in the form of future claims on Microsoft or Mitsubishi products, effectively displacing national governments' monopoly over the supply of money. Between these corporate monies and local exchange systems many hybrids are possible that could strengthen the bonds holding the economy of a city or a neighbourhood together. So for example a local employer could pay a tranche of their employees' salaries in the form of electronic vouchers that are held on a card and are redeemable against training courses or locally purchased domestic services. Unemployed citizens could exchange goods and services with each other, and gain access to public services, without having to use dollars or pounds. College courses could be repaid by giving time for community service rather than money. Twin monies could even be used as a tool of demand management in local areas when the formal economy turns down.

The rise of new forms of ownership and new forms of money offers the prospect of a change in the characteristic form of economic relationships away from one-way provision and towards greater reciprocity. Twentieth-century economies were built around mass production for the mass market, driven by economies of scale and made possible by the standardisation and interchangeability of parts. More recently, in many industries, specialised production for niche markets has become the norm, again based on some standard elements but tailoring these to more varied needs. But the examples set out here are more like clubs. Clubs are based on members, and share values and mutual commitment. They are, almost by definition, reciprocal. Charles Handy wrote about the club cultures that he had observed in organisations of less than twenty people, as 'based on trust and communicating by a sort of telepathy, with everyone knowing each other's mind'. Others achieve only a fraction of this intimacy, like the clubs in marketing, those in advanced telecommunications where users play as large a role in defining 'the product' as the producer, or the joint ventures in which groups of firms seek to cultivate a sense of common mission. But what all are trying to create is a stable ordering of relationships to achieve better mutual understanding and higher orders of intensionality than in classical markets.

These new economic forms all defy the logic of organisations formed in the industrial age. They define their strength by the number and quality of their connections and the resilience of their values. They reverse the tendency of the system to emphasise the abstract over the concrete, quantities over qualities. They mitigate the blindness of the classic market by reconnecting business to real localities, real needs and real lives.

14

GLOBAL ORDERS WITHOUT A
GLOBAL GOVERNMENT

A CASUAL OBSERVER OF the modern media would be justified in believing that the world is falling apart. A tiny terrorist incident or a hurricane count for more than a dull committee on trading arrangements. Wars seem to be rampant, human misery unlimited, genocide the norm, and international bodies look like a cacophony of mutually deaf voices making demands. Yet the remarkable fact of the end of the twentieth century is the degree of global order, not disorder. It is this order that makes it possible to travel, to trade and to communicate far more widely than before. It is an order under which wars between nations have been largely suppressed, even though wars within nations are many. Expeditions across deserts and jungles take it for granted that they will be plucked out instantly if things go wrong. A panoply of international laws and rules protect us from dangers.

In the past, order meant empire. If you did not live in an empire you probably lived in chaos, and empires brought law, civilisation and culture. As a rule you were better off living under the umbrella of the Chinese, Persian or Roman empires rather than outside them. This long historical experience meant that the idea of a single source of order has resonated down the ages. The Holy Roman Empire, and more recently the idea of world government, or a United States of Europe, all shine out as aspirations, political solutions to any number of problems. One vision of the twenty-first century is of just such a global government evolving as the institutions of the

United Nations gradually gain power and legitimacy, building a world army to punish miscreants and make peace, a world environmental agency to guarantee biodiversity and climate controls, a world emergency service to intervene when disasters happen, and a world parliament for the peoples of the world to deliberate in.

Such a vision seems like a logical result of a more connected world. But these are misplaced hopes, and not primarily because of the persistence of national sentiments. Over the last few centuries grand empires and superstates have turned out to be the problem, not the solution. Too much of their energy went into holding themselves together, too many of their resources were soaked up financing armies, and those armies in turn spent more of their time tied up in maintaining internal order rather than providing the external protection that was the reason for existing. In the modern era smaller nations turned out to be the powerhouses of history, or at least nations which did not exhaust themselves trying to contain subject peoples. So the Austro-Hungarian and British Empires broke up, and the USA prevailed where the Russian Empire failed. The smaller nations like those of Scandinavia succeeded over the big nations. The city states of East Asia grew faster than the mainland.

Some have interpreted this as proof that the world is reverting to a pre-imperial model, with the nation-state as a way-station. Ultimately they predict that we will live in a world where the favoured form is the self-governing city or region: fiercely independent and energetically competitive, but built on a human scale and so able to tap into an intensity of belonging that eludes the bigger units. Andorra and Liechtenstein represent the future, the optimum scale for belonging, and perhaps for being creative, where the nation was the optimum size for military defence.

There is more than a grain of truth in this hope. Big nations with forty or a hundred million people are ideal for marshalling large armies, but they are too big to sustain village-scale numbers in their elites. They need to be more formal, more rule-driven, less subtle in their understandings than the smaller units. They often spend their energies trying to keep peripheral provinces from seceding, or stopping the richest provinces from opting out of their fiscal support for the poorer ones. But the vision of a world made up of micro-states, most of them based on cities, is at best partial. It leaves out the most important dimensions of the emerging order and it transfers the kinds of sovereignty that made sense in ancient Greece, or the city states of the Holy Roman Empire, to a world of dramatically different forms of organisation and technology.

To understand what might be a more realistic goal we first need to be clear about the international order that we in-herited. The Cold War order, which provided the umbrella for the spread of the telephone and the television, and gener-ated the finance for the semiconductor and the satellite, was based both on mutual fear and mutual understanding that the main protagonists would not fight each other and would not use nuclear weapons except in retaliation. With this conven-tion in place either side was free to behave as it wished in its own sphere of influence. The USA could have free rein in Central America, the Soviet Union in Eastern Europe, and where there were contested territories like the former Portuguese colonies of Angola and Mozambique, Ethiopia or Turkey, there were clearly understood rules of engagement.

As an order, the Cold War proved remarkably stable. There were many wars under its umbrella but none with the destruc-tive force of the world wars. Yet it was also, in another sense, unstable, and for two reasons. The first was that the balance of terror was morally doubtful: how could a political or military leader honestly commit themselves to killing tens of millions of people in vengeful retaliation, given that once the retaliation was needed it would already be redundant? The second was that both sides were ideologically committed to domination. Both had to win the war, and could only accept the status quo as a temporary arrangement, a breathing space.

The fall of the Berlin Wall brought that Cold War order to an end. It was followed first by high hopes that the United Nations would establish a new world order based on common and transparent rules of behaviour, and then by low despair when events in Somalia and Bosnia revealed the divisions and inadequacies of the leading nations. Some interpreted the 1990s as the dawn of a new age of chronic disorder. The rise of dozens of civil wars, the prevalence of terrorism even in the heart of the USA, on the streets of Tokyo and in Moscow, the chaotic powers of hackers: all seemed to presage a descent into apocalypse. But these lurid accounts misread the situation. Connexity has made new kinds of order possible, at least for some, and has created the conditions for what is potentially a more stable and morally justifiable system than what went before.

Today's world order has a very different structure to the world before 1989. Parts of the world are best described as pre-modern: these are the areas where there is no functioning state, and thus no functioning social order. An earlier government may have had it and lost it. An earlier empire may have been replaced by warlords rather than nations. The important point is that in these areas the state no longer has the monopoly over the legitimate use of force. Parts of West Africa fit this description, as do parts of the former Soviet Union, and Somalia. They were memorably described by Robert Kaplan in his influential essay on 'The Coming Disorder', which depicted a future of social breakdown, terrorism, organised crime and drugs, with the West African model as one that was already being echoed in the inner cities of America and Europe.[1]

The second element of the new world structure consists of the nation-states. These are the classic political entities that believe themselves to be self-contained and sovereign. Their sense of themselves is bound up in their own territory, they run their own armies, and see themselves in a complex pattern of balance of power with other nation-states. They live in their boxes and are concerned most of all with threats to the integrity of those boxes, whether they come from invasions or secessions. These are the states that still often initiate wars, partly to shore up internal unity, partly to win territory, partly to sharpen their own reflexes.

The third element of the new structure is the post-modern, the parts of the world most shaped by connexity. In these areas the old state structure is collapsing, but into more order rather than less. Where older orders were founded on the balance of power, the post-modern order rests on mutual interference and transparency, and pooled powers, rather like the order within states. The simplest reason for this is that borders no longer count for much. Objectively few economies are national in any meaningful sense, but the steady effect of the telegraph, the motor car, the satellite and the missile has been to make a mockery of the idea of a self-contained sovereignty. Changing your borders is both less necessary and less important than accumulating economic and cultural power, power over knowledge, and above all power for citizens rather than pieces of land. In practice, all of the most advanced nations on earth see the world in this way, even if they pay lip-service to an older ideal of territorial sovereignty.

The clearest example of the coming new order is the European Union. This is neither a union of nation-states nor an embryonic superstate. It can only be understood as a new species of governance made for an information age, since its main principles are the common acceptance of rules and openness about decisions on everything from public budgets to the contents of sausages. These types of state have emerged because force is such an inefficient way of resolving disputes. Instead the new rules function because everyone has an interest in making the system work, even when particular rules, particular judgements of courts like the European Court of Justice, or particular limits on conventional military forces, are disliked. Disputes are resolved by a mix of law, bargaining and arbitration. The EU represents 'the most developed example of a post-modern state. It represents security through transparency, and transparency through interdependence.'[2] Governance is coming to work like a system, delivering benefits systemically and therefore requiring systematic adherence. It does not require a new hegemonic world power to keep national states in check, but rather a system that cumulatively increases confidence internally, and the capacity to cooperate to restrain those nations that remain expansionist.

Even many of the people closely involved in the European Union still see it as nothing more than an evolution of the sovereign nation-state. But, as Robert Cooper, a leading diplomat and geopolitical thinker has written, 'it is important to realise what an extraordinary revolution this is. The normal, logical, behaviour of armed forces is to conceal their strength and hide their forces and equipment from potential enemies. Treaties to regulate such matters are an absurdity in strategic logic. In the first place you do not reach agreements with enemies since if they are enemies they cannot be trusted. In the second place you do not let the enemy come snooping around your bases counting weapons.'[3]

The reason why these normal behaviours have been thrown into the dustbin of history lies in the logic of the nuclear age: the need to avoid catastrophe was enough to overcome the normal strategic logic of suspicion and distrust. But the same principles now apply in other fields. There are many global examples: the IMF and OECD, which keep detailed track of economic behaviour and warn and cajole national governments, even the richest ones; the Non-Proliferation Treaty and International Atomic Energy Authority, which try to police behaviour by requiring openness to inspection teams; the various arrangements for controlling chemical and biological weapons, which, against expectations, have succeeded in keeping them out of wars.

These new orders rest on a structure of information and on coevolutionary principles. If one side unilaterally disarms it makes it harder for the other side to maintain arms, and so sets in motion a cycle that leads towards greater security. One might say that some of the principles of Gandhian *satyagraha* have found a technological logic to support them. Robert Axelrod puts it well: 'In zero sum games you always try to hide your strategy but in non zero sum games you might want to announce your strategy in public so the other players need to adapt to it.'[4]

The post-modern model also brings a new kind of democracy. Traditional realpolitik kept the public out of decisions.

It could not be expected to understand the complexities of balances of power and national interests. But in a more open climate of information, where the public expects to exercise more sovereignty, this separation ceases to be viable. Publics respond with emotion to international events and put pressure on their governments to act even where there is no national interest involved. In effect all international events become part of domestic politics in many different countries. By the same token, in matters of environmental policy or science there is no clear distinction between domestic and international issues, and constitutional experts are increasingly hard-pressed to describe just where national sovereignty begins and ends.

The essential idea of this emerging order is that openness makes you more secure. If you cede sovereignty you can gain rather than losing. If you can create structures based on mutual interests and reciprocity you gain more than by asserting your might. In global historical terms this is an extraordinary achievement. It mirrors the logic of a post-nuclear world, and a connected world, and reflects public values that have evolved beyond militarism. It reflects, too, the demise of the great collectives of the nation, class and race, since war is the ultimate collective act, and it reflects the fact that for the first time ever most of the world's powerful nations do not want to conquer territory, and do not want to take responsibility for large subject peoples. The trend which began when Britain invented dominion status in the nineteenth century, and which led Sweden to cooperate with Norwegian independence in 1905, has now become a norm.

Peace does not come solely from common interests, or from industrial integration (as Yugoslavia demonstrated). But it does come when common interests are amplified by confidence-building, deliberate policies to increase trust, and the ethos of cooperation that flows from these. In the military field, joint exercises, the disclosure of confidential information and the sharing of technologies achieve this. In economics, revealing the rules that will be followed by a central bank or a government makes it easier for other governments and firms to run efficiently. In policing, the sharing of information increases mutual confidence which makes it easier to fight organised crime.

The same rules can apply in any part of the global order. One is the environmental order, which is peculiarly complex because the interests being protected, such as future generations or habitats, have no voice. But the shared ethical commitment to protecting the environment can translate into similar rules of common responsibility and inspection, for example of emissions into the air or seas. This is not to discount the difficulties: not unreasonably, the poor nations want the rich to pay them for giving up on more resource-intensive paths of development, and in an open economy the incentives to cut standards and dump environmental problems on to others are strong. But the opportunities for parasitism of this kind strengthen the reasons for wanting to settle an agreed order. And whereas in the past punishment for infringing international rules might have been carried out by gunboats, today it is more likely to take the form of being excluded from the world's exchange systems, from trade and capital flows.

Another of the new orders is that governing information itself. Intriguingly the very first global institution grew out of communications. Following the adoption of rules on river trade on the Rhine and Danube, the new technology of the telegraph demanded common rules on what messages meant, and how they should be paid for. The International Telegraphy Union was the result, and over time evolved into the International Telecommunications Union, which organises the frequencies for radio and television stations, navigation and war, defines what technological standards will be used, and fixes the payments systems for messages that may pass through dozens of different countries.

The ITU is a body for the forms of messages, not their contents, but the infosphere is made up of meanings as well as bits. With integrated digital communications systems the capacity of any agency to control who says what to whom is limited. Since so many of the battles this century were fought

231

to remove restrictions and prise governments off newspapers and broadcasters, this represents progress, and a natural step beyond the erosion of national sovereignty caused by propaganda broadcast over frontiers by international radio stations and the illegal trades in cassette tapes and samizdat journals. But the battles to achieve a more open international infosphere have taken a more complex turn. Just as it used to be assumed that the natural environment had an infinite absorptive capacity, so did earlier debates about information assume that it can have no harmful effects, or that any restriction on information would be worse than any harm information could do. But in an environment saturated with signals ranging from child pornography to instruction kits on making bombs, this laissez-faire viewpoint loses conviction, and attention turns instead to how information can influence ecologies of mind that may be just as fragile as natural ecologies.

It is legitimate to be worried about who will decide what constitutes a 'toxic' message, but fierce struggles are already under way over who should have access to the Internet, with national and state governments placing the onus of responsibility on to service providers to restrict pornographic and other materials. Although technically it is not easy to regulate contents on interconnecting networks, for most of the mainstream networks, and most of the networks within easy access of children, some rules are viable, just as it would be viable to cut off those centres, like data havens, that do not accept responsibility for the information they provide. Even if on the margins a wholly unregulated hinterland survives unscathed, those using the networks have surprising power to self-regulate, punishing people who deliberately lie or deliberately corrupt by retaliating with waves of disruptive communications. Moreover the economic interest in policing intellectual property seems likely to encourage technologies that will make it easier to track and hold to account providers of information, or abusers of personal privacy.

Each of these new global orders of governance is paralleled by the informal orders of civic society. There are the global tribes, the transnational networks based on ethnic identities that have been organised so successfully by the Chinese, Indian, Jewish and Palestinian diasporas. Politics too has gone global, although global political institutions are not new in themselves. There have been those associated with the Catholic Church (like the Jesuits), the First, Second and Third Internationals, the Comintern, the Muslim Brotherhood, and more recently the Socialist International and the various groupings in Europe of Conservatives and Liberals. But today's global civil society is distinct in its breadth and scale. It includes environmental groups, religious organisations, human rights campaigns, all competing in a global public space to shape a global moral argument about issues like abortion or biodiversity. Whereas in 1909 there were 37 intergovernmental and 176 international nongovernmental organisations, by 1989 there were 300 intergovernmental and over 4,200 nongovernmental organisations; and whereas in the nineteenth century only two or three conferences and congresses were held each year by international governmental organisations, today the figure is around 4,000.[5] For the citizen perhaps the clearest expression of this web of new orders is tourism, which has risen nearly twenty-fold since 1950, and is set to rise even faster with the booming purchasing power of the middle classes of India and China.

Together these overlapping orders of military security, economic trade, environmental protection and information offer the hope that they will lock the world into peaceful conduct and that the costs of opting out of a single, connected system will become prohibitive. But this ethos of peace founded on mutuality, transparency, visible responsibility, is not bound to prevail. A powerful nation which holds to traditional notions of what its power is, and how it wants to use it, could be a major threat. A China that is set to be the world's most powerful economic and military power could challenge this embryonic order, while the danger for more pacific regimes is that they lose the capacity to defend themselves and that they wish themselves out of seeing threats.

Yet on balance the pressures towards peace appear stronger

than those towards conflict because of the mutual advantages to be gained in a world no longer so constrained by the zero-sum logics of territory and material goods. This takes us to the general point. In the past, global orders could have a radically different character to national or local ones. The most democratic nations often assumed that in international affairs they would have to behave with the ruthless realpolitik of an empire or tyranny. Secrecy and deception were legitimate, and the guiding principle was that my enemy's enemy is my friend, an ethic of distrust of others that sees all alliances as temporary and contingent. But the global order of connexity has almost the opposite character. It is almost fractal, in that the same principles and forms that make sense in the smallest scale in connexity – transparency, ethos, responsibility, mutuality – also work at the very largest scale too. If there is to be a form for global governance, and for an overarching intelligence to guide the world through the huge challenges of the twenty-first century, it will surely embody these principles rather than looking like a national government writ large.

15

HOPE AND FEAR

WHEN SOMEONE ONCE remarked to T.S. Eliot that we know far more than previous generations, he replied: 'Yes, but they are what we know.' In so far as their knowledge included answers to the question 'How should we live?' he was probably right. The guides to living a fulfilled and meaningful life that can be found in the great religions and literatures have not dated much, which is why there is little need for yet another guidebook or a self-help menu of therapies. But the ways in which we live together do change in every age. They are shaped by the prevailing technologies and institutions, by values and by weights of numbers and connections, and past insights are of only limited use. That is the justification for focusing in this book on the structures and institutions, the social and economic orders, within which people live their lives: the radically novel context of a more densely connected world.

In the preceding chapters I have argued that although the task of reconciling freedom and interdependence is not in itself new – everyone who becomes a parent, takes on a job or joins a community lives with it – the tension between them has been sharpened as the world has become more interdependent and more closely connected. This tension now poses the most acute challenge to the thinking and practice of politicians, business leaders and citizens all over the world.

If we are to resolve this question, we need a new way of thinking about progress. Instead of seeing it as an accumulation of technical prowess or material goods, or an expansion of freedom, we need to understand it as a transition that parallels the one that every individual life passes through, from dependence through independence to interdependence. Where the child passes from dependence on its parents and family, through adolescence to taking on new responsibilities and relationships of trust in adulthood, societies are passing from the dependence on tradition and hierarchy, through the independence of liberal individualism, to the interdependence of connexity. In philosophical terms this transition can be understood as a process whereby the tension between freedom and dependence resolves itself through a change from quantities to qualities, from the quantities of freedoms and connections to a qualitative improvement in the nature of human relationships.

If this analysis is correct, our challenge today is two-fold: on the one hand to cultivate mentalities that make people genuine moral subjects, able to make decisions, bear responsibilities and exercise moral judgements, and on the other, to develop new social orders based on laws and institutions that are better suited to an interdependent world.

This might all be of only academic interest. But in fact we have little choice but to make a transition of this kind. The extraordinary advance of industrial society has rendered the systems on which we depend much more vulnerable. We walk more heavily on them, we subject them to new and uncharted risks, and as the world's population continues its vertiginous climb, their fragility is likely to become increasingly apparent.

There are many reasons why people are likely to want to ignore these uncomfortable facts. It is easier to think of yourself as living in a box, whether that box is a firm, a community or a nation, than it is to grasp all of the ways in which your life connects with others beyond your box. If societies remain chronically divided into rich and poor, ins and outs, the common good is bound to be sacrificed to struggles over who gets what. If technologies foster isolation and passivity (as television has probably done) then it will be easier to ignore the facts of interdependence. The reason for optimism is that there are so many signs of new principles becoming second nature, slowly embedded in mentalities and institutions: the principle that difference is something to be welcomed, not feared; that authority is unavoidable but that it must be always ready to answer for itself; the principle of mutual transparency as the basis for feeling secure; the principle that mutual, reciprocal relationships are always preferable to dependent ones. These are simple principles, even if complex in their implementation, and they go with the grain of human nature.

The ends of centuries and millenniums lead many to be attracted to finality. We have been promised the end of history, geography, politics, and of the good. Erudite thinkers tell us why there is no possibility of progress or of common understanding. Nations and social groups in relative decline invariably project their own condition on to the world at large, and opt for a comfortable pessimism. What George Orwell called the 'pensioned oppositions' never have to worry too much about what they would do otherwise, and so can pass their time in peaceful negativity.

There is no absence of good reasons for being pessimistic. It is far from clear that human societies are able to evolve their mentalities and institutions fast enough to adapt to the changes they inflict on their environments. Many of the indicators of change are now moving at faster rates than ever before, tending towards the hyperbolic. This is certainly true of messages, and financial transactions, but also of physical quantities like the number of people on the planet, the use of raw materials or the destructive power of weaponry. But in making an overall judgement between hope and fear, optimism and pessimism, the rational weighing of facts is of only limited help. At no time in history has it been possible to make an objective judgement, and in retrospect even the most worldly-wise got most of their forecasts wrong.

Today too, there are few easy ways of, for example, weighing the balance between rising longevity and the emergence of new diseases, between the rise of civil wars and the decline of wars among nations, between rising living standards in China and stagnation and famine in Africa, or between science's success in understanding the human genome and its ignorance of the new risks it is generating. The same is true of the particular characteristics of connexity. The optimists focus on the runaway qualities of knowledge and information that seem able to grow beyond the norms of material things, the rise of mutual understanding and capacities to communicate, the emergence of a global public space in which to debate questions of morality and survival. The pessimists stress the tendencies towards myopia, disconnection from responsibility, cultural imperialism, economic inequality, and the collapse of authentic cultures. It is just as possible that we will end up with a Tower of Babel, in which the peoples of the world berate each other in mutual incomprehension and drive each other into sullen isolation, as it is that they will find a common meaning, a set of bigger goals that in turn make them feel stronger.

Most people choose on the basis of taste as much as reason, but given a choice, the advantages of choosing hope, of an optimism tempered by realism, are overwhelming. At a personal level hope releases all sorts of energies. What one psychologist defined in his study of hope as 'believing you have both the will and the way to accomplish your goals' is one of the keys to success in life.[1] It is the best thing that an education can give to its pupils, the most valuable thing a family can give to its children, and the most useful service provided by political leaders. At a societal level, hope justifies itself because it creates the conditions for problems to be solved. Without hope no human groups stretch themselves to their limits and realise their full potential. This is why hope is functional rather than naive.

Yet it goes without saying that no progress is determined, inevitable or irresistible. The classical idea of progress as the unfolding of a grand plan, or the expression of a higher intelligence, is as doubtful as the much more recent faith that the world might have immanent properties that drive it towards complexity, integration and self-organisation. But even if history is no longer providence it can still be infused with hope, and hope shared across the myriad of connections that now join our feelings and fears to those of so many others. There may be no destiny, and no certainty, nothing determined, only choices and chances. But life is all the better for that, because that is what leaves the room for people to make their own history.

Earlier this century, E.M. Forster wrote that we should 'only connect'. The world has followed his injunction. Now all we have to do is to learn to live with the connections that we have made.

NOTES

Introduction

1. The contradictions at the heart of capitalism were most coherently set out by Daniel Bell in *The Cultural Contradictions of Capitalism*, New York, Basic Books, 1978, although he did not draw out the implications of his argument.

Chapter 1

1. Instead of perfect competition, temporary monopolies result, both to exploit economies of scale and to ensure sufficient returns to finance new investment. This is one of the reasons why the market dominance of firms like Intel and Microsoft is greater than that of previous leading industries. They are engaged in Schumpeterian rather than Ricardian competition.
2. This was the argument made by Marcel Gauchet in 'Tocqueville, l'Amerique et nous' *Libre*, 7, 1980, pp.116–7. As Albert Hirschman points out, there is a long tradition of seeing the virtues of conflict, notably in Georg Simmel, *Soziologie*, 1908, and Lewis Coser *The Functions of Social Conflict*, 1956.
3. Daniel Dennett, 'Intentional Systems in Cognitive Ethology: the "Panglossian Paradigm" defended', *Behavioural and Brain Sciences*, 6, 1983, pp.343–90.

4. Robin Dunbar, *Grooming, Gossip and the Evolution of Language*, London, Faber & Faber, 1996, pp.83–6.

Chapter 2

1. And in economic life too, freedom manifests itself in the power to exit. As Fernand Braudel pointed out, the earliest freedom of the modern world was won by the holders of capital, who could move it from place to place, making kings more beholden to bankers than vice-versa.
2. Ithiel de Sola Pool, *Technologies of Freedom*, Cambridge, MA, Harvard University Press, 1983, is the classic argument of technologies as liberators.
3. Oscar Patterson, *History of Freedom*, New York, Basic Books, 1991, p.41.
4. Paul Abramson and Ronald Inglehart, *Value Change in Global Perspective*, Ann Arbor, University of Michigan Press, 1995.
5. Michael Mann, *Sources of Social Power*, vol.1., Cambridge University Press, 1993, p.53.
6. Alan McFarlane, *The Origins of English Individualism*, Oxford, Basil Blackwell, 1978.

Chapter 3

1. Lionel Tiger, *The Pursuit of Pleasure*, Boston, Little, Brown, 1992.
2. Paul Ricoeur, 'The Critique of Religion', in *The Philosophy of Paul Ricoeur: an Anthology of his Work*, Boston, Beacon Press, 1978, p.214.
3. Robert Kegan, *In Over Our Heads: the Mental Demands of Modern Life*, Cambridge, MA, Harvard University Press, 1994.
4. Japanese appears to have a less fixed idea of the self. Robert Smith writes that 'the large number of referents and the manner in which they are employed indicates that

even the question "who is self; who is other" is not unambiguously settled . . . some common terms such as boku and temae may mean 'I' or 'you' . . . in English usage by contrast, the speaker stands at the centre of the set of referents he or she will employ.' *Japanese Society*, Cambridge University Press, 1983, p.81.

Chapter 4

1. Sceptics argue that globalisation is not a new phenomenon and that the world economy is no more global than before 1913. There is a grain of truth in this, but even taking the sceptics' chosen indicator, the ratios of world trade to GDP, the 1913 levels had been clearly overtaken by the 1980s.
2. Michael Walzer, *Spheres of Justice, A Defence of Pluralism and Equality*, Oxford University Press, 1983, pp.101–3 provides a comprehensive list of things which cannot be exchanged.
3. Matt Ridley, *The Origins of Virtue*, London, Viking, 1996.
4. Johann Huizinga, *Homo Ludens: the Study of the Play Element in Culture*, New York, Harper & Row, 1970.
5. Adam Smith, *The Theory of Moral Sentiments*, Oxford University Press, 1976, p.183.

Chapter 5

1. Jane Jacobs, *Systems of Survival*, London, Hodder & Stoughton, 1993.
2. Norbert Elias, *Court Society*, New York, Pantheon, 1983.
3. and 4. Francis Bacon and Heinrich von Treitschke both quoted in Theodore Zeldin, *An Intimate History of Humanity*, London, Sinclair Stevenson, 1994.
5. The best account of these cities is provided by Peter Hall in his book on creative cities, forthcoming from Routledge.

6. Howard Gardner, *Creating Minds*, New York, Basic Books, 1993.
7. Daniel Bell, 'Technology, Nature and Society'. In *The Winding Passage*, New York, Basic Books, 1980.
8. Theodore Zeldin, op.cit.
9. Fred Hirsch, *The Social Limits of Growth*, London, Routledge Kegan Paul, 1977.

Chapter 6

1. Leda Cosmides and John Tooby, 'From Evolution to Behaviour: Evolutionary Psychology As the Missing Link', in J. Dupre, *The Latest on the Best*, Cambridge, MIT Press, 1987.
2. Peter Drucker, *Managing the Non-Profit Organisation*, London, Butterworths, 1990, p.89.
3. Mary Douglas, *How Institutions Think*, New York, Harper Row, 1984.
4. Amartya Sen, *Poverty and Famines*, Oxford University Press, 1986.
5. Richard Wilkinson, *Unhealthy Societies*, Routledge, London, 1996, p.150.
6. D'Arcy Thompson, *On Growth and Form*, Cambridge University Press, 1963.
7. Much of this is drawn from Robin Dunbar, *Grooming, Gossip and the Evolution of Language*, London, Faber, 1996.
8. A good source of this in the UK is the Henley Centre's *Planning for Social Change 1996/7*, which shows a long-term decline in the influence of big institutions and a rising influence from friends, siblings, partners and work colleagues.
9. Also in *Planning for Social Change*, op.cit.
10. Like those expressed by Daniel Bell in his classic *The Cultural Contradictions of Capitalism*, New York, Basic Books, 1978.
11. Robert Puttnam, *Making Democracy Work*, Princeton,

NJ, Princeton University Press, 1993; and subsequent articles.

12. Although both groups tend to do the least volunteering.

13. Jane Jacobs, *The Death and Life of Great American Cities*, Cape, London, 1961.

14. The fullest exposition of James Coleman's ideas is to be found in *Foundations of Social Theory*, Cambridge, MA, Belknap Press, 1990.

15. Francis Fukuyama, *Trust*, London, HarperCollins, 1996.

16. Charles Hampden-Turner, 'Finite and Infinite Games', *Demos Quarterly 6*.

Chapter 7

1. Mihalyi Csikszentmihalyi, *The Evolving Self*, London, HarperCollins, 1993, p.19.

2. Clifford Geertz, 'On the Nature of Anthropological Understanding', *American Scientist*, 63, 1975, pp.47–53.

3. There is also a long tradition of seeing all moral engineering as futile hubris. Edmund Burke once wrote that 'an ignorant man, who is not fool enough to meddle with his clock is however sufficiently confident to think he can safely take to pieces and put together at his own pleasure a moral machine of another guise, importance and complexity, composed of far other wheels and spins and balances and counteracting and cooperating powers. Men little think how immorally they act in rashly meddling with what they do not understand.'

4. It is significant that the conservative critique of welfare moved on to this ground, rather than argue on the ground that it means unfair taxes on those in work.

5. James Q. Wilson, *The Moral Sense*, New York, Free Press, 1993, p.45. Wilson draws on Nancy Eisenberg and Paul Musen, *The Roots of Prosocial Behaviour in Children*, Cambridge University Press, 1989.

6. Diana Baumrind, 'Parental Disciplinary Patterns and Social Competence in Children', *Youth and Society*, 9,

1978.
7. Arthur Kornhaber and Kenneth Woodward, *Grandparents/Grandchildren*, cited in James Q. Wilson, op. cit.
8. Ulrich Beck, *Risk Society*, Cambridge, Polity Press, 1991, p.118.
9. Shoshanna Zuboff, *The Age of the Smart Machine*, New York, Basic Books, 1988.
10. Francis Ianni, *The Structure of Experience*, New York, Free Press, 1988.
11. Amitai Etzioni, *The Spirit of Community*, New York, Crown, 1993.

Chapter 8

1. Robert Wuthrow, *Acts of Compassion*, Princeton, NJ, Princeton University Press, 1991, p.20.
2. Rudolf Otto, *Das Heilige*, (The Sacred), 1917.
3. Anne Glyn-Jones, for example, drawing on Pitirim Sorokin, has argued that all civilisations tend to follow a similar path, from domination by belief in a non-material order to which people are subordinate, through concerns for human well-being that combine with a more benign transcendent realm of religion, to a final stage in which materialism and hedonism are left as the only values. Once there, such civilisations have to pile on ever greater extremes of pleasure or horror to feed their desire for sensation, until finally they collapse (*Holding up a Mirror: How Civilisations Decline*, London, Century, 1996). Bishop Tom Butler had the idea that morals without faith are like the smile on the Cheshire cat's face, the last thing to fade.
4. Marcel Mauss, *The Gift: Forms and Functions of Exchange in Archaic Societies*, London, Cohen and West, 1970.
5. Alasdair MacIntyre, *After Virtue*, London, Duckworth, 1981.

6. See Donald Pfaff, *Estrogens and Brain Function*, New York, Springer-Verlag, 1980, and Paul MacLean, 'Brain Evolution Relating to Family, Plan and the Separation Call', *Archives of General Psychiatry*, 42, 1985, pp.405–17.
7. James Q. Wilson, *The Moral Sense*, New York, Free Press, 1993.
8. May and others (ed.), *Mind and Morals*, Cambridge, MA, MIT Press, 1996, p.7.
9. Owen Flanagan, *Varieties of Moral Personality*, 1991, p.32.
10. Roger Scruton, *Animal Rights and Wrongs*, London, Demos, 1996, p.56.
11. Iris Murdoch, *The Sovereignty of Good*, London, Routledge Kegan Paul, 1970.
12. Mary Midgeley, 'Can Education Be Moral?', *Prospero*, 1/2, March 1995; Mark L. Johnson, 'How Moral Psychology Changes Moral Theory', in *Minds and Morals*, Cambridge, MA, MIT Press, 1996.
13. Benjamin Lee Whorf in *Language, Thought, and Reality*, ed. J.B. Caroll, Cambridge, MA, MIT Press, 1956.
14. There are many professions for which truth and falsehood are purely instrumental: like marketing and advertising, politics or even the media, professions which have lost any of the sense of honour that comes from fulfilling the obligations associated with a position.
15. Derek Parfitt, *Reasons and Persons*, Oxford, Clarendon Press, 1984.

Chapter 9

1. Stuart Kauffman, *At Home in the Universe*, Oxford University Press, 1995.
2. Ludwig von Bertalanffy, *General Systems Theory*, Braziller, New York, 1968.
3. W.R. Ashby, 'Principles of the Self-organising Systems', in Heinz von Foerster and George W. Zopf (eds),

Principles of Self-Organisation, New York, Pergamon, 1962.

4. There are exceptions to this rule: Ursula Le Guin's *The Dispossessed* is a good example.

5. Heinz von Foerster and George E. Zopf, op. cit.

6. From 'Lessons from Geese' a speech given by Angeles Arrien at the 1991 Organisational Development Network.

7. Humberto Maturana and Francisco Varela, *The Tree of Knowledge: The Biological Roots of Human Understanding*, Boston, 1992.

8. Niklas Luhmann, *Social Systems*, Stanford, CA, Stanford University Press, 1995.

9. Stuart Kauffman, *The Origins of Order: Self-organisation and Selection in Evolution*, Oxford University Press, 1993.

10. Ilya Prigogine and I. Stengers, *Order out of Chaos*, London, Heinemann, 1984.

Chapter 10

1. Although there are exceptions, such as the state of Texas which moved to weeklong voting, Oregon, which doubled turnout by holding an election by post, or Ross Perot's staging of a virtual party convention in 1996.

2. C.J. Jung, *Collected Works*, vol.7, sect. 78, Princeton, NJ, Princeton University Press, 1953.

3. James Hillman, *Kinds of Power*, Doubleday, New York, p.37.

4. A summary of these methods and the arguments used for them is in Andrew Adonis and Geoff Mulgan, 'Back to Greece', in *Lean Democracy*, Demos, 1994.

Chapter 11

1. Mancur Olson, 'Big Bills Left on the Sidewalk: Why Some Nations are Rich and Others Poor', *Journal of Economic Perspectives*, Spring 1996.

Chapter 12

1. Philip Selznick, 'Personhood and Moral Obligation' in A. Etzioni (ed.), *New Communitarian Thinking*, University of Virginia Press, 1995.
2. Thomas Nagel, *The Possibility of Altruism*, Princeton, NJ, Princeton University Press, 1970, p.145.

Chapter 13

1. Much of this section draws on work by Perri 6 at Demos.
2. Manuel Castells, *The Network Society*, Oxford, Blackwell, 1996, p.165.
3. *The Economist*, 1.7.95.
4. *Visa International: the Management of Change*, Cambridge, MA, Harvard Business School, 1981, p.2.
5. Dee Hock, 'The Chaordic Organization: Out of Control and Into Order, *World Business Academy Perspectives*, vol. 9, No. 1, 1995.
6. Kevin Kelly, 1994, *Out of Control*, London, 4th Estate, 1994, p.607.
7. The Wuppertal Institute has proposed between a fourfold and tenfold improvement in the economy's performance in terms of MIPS: material intensity per unit of service or function.
8. One example is the US Pacific Gas and Electric company, which in the mid-1980s was planning to build 20 new power plants, and instead devoted its resources towards energy efficiency or purchases from private-built renewable energy sources.

9. One way of doing this, which also suggests a possible evolution for trade unions, would be through developing employee mutuals which are jointly owned by their members and sell their labour on to business. Cooperatives of actors, computer programmers, and firms like Manpower which deploy labour rather than employing it are pointers in this direction. See 'Employee Mutuals: the 21st Century Trade Union' by Geoff Mulgan and Tom Bentley, Demos, 1996.

10. This is not such a leap as is supposed. The theoretical obsession with property rights in modern capitalism is misleading since only in rare cases is there the clear exchange of property rights that economics describes. For example, if someone buys a drink in a bar they are not simply purchasing ownership of the drink but also a cluster of other properties – for example, the right to enjoy the atmosphere – defined by various social norms, about acceptable behaviour.

11. See my 'Twin Economies' in *Reconciling Society and Economy*, OECD, 1996.

Chapter 14

1. Robert Kaplan, 'The Coming Disorder', *Atlantic Monthly*, 1992.
2. Robert Cooper, *The Postmodern State and the World Order*, Demos, 1996.
3. ibid.
4. Quoted in Kevin Kelly, *Out of Control*, London, 4th Estate, 1994, p.116.
5. Figures taken from David Goldblatt, 'The Paradox of Power: Globalisation and National Government in Missionary Government', *Demos Quarterly*, 7/95, p.28.

Chapter 15

1. 'The Will and Ways: Development and Validation of an Individual-differences Measure of Hope', *Journal of Personality and Social Psychology*, 60, 1991, p.579.

INDEX

ABOUT THE AUTHOR

Geoff Mulgan is the founder and director of Demos, an independent think-tank set up in 1993 in London. He is visiting professor at University College London, and has published books on broadcasting, telecommunications and culture. He has been a reporter for both BBC TV and Radio, and contributes regularly to the *Guardian* and the *Independent*.